RENEWABLE ENERGY FINANCE
Powering the Future

RENEWABLE ENERGY FINANCE
Powering the Future

Edited by

Charles W. Donovan
Imperial College Business School

Imperial College Press

ICP

Published by

Imperial College Press
57 Shelton Street
Covent Garden
London WC2H 9HE

Distributed by

World Scientific Publishing Co. Pte. Ltd.

5 Toh Tuck Link, Singapore 596224

USA office: 27 Warren Street, Suite 401-402, Hackensack, NJ 07601

UK office: 57 Shelton Street, Covent Garden, London WC2H 9HE

Library of Congress Cataloging-in-Publication Data
Renewable energy finance : powering the future / edited by Charles W. Donovan, Imperial College
Business School, UK.
　　pages cm
　　ISBN 978-1-78326-776-7 (hardback) -- ISBN 1-78326-776-3 (hardback)
　　1. Renewable energy sources--Finance. I. Donovan, Charles W.
　　HD9502.A2R444 2015
　　333.79'4--dc23
　　　　　　　　　　　　　　2015016677

British Library Cataloguing-in-Publication Data
A catalogue record for this book is available from the British Library.

In-house Editor: Thomas Stottor

Typeset by Stallion Press
Email: enquiries@stallionpress.com

Printed in Singapore

Contents

Foreword

I joined the energy industry in 1969, working as a reservoir engineer on the North Slope of Alaska. In 1969, oil companies were still national champions, steeped in the history of colonial exploration and conquest. Energy meant hydrocarbons, primarily oil, and the 'energy problem' was simply defined: how to obtain more oil, at the lowest cost, with little regard for the consequences. Renewable energy was not part of the industry's lexicon.

Two changes in the 1970s marked the beginning of a fundamental shift in the energy industry. The first was the oil shock of 1973 and the rise of OPEC, which demonstrated that OECD countries no longer had full control over their energy supplies. The world was reminded that oil can be a scarce commodity, and that it was subject to market and non-market forces which were starting to operate to the advantage of producers over consumers.

The second change was the rise of environmentalism. Concern for the natural environment has a long history, but only in the 1970s did it reach the mainstream political agenda. Reports like the Club of Rome's 'The Limits to Growth' attract scorn today for their outlandish predictions of catastrophe, but they set the scene for today's justified concerns about climate change.

The events of the 1970s recalibrated the world's approach to energy. Advanced economies entered a period of steadily declining energy intensity, as governments and consumers sought to mitigate the effects of rising energy prices. Oil companies responded to higher prices by exploring new frontiers, such as the North Sea and Alaska, and work began in earnest on developing alternatives to fossil fuels.

But it was not until the 1990s that a viable renewable energy alternative emerged. When I became the CEO of BP in 1995, just over one percent of the world's electricity was generated from renewable sources like wind and solar. But thanks to rapid declines in the cost of technology, that figure doubled over the twelve years that I led the company, and it has doubled again in the eight years since I left. Most supermajors now call themselves *energy* companies rather than *oil and gas* companies, reflecting their need to diversify beyond hydrocarbons. That represents remarkable progress from the days of Standard Oil and British Petroleum.

As chief executive of BP, and afterwards as co-head of the world's largest renewable energy private equity fund, I witnessed this evolution and its impact first hand. The rise of renewable energy requires new perspectives on risk, an appreciation of the interaction between energy markets and government policy, and a willingness to develop creative solutions to new problems. It calls for people with a new combination of scientific, political and financial skills, and a strong understanding of the external forces driving change in the energy sector. It requires a willingness to adapt to new circumstances.

This book sets out the foundations for success in a rapidly evolving industry, and I hope it will serve as a reference manual for investors in this increasingly important sector. With contributions from a range of experts and practitioners, *Renewable Energy Finance* is an essential reference point for professionals working in the energy industry today.

Lord Browne of Madingley,
former group chief executive, BP

Author Biographies

Philip Andrews-Speed is a principal fellow at the Energy Studies Institute of the National University of Singapore. He has 35 years in the field of energy and resources, starting his career as a mineral and oil exploration geologist before moving into the field of energy and resource governance. Until 2010, he was professor of Energy Policy at the University of Dundee and director of the Centre of Energy, Petroleum and Mineral Law and Policy. While a fellow at the Transatlantic Academy of the German Marshall Fund of the US, he co-authored the report *The Global Resource Nexus: The Struggles for Land, Food, Water and Minerals*. Recent books include *China, Oil and Global Politics* with Roland Dannreuther and *The Governance of Energy in China: Transition to a Low-Carbon Economy*. His current research focuses on the development of unconventional gas in Asia and on the governance of energy in China and Asia.

Derek W. Bunn is professor of Decision Sciences at London Business School. Author of over 200 research papers and books in the areas of forecasting, econometrics, decision analysis and energy economics, he has been editor of the *Journal of Forecasting* since 1984, a previous editor of *Energy Economics*, and founding editor of the *Journal of*

Energy Markets. He has advised many international companies and government agencies in the energy sector as well as giving evidence in arbitration and litigation.

Alejandro Ciruelos is an executive director at Santander Global Banking and Markets, the international wholesale banking division of Banco Santander. Alejandro joined Santander Global Banking and Markets' Project and Acquisition finance department in 2006 as part of the global energy practice of the bank. He is currently the head of Santander's Project and Acquisition department in London and responsible for the origination, execution and distribution of non-recourse project finance loans across the energy and infrastructure sectors in the UK, Ireland, and Scandinavia. During his tenure at Santander, Mr. Ciruelos has led the structuring, execution and negotiation of over 25 transactions in the renewable energy sector in numerous regions of North America and Europe. Prior to joining Santander, Mr. Ciruelos was a management consultant in the energy sector with Diamond Cluster International (now Oliver Wyman). Alejandro holds a BSc in Business Administration from Universidad Pontificia Comillas-ICADE, and an MSc in Applied Economics from Marquette University.

Alexandre Chavarot is a project and climate finance banker with more than 20 years' experience in financial structuring, capital raising, acquisitions and divestitures. Mr. Chavarot spent the first 15 years of his career as a banker with Crédit Commercial de France and Lazard, where he was involved in a number of groundbreaking infrastructure transactions in emerging markets. In 2011, he co-founded Clean Infra Partners, a financial advisory firm focused on energy, water and waste-related infrastructure projects with a strong focus on developing countries. Prior to starting Clean Infra Partners, he was head of project finance and solar program coordinator at the Clinton Climate Initiative. Mr. Chavarot is a graduate of the Institut d'études politiques de Paris ('Science-Po'), and holds a Master's in Public Policy from the Harvard Kennedy School of Government and an MBA from INSEAD.

Charles Donovan is principal teaching fellow at Imperial College Business School in London. He was most recently head of Structuring and Valuation for Alternative Energy at BP plc, where he was responsible for investment evaluation and project financings in North America, Europe, and Asia. He began his career as an energy policy analyst with the US Environmental Protection Agency during the Clinton Administration and subsequently worked for the Enron Corporation. His experience includes several years in private sector consulting, advising national governments and multinational energy companies on the impacts of governmental policy on investment. Dr. Donovan holds a BA in Psychology from the University of Washington, an MBA from Vanderbilt University, and a DBA in Management from IE Business School.

Sam Friggens is an economist and writer. He specializes in technology innovation, energy system transformation and renewable energy crowdfunding. After giving up a career managing urban regeneration projects in East London, he earned an MSc in Environmental Change and Management at the University of Oxford, graduating with distinction in 2012. Since then he has worked as a consultant, leading assessments of new renewable energy and nuclear technologies, as well as supporting clean technology start-up companies bring their products to market.

Albert Gore III is an MBA candidate at Columbia Business School. Before school he was the vice president of Business Development at Strategic Capital Partners, a privately held real-estate investment firm, specializing in the development and acquisition of industrial, office, mixed-use and multi-family properties nationwide. Prior to that he was the associate publisher of *Good* magazine, a media platform that highlights and promotes individuals, businesses, and non-profits driving change in the world. He is a board member of the Sustainable Furnishings Council, a non-profit industry organization focused on promoting sustainable practices amongst manufacturers, retailers, and consumers.

Richard Green is the Alan and Sabine Howard Professor of Sustainable Energy Business at Imperial College Business School. An economist, he has been studying the economics and regulation of the electricity industry since 1989. He started his career at the Department of Applied Economics, University of Cambridge, and has been a professor at the University of Hull and the University of Birmingham, where he was director of the interdisciplinary Institute for Energy Research and Policy. Dr. Green has held visiting positions at the World Bank, the Office of Electricity Regulation (UK), the University of California Energy Institute, and at MIT. Most of his recent work is on the economic implications of low-carbon electricity, particularly in terms of its impact on electricity wholesale markets.

Karl Harder started out as a parliamentary researcher on renewable energy. He subsequently ran a successful social enterprise, which he left in 2007 to pursue the idea that eventually became Abundance Generation. Abundance was the world's first renewable energy crowdfunding platform and was also the UK's first regulated crowdfunding platform. The business was founded in 2009 by Mr. Harder, Louise Wilson and Bruce Davis and launched to the public in 2012. He currently serves as a managing director of Abundance Generation, which now operates across Europe and has raised over £10 million for renewable energy projects.

Thorsten Helms is a Nagelschneider Foundation Fellow and PhD candidate at the University of St. Gallen, Switzerland. He graduated in Management Science and Engineering from Karlsruhe Institute of Technology in 2009 and worked as a strategy development associate for Switzerland's largest electric utility between 2010 and 2013. His dissertation focuses on business model innovation and investment decisions in light of the energy transition.

Chris Hunt is a managing director of Riverstone. Throughout the course of his career, he has developed, constructed, financed, and/or operated renewable and conventional energy businesses in over 25 countries, involving more than 30 GWs of power capacity. Prior to joining Riverstone, Mr. Hunt was one of the principals leading the creation and growth of the Alternative Energy division at BP plc. He was also an executive at Enron, where he was responsible for the acquisition, development, operations, and/or financing of a multi-billion dollar portfolio of 16 coal, gas, wind, and distribution businesses. Prior to Enron, he was a founding member of a privately held international private power company that developed multiple wind and gas-fired power assets across Latin America, Europe, and Asia. Mr. Hunt currently serves on the boards of directors of Pattern Energy Group LP, Silver Ridge Power, and Velocita Energy Developments. He received his BA, with high departmental honors, from Wesleyan University in Connecticut and his MBA, Beta Gamma Sigma, from Columbia University.

Matthew Konieczny is a vice president at Clean Infra Partners, a climate finance advisory firm focused on renewable energy infrastructure, primarily in emerging markets. He worked previously at the William J. Clinton Foundation, where he advised foreign governments on their energy sectors, developing policy-and finance-based solutions for deploying utility-scale renewable energy. Mr. Konieczny has advised clients in Europe, Asia, Australia, Brazil, North America, the Caribbean, East Africa, and the Middle East. Mr. Konieczny started his career in investment banking at Lehman Brothers and Nomura in London, where he specialized in mergers and acquisitions in the mining sector. He holds a degree in Economics from Yale University.

Celine McInerney has been a finance lecturer at University College Cork (UCC) since 2009. Prior to joining UCC she spent 12 years working as a corporate finance advisor. Her last position in industry was as director of corporate finance at boutique advisor Merrion Capital where she focused on the energy sector. Prior to this, she spent three years working for Ireland's largest private wind farm developer SWS Group where she was responsible for acquisitions and fundraising. Previously she worked in mergers and acquisitions at Deutsche Morgan Grenfell and Lehman Brothers in London and New York. Dr. McInerney holds a BSc in Finance from Dublin City University, an MLitt in Finance and a graduate diploma in Statistics from Trinity College Dublin and a PhD in Energy Finance from University College Cork completed under the external supervision of Professor Derek Bunn at London Business School.

Brian Potskowski is responsible for policy and strategy at Riverstone, an energy and power-focused private equity firm, based in London. Prior to joining Riverstone, Mr. Potskowski was a senior analyst at Bloomberg New Energy Finance, where he conducted analysis of the European power markets. Before joining New Energy Finance, Mr. Potskowski worked as an analyst in the UK Mergers and Acquisitions team for Citigroup in London on over £2.5bn of transactions for clients in the energy, healthcare and leisure sectors. Mr. Potskowski graduated *magna cum laude* with a BA in Political Science from Tufts University. He received his MSc from the University of Edinburgh in Carbon Management with honors, specializing in climate change and environmental finance.

Sarah Salm is a PhD candidate and research associate at University of St. Gallen's Institute for Economy and the Environment (IWOE-HSG). In her role as research associate, she holds the function of program manger for the Executive Diploma in Renewable Energy Management (REM-HSG). During her academic studies of finance and power engineering in Munich and Buenos Aires, she focused on capital market related aspects of energy financing. She gained practical experience from large German and non-European companies in the financial sector. Within her research at the Chair for Management of Renewable Energies, she focused on financial investment behavior and requirements of strategic and institutional investors.

Gireesh Shrimali is a professor of Energy Economics at the Monterey Institute of International Studies, a graduate school of Middlebury College. He is concurrently a faculty fellow at the Steyer–Taylor Center for Energy Policy and Finance at Stanford University and a fellow at Climate Policy Initiative (CPI). Previously, he taught at the Indian School of Business (ISB), where he helped found the CPI–ISB Energy and Environment Program in collaboration with CPI; he still co-manages the CPI–ISB Program. His current research focus is on renewable energy finance and policy in developing countries — in particular, on analytical frameworks for identification of effective policies as well as on instruments for provision of low-cost, long-term capital. He has over nine years of industry experience. Dr. Shrimali holds a PhD from Stanford University, an MS from the University of Minnesota, Minneapolis, and a BTech from the Indian Institute of Technology, New Delhi.

Jim Skea is professor of Sustainable Energy at Imperial College London and a Research Councils UK Energy Strategy Fellow. Until June 2012, he was research director of the UK Energy Research Centre (UKERC). Dr. Skea has research interests in energy, climate change and technological innovation. He has previously been director of the Policy Studies Institute, Director of the Economic and Social Research Council's Global Environmental Change Program, professorial fellow at the Science Policy Research Unit, Sussex University and visiting assistant professor at the Department of Engineering and Public Policy, Carnegie-Mellon University. He is a founding member of the UK's Committee on Climate Change and is vice-chair of Working Group III (Mitigation) of the Intergovernmental Panel on Climate Change. Dr. Skea was awarded an OBE for services to sustainable transport in 2004 and a CBE for services to sustainable energy in 2013.

Guy Turner is formerly chief economist at Bloomberg New Energy Finance. His professional experience spans two decades of consulting and business management in the energy and environmental sector. On the advisory side, he has worked with governments and their agencies on a wide range of environmental policies, covering carbon trading, clean energy, power markets, gas markets, water, waste, and air quality. In the private sector, he has led projects to advise some of the largest companies on strategic activities in the alternative energy and environmental space. Mr. Turner was a director at Enviros Consulting where he founded and successfully grew the firm's economics and policy practice. He holds degrees in Mechanical Engineering and Economics from Birmingham University, an MSc in Environment and Pollution Control from Manchester University and is a graduate of the Corporate Finance Evening Program at London Business School.

Bruce Usher is the Elizabeth B. Strickler '86 and Mark T. Gallogly '86 Faculty Director of The Tamer Center for Social Enterprise at Columbia Business School in New York City, where he teaches MBA students on the intersection of finance, social and environmental issues. Mr. Usher is a recipient of the Dean's Award for Teaching Excellence. From 2002 to 2009, Usher was CEO of EcoSecurities Group plc, during which time he built it into the world's largest carbon credit company. Usher led EcoSecurities through an IPO, a secondary public placement and strategic investment, and the sale of the entire company to JP Morgan in December 2009. Mr. Usher was co-founder and CEO of TreasuryConnect LLC, which provided electronic trading solutions to banks and was acquired in 2001. Mr. Usher is on the Board of Community Energy Inc, a US solar project development company, and the United Nations Fund for International Partnerships. He earned an MBA with distinction from Harvard Business School.

Rolf Wüstenhagen is the Good Energies Professor for Management of Renewable Energies and head of the Center for Energy Innovation, Governance and Investment at the University of St. Gallen, Switzerland. He has held visiting faculty positions at University of British Columbia, Copenhagen Business School, National University Singapore and Tel Aviv University, and served as a lead author on the chapter on policy, financing and implementation of the IPCC special report on renewable energy sources and climate change mitigation. His research focuses on decision-making under uncertainty by energy investors, consumers and entrepreneurs, and how such choices are influenced by energy policy. Prior to his academic career, Dr. Wüstenhagen worked for one of the leading European energy venture capital funds.

Sufang Zhang is a professor of Energy Economics and Energy Policy at the School of Economics and Management, North China Electric Power University (NCEPU). She is also an energy policy consultant of the Asian Development Bank and a research fellow at the Research Centre for Beijing Energy Development. Before joining the NCEPU in 1993, she had several years of working experience in government as a project officer in charge of international programs. Dr. Zhang's current research focuses on wind power and solar PV power policy in China.

Section I

Introduction to Renewable Energy Finance

Charles Donovan, Principal Teaching Fellow,
Imperial College Business School

Following a steep fall in the oil price in the early 1980s, the renewable energy industry was nearly decimated. Significant investments by large oil companies such as Exxon in solar photovoltaics (PVs) were sold off or abandoned and interest in the sector stagnated for nearly two decades. At the end of the last century, only two countries, Japan and the US, were producers of solar PV panels and total investment in the renewable energy sector as a whole bordered on trivial.

Fast forward to the present day and we see a much more promising landscape. Rising energy security concerns, mounting ecological problems, and remarkable technological innovation have reshaped perceptions about solar and other forms of renewable energy. Countries are now competing fiercely to establish themselves as players in the global supply chain for renewable energy equipment. China, nowhere on the scene 15 years ago, now invests more in renewable energy than the whole of Europe. Renewable energy, excluding large hydropower, attracts more than US$200 billion in annual investment (BNEF, 2014), within striking distance of the gross amount invested in fossil fuel power generation plants each year. Yet despite many positive indicators, there remains a real risk of a reversal in fortunes. Will lower oil prices, government austerity, and the lack of a meaningful international political agreement on climate change yet again darken the outlook for renewables?

The core motivation for *Renewable Energy Finance* is to bring to a wider audience the challenges associated with continued growth of investment in non-fossil fuel energy. Lofty goals, such as those made by the United Nations, calling for a tripling of the annual rate of investment in renewable energy within the coming decade, will not in of themselves deliver results. Numerous stakeholders, including government, industry and civil society, are responsible for the work needed to make a transition towards a clean energy future. The perspectives of leading academics and finance executives contained in this book will contribute to a deeper understanding of the magnitude of the task ahead and a sense of optimism that the job can be done.

This introductory chapter is intended as a primer on renewable energy finance for non-specialists. As such, it provides useful background and helps frame information for the ensuing chapters. It has been written with the following objectives:

- Define recurring terms used throughout the book.
- Describe the concept of risk and return and its role in financial decision-making.
- Identify some of the key difficulties of financing renewable energy at scale.
- Highlight the major topics to be explored by other chapter authors.

Historically, the energy sector has been comprised of state-owned companies. This situation began to change in the 1990s, as privatization and liberalization induced a shift from governments to companies as the primary source of sector investment. The trend is highly pronounced in the field of renewable energy, where it is private sector investors, generating profits for shareholders, who are the major actors in financing new renewable energy projects. The renewable energy industry is still in the process of building relationships with these providers of capital. Making green energy the mainstream choice for new energy infrastructure will require expanding access to a diverse spectrum of private sector investors around the world. An important premise of this book is that a better understanding of investors and their motives may help reduce the risk of another false dawn for a future powered by renewable energy.

Defining the Landscape

Understanding renewable energy from a financial point of view requires the definition of key terms. Finance has its own language, and it seems no matter where you go in the world these days, that language reflects the trends of globalization. In short, money speaks English. But although the language of finance has a common tongue, it remains poorly understood and commonly confused. Academics, practitioners, and the media may use the same words, but often mean different things.

An **investment** involves an exchange of money for a claim on benefits to be generated by some asset. Investments can be made as **equity** (a form of partial ownership) or as **debt** (money loaned by one party to another). Assets can be defined in many different ways, following academic or popular conventions. For the present discussion, we shall identify assets in one of two ways, as either real or financial. **Real assets** are those which come most readily to mind: steel structures, tracts of land, and heavy machinery. They are the foundations upon which all economic activity is built. **Financial assets** are less tangible, often having no physical properties whatsoever. Financial assets constitute a form of agreement between parties. They range from the straightforward (a certificate of deposit at your local savings bank) to the highly exotic (equity derivatives structured by a global investment bank).

Investors are buyers of real and financial assets. While investors may be government or private sector entities, the primary focus in this book is on those in the private sector. Examples of private sector investors include:

- Corporations (electric utilities, oil and gas, consumer-facing industries).
- Retail Investors (individuals, family offices).

- Investment partnerships (hedge funds, private equity firms).
- Financial intermediaries (banks, insurance companies, pension funds).
- Endowment funds (foundations, universities).

Private sector investors in renewables have, historically, been made up of companies with an existing presence in the energy sector. Commonly referred to as **strategic investors**, these market participants often see a tight pairing between renewable energy and their core lines of business. Strategic investors may also refer to newly established companies for whom renewable energy *is* their core activity. **Financial investors** have also been involved since the early days of the industry, but their involvement was often limited to project-based loans offered by commercial banks. One of the most important developments in the renewable energy sector over the past decade is how this situation has begun to change. Hedge funds and private equity firms are now frequent participants, and there is increasing action amongst insurance companies, pension funds, and endowment funds. Unlike strategic investors, financial investors usually have no specific impetus for getting involved in renewable energy and have not been obligated by governments to do so. As funding sources, they are quickly prone to flight during turbulent market conditions.

The key factor that sets financial investors apart from strategic investors is their preference for financial assets versus real assets. Financial investors also typically maintain a portfolio of investments in more than one asset class. An **asset class** is a grouping of assets that share similar risk/return characteristics. Major asset classes include:

- Equities.
- Fixed income.
- Real estate.
- Commodities.
- Derivatives.

Investments in the renewable energy sector span multiple asset classes. Investors may, for example, buy shares in publicly traded renewable energy companies (equities), lend directly to clean energy projects (fixed income), have ownership in manufacturing and production facilities (real estate), and speculate on the price of outputs such as electricity, liquid fuel or emissions allowances (commodities). Renewable energy is, therefore, not as an asset class itself, but rather a sub-category within several asset classes. Thinking of clean energy investment as a set of **asset class categories** is helpful in positioning the sector more exactly within the universe of investment opportunities available to large capital providers.

The Guiding Principles of Risk and Return

Investors use risk and financial return as their primary criteria for deciding whether to invest in a particular asset class. Some market participants are constrained by strategic aims or may have specific fiduciary responsibilities preventing certain types of investments. Many more will simply be on the sidelines, waiting for the data about risk and return in an asset class to become clear. For all investors, the key question about a new investment prospect is one of valuation: *Does the price at which the asset is trading today offer a good prospect for capital appreciation over time?* To answer this question, investment decision-makers choose an appropriate means of **asset pricing**.

Asset pricing methods differ according to the asset class being analyzed, and investor sophistication. A large hedge fund does not, for example, evaluate sovereign bonds in the same way that a retiree would examine equities. Nonetheless, there is a generalized analytical process undertaken in asset pricing, represented by Cochrane (2005) as follows:

$$P_t = E\,(m_{t+1}\,x_{t+1})$$

Where
P_t = asset price,
x_{t+1} = asset payoff, and
m_{t+1} = stochastic discount factor.

The equation describes the price of an asset as a function of its expected payoff (i.e. the anticipated cash flows) and a **discount rate**.

There are a range of analytical techniques for estimating a discount rate, some employing mind-boggling computational methods. But regardless of how complicated, a discount rate has embedded within it two basic judgements. The first is an estimation of the **time value of money**. This element of the discount rate compensates an investor for receiving a secure payment at some date in the future, rather than today. The second judgement is about the likelihood and timing of receiving the expected future payment[1]. We refer to this as the **risk premium**.

While there is broad consensus that risk and return are the primary measures used by investors to evaluating investment attractiveness, there is considerable debate about the precise method for accurately measuring investment risk. We summarize here two of the most well-known schools of thought.

Among the most basic tenets of **portfolio theory** (Markowitz, 1959) is that investors hold a diversified bundle of financial assets and that investment risk is shaped by this diversification. Portfolio theory later gave rise to the **capital asset pricing model** (Sharpe, 1964; Lintner, 1965), in which investment risk is represented by a single mathematical coefficient. This coefficient, known as *Beta*, measures how the financial payoff from a specific asset varies in relation to the payoff from all assets in the market as a whole. Beta represents an asset's sensitivity to systematic risks faced by all investors. The capital asset pricing model (CAPM) is an analytical tool taught to nearly all aspiring finance practitioners around the world and cited as the most popular method amongst corporate finance directors for estimating company discount rates (Bruner *et al.*, 1998).

In contrast to the CAPM approach, **arbitrage pricing theory** (Ross, 1976) holds that discount rates are a function of multiple risk factors. Whereas using CAPM, investment risk varies according to just a single Beta term, arbitrage pricing theory (APT) places no restrictions on the number of risk factors to be used. The factors of an APT asset pricing model may include generic macroeconomic indicators

---

[1] In the interest of simplicity we do not differentiate between payments in the form of interest, dividends or capital gains.

such as government bond rates, oil prices and various forms of inflation, as well as asset-specific risk indicators, such as liquidity. Arbitrage pricing theory allows greater analyst discretion in representing the complexity of the real world of investing. This analytical discretion does, however, come with a cost — namely the loss of simplicity, replicability and standardization.

No matter what approach one takes to asset pricing, the basic analytical challenge remains the same. Investors must estimate their financial payoff by forecasting future cash flows from the asset. They must also compute an appropriate discount rate for the investment, taking into account investment risk. Stated most simply, the question of valuation asks whether the expected financial return is sufficient to compensate for the prevailing level of risk.

Renewable Energy as an Investment Type

Due to the numerous ways in which investments in the sector can be made and overlaps with other industrial sectors, renewable energy is challenging to characterize as an investment type. Renewable energy bears resemblance to other types of infrastructure investment, such as those in the water and transportation sectors. Like all these public services, the supply of energy from wind, solar, and biomass resources is regulated and subsidized. Renewable energy also has aspects in common with conventional energy developments, like oil and gas exploration. As with conventional energy, non-fossil fuel projects are capital intensive, requiring much of the life-cycle investment costs to be made upfront.

As an asset class category, renewable energy is most often compared to the conventional electric power sector. For some investors, electric power still carries the legacy of a chequered past. High-profile debacles such as the Dabhol gas-fired power project in India and the spate of bankruptcies that followed in the aftermath of the implosion at Enron have created long-lasting memories about getting burned in the power sector.

In addition to perceptions that spill over from other sectors, renewable energy has its own characteristics. By and large, investors are still in the process of recognizing the unique facts about renewable energy technologies, such as:

- With the exception of biomass, they have no fuel costs, leading to complex price interactions with fossil fuel technologies in marginal cost-driven markets.
- They generate commodities that may be costly to transport and/ or difficult to store.
- They encompass a broad range of technologies, each with distinct value chains, often having little technical resemblance to one another.
- Some rely upon the highly centralized energy networks for their viability, while others pose a competitive threat to them.
- Each renewable energy technology is at a different level of commercial readiness and cost competitiveness.

There are numerous implications that investors can draw about renewable energy in reaction to its inherent diversity and complexity. In the long term, many of these characteristics are what give renewable energy the potential to induce a radical shift in the current energy market paradigm. But in the short term, these sources of complexity have created confusion amongst investors regarding the predictability of risk and return for renewable energy investments.

Financing Renewable Energy at Scale

Strategic investors, such as electric utilities, do not have the scale of financial resources at their disposal to meet the challenge of scaling up investment in clean energy at three to four times its current level. It is also becoming clear that renewable energy poses a direct competitive threat to the conventional utility business plan, straining the financial position of traditionally large players (Gillis, 2014). Awareness is growing that increased funding by financial investors will be necessary to meet renewable energy investment goals. But rather than replacing the investments being made by energy companies, direct funding from the capital markets should be viewed as complementary.

Increased participation by financial investors will help unburden utility balance sheets and encourage redeployment of funds into early-stage development projects.

Packaging mature investments with relatively stable risk–return profiles to large financial investors, while still embryonic, is a rapidly growing area of renewable energy finance. As stated previously, many large investors — regulated financial intermediaries, in particular — tend to prefer financial assets, as these assets tend to offer important benefits to investors, namely:

- Scale (the capacity to absorb sizable capital inflows/outflows).
- Liquidity (frequent trading that allows securities to be bought or sold immediately).

Investing in real assets, for example via direct ownership of an offshore wind farm, does not offer the necessary scale or liquidity that many investors need to adequately manage an investment portfolio. While an offshore wind farm may be quite large, the investment opportunity is capped by the size of a single project. Furthermore, the investor is effectively stuck in the project until a subsequent buyer can be found. Contrast this situation with the market for large government bonds, which offer supply far greater than any single investor could absorb, and transactions to buy or sell occur in a matter of seconds.

A growing trend in the renewable energy investment is for real assets to be transformed into financial assets. It is a form of commoditization playing out across nearly all fields of environmental protection and ecological restoration (Sandor *et al.*, 2013). Making investment in clean power and renewable fuels available to investors as financial assets has the potential to unlock access to a US$600 trillion pool of global finance capital, nearly three times greater than the stock of real assets that underpin all economic activity in the global economy (Bain & Company, 2012).

The transformation of geothermal power stations, biofuel refineries and solar energy facilities into financial assets can be accomplished through packaging of asset backed securities (ABS). As their name implies, ABS are financial assets whose income is generated from a collection of real assets. They are difficult to define precisely, as their exact nature depends upon the regulations of the country in which they are issued. In the US, the world's deepest capital market, renewable energy assets have been used as collateral to create real estate investment trusts (REIT), C-Corporations ('Yield Co'), and sector-specific debt securities (climate bonds). Common to all these forms of financing is their direct link to the capital markets.

Having stable cash flows and no fuel price risk, the returns from renewable energy financial assets may be weakly correlated or entirely uncorrelated to those of the major asset classes. For portfolio inves-tors, weak correlations are a favorable indicator of attractiveness as they reduce measured risk. It is incumbent upon the industry to dem-onstrate a track record of performance that firmly establishes whether it offers a diversification benefit to portfolio investors. To the degree it does, renewable energy will be attract sizable investment at extraor-dinarily low discount rates (Awerbuch, 2007).

Laying Conceptual Foundations for a Renewable Energy Future

One of the key messages of this introductory chapter is that the required rate of return for private sector investors is a function of risk. Although most investors have by now turned over the task of risk assessment to highly intelligent machines, risk will never be defined solely by data. Risk is a product not just of numbers, but also of ideas. Even in the realm of highly quantitative finance, it remains a judge-ment shaped by interpretations and beliefs. No amount of data or sophisticated modelling will ever provide a complete answer to the question about what rate of return investors will demand from renew-able energy projects in exchange for their money. Policymakers, aca-demics, the investment community and the general public all play a role in shaping the idea of risk that ends up being held in an invest-ment decision-maker's mind.

There is nonetheless, a purely objective aspect of risk assessment that cannot be avoided. Information about risk and return on common asset classes such as equities, bonds and commodities are available to investors instantaneously at any time of day, in any language, all over the world. As an asset class category, renewable energy is still in the very early days of establishing itself. A key task ahead is for the industry to generate a history of investment performance. Although historical returns are not always a reliable guide to the future, transparency about past investment performance will be necessary for investors — financial investors, in particular — to understand and articulate a story about risk and return in the renewable energy sector to their investment committees.

Looking Forward

The volume of capital needed for a widespread transition towards a renewable energy economy will require increasing participation of financial investors and continued adoption of innovative financing techniques. This need not undermine the importance of the continued role for strategic investors. It is, after all, within utilities, project development companies, and network operators that most of the technical knowledge about renewable energy is to be found. But it is also evident that for a step-change to occur in capital flows to the sector going forward, funding must increasingly come from financial investors. These new players will need to be brought into the game, while retaining the core investors who have brought the industry to its current level. The thirteen chapters of *Renewable Energy Finance* tell important elements of the story of how to achieve this new balance.

The chapters in Section One lay the groundwork by defining key terms and exploring the major drivers for the expansion of renewable energy. Section One will be of particular interest to readers looking for an in-depth explanation of the characteristics of the heterogeneous set of technologies that make up renewable energy. These initial chapters consider the costs of different forms of renewable energy and their prospects for competitive dominance in wholesale and retail energy markets.

A common theme to all the chapters in Section Two is the inextricable link between energy markets and government policy. The authors describe the main ways in which governments support renewable energy, and identify general principles of how policy influences investment decisions. Lessons learned over two decades of government support for renewables are drawn out, with a particular focus on experiences to date in China and developing countries. The section closes with a study of the impact of carbon pricing policies on investors in Europe.

Section Three delves into the real world of investing and considers the challenges and opportunities for commercial banks, private equity funds, institutional asset managers, and retail investors. The authors of these chapters take up the difficult work of sorting through the changes that have occurred since the financial crisis of 2008 and charting the future direction for specific of investors. The collection of chapters in Section Three touch upon recent innovations in renewable energy financing such as leasing and crowdfunding, as well as the adaptation of long-time corporate and project funders to the evolving dynamics of the financing market.

In all, the three sections of this book seek to illuminate the foundations upon which a renewable energy future can be built. There are many actions to be taken in the years ahead to broaden the investor base for renewable energy in the future. We hope that readers will find *Renewable Energy Finance* to be a resource that they return to many times over the ensuing years to deepen their understanding of this important topic — and hence, their courage to act.

References

Awerbuch, S. (2007). Unpublished book manuscript. Available at: http://www.awerbuch.com [accessed 17 April 2012].

Bain & Company, Inc. (2012). 'A World Awash in Money: Capital Trends through 2020'. Available at: http://www.bain.com/publications/articles/a-world-awash-in-money.aspx [accessed 19 December 2014].

Bloomberg New Energy Finance (2014). 'Global Trends in Renewable Energy Investment 2014'. Available at: http://fs-unep-centre.org/publications/gtr-2014 [accessed 22 December 2014].

Bruner, R. F., Eades, K. M., Harris, R. S. and Higgins, R. C. (1998). 'Best practices in estimating the cost of capital: Survey and synthesis', *Financial Practice and Education*, **8**, 13–28.

Cochrane, J. (2005). *Asset Pricing (Revised Edition)*, Princeton University Press, Princeton.

Gillis, J. (2014). 'Sun and Wind Alter Global Landscape, Leaving Utilities Behind', *The New York Times*. Available at: http://www.nytimes.com [accessed 10 October 2014].

Lintner, J. (1965). 'Security Prices, Risk, and Maximal Gains from Diversification', *Journal of Finance*, **20(4)**, 587–615.

Markowitz, H. M. (1959). *Portfolio Selection: Efficient Diversification of Investments*, John Wiley and Sons, New York.

Ross, S. A. (1976). 'The Arbitrage Theory of Capital Asset Pricing', *Journal of Economic Theory*, **13**, 341–360.

Sharpe, W. F. (1964). 'Capital Asset Prices: A Theory of Market Equilibrium under Conditions of Risk, *Journal of Finance*, **19(3)**, 425–442.

Sandor, R., Clark, N., Kanakasabai, M. and Marques, R. (2013). 'Environmental Markets: A New Asset Class', CFA Institute Research Foundation. Available at: www.cfainstitute.org/foundation [accessed 5 November 2014].

Chapter One

The Clean Energy Imperative

Jim Skea, Professor of Sustainable Energy,
Imperial College London

Introduction

Some forms of renewable energy are well established and are playing a growing role in global energy markets. This growth is being driven by a mixture of market forces and policy intervention. It is vital to understand how these forces interact.

This chapter starts with an overview of drivers for the expansion of renewable energy, focusing particularly on climate change and the reduction of carbon dioxide (CO_2) emissions. The chapter then moves on to look at the status and characteristics of the heterogeneous set of technologies that make up renewable energy, focusing on technical characteristics, the maturity of technology and environmental and other impacts. Next, we look at the changing role of renewables in energy markets, noting in particular the rapidly growing deployment of wind, solar photovoltaics (PV) and transport biofuels. While there is a universal perception that renewable energy will continue to grow, the assessment points out that there is less agreement about the rate of deployment and the balance between different forms of renewable energy. A key differentiator between different scenarios is the level of commitment to ambitious climate change policies. The next section looks at trends in the costs of different forms of renewable energy, noting that, while emerging renewable technologies are cost-competitive in some markets, most renewable investments still require policy support. The final section reviews, at a high level, existing policies to support renewable energy, plans proposed for the future, and potential risks for investors in this changing landscape.

The Challenge of Fossil Fuels and the Promise of Renewable Energy

Three factors are traditionally cited as driving the move towards clean, renewable and non-depletable energy sources. They are environmental considerations (notably, climate change), security of supply and resource scarcity. The latter justification is weakening: innovative approaches for extracting oil and gas from once unyielding geological formations have transformed the resource situation. Tight gas and shale gas, especially in the US, have taken resource scarcity out of the energy debate for a very long time. Figures 1.1 and 1.2 show global resources of technically recoverable oil and gas (International Energy

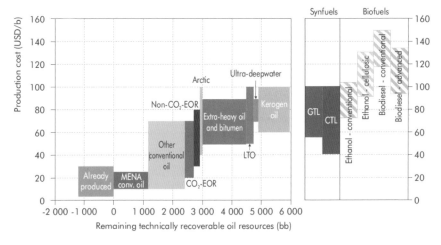

Fig. 1.1:   Oil production costs for various resource categories (Source: International Energy Agency, 2013c)

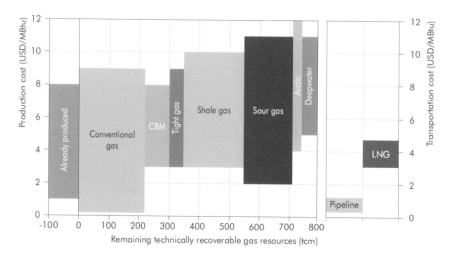

Fig. 1.2: Long-term gas supply cost curve (Source: International Energy Agency, 2013c)

Agency, 2013c). Oil resources, excluding synfuels and biofuels, are equivalent to 180 years consumption at current levels and gas resources equivalent to 230 years consumption. The world's pursuit of clean energy must be based on motivations other than resource scarcity.

Environmental challenges, particularly climate change, provide the most enduring policy motivation for promoting renewable energy. The Intergovernmental Panel on Climate Change (IPCC) Fifth Assessment Report (AR5) has concluded that 'warming of the climate system is unequivocal' and that 'human influence on the climate system is clear' (Intergovernmental Panel on Climate Change, 2013). The IPCC has drawn attention to a clear correlation between cumulative emissions of CO_2 into the atmosphere from human activities and global temperature increases, both historically and based on modelling of future emissions (Fig. 1.3).

Signatories to the UN Framework Convention on Climate Change (UNFCCC) have recognised that, in order to meet the Convention objective of 'avoiding dangerous anthropogenic interference with the atmosphere', 'deep cuts in global greenhouse gas emissions are required ... with a view to reducing global greenhouse gas emissions so as to hold the increase in global average temperature below 2 °C above pre-industrial levels'. Fig. 1.3 shows that total

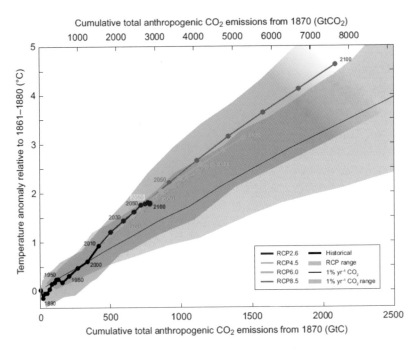

Fig. 1.3: Global mean surface temperature increase as a function of cumulative total global CO_2 emissions (Source: Intergovernmental Panel on Climate Change, 2013)

future CO_2 emissions will need to be limited to about 1,000 Gt CO_2 if this goal is to be attained. Anthropogenic CO_2 emissions in 2010 were about 38 Gt CO_2 with 32 Gt (or 86%) originating in the energy sector (Victor and Zhou, 2014). Without new action on climate change, the world could warm by 3.1–4.8 °C during the 21st century (Intergovernmental Panel on Climate Change, 2014a), with major consequences for physical systems (glaciers, rivers, coasts), ecosystems and human systems (food production, health, livelihoods).

Meeting the 2 °C goal requires cuts in global emissions of between 40% and 70% by 2050 from 2010 levels (Intergovernmental Panel on Climate Change, 2014b). This requires a major up-scaling of low emissions energy supply such as renewables. Even if mitigation efforts were to fall short of the 2 °C goal, significant increases in renewable energy deployment are required.

The Status of Renewable Energy

Overview

The terms *clean* and *renewable* energy need to be approached with caution. Nor are the terms synonymous. Renewable energy covers a diversity of energy sources, joined only by the common feature that they rely directly on solar radiation, either directly, as it falls on the Earth, or indirectly, through interactions with hydrological, marine and biological systems. Even this is not entirely true — geothermal energy relies on heat from deep within the Earth's core. Nor can renewable energy unambiguously be said to be clean, although there are manifest environmental advantages compared to fossil fuels. The other characteristic of renewable energy is that resources are usually geographically specific. Some forms of renewable energy, such as solar, wind and bioenergy, are quite ubiquitous and can be exploited in many different regions. Other forms of renewable energy such as hydro, geothermal and tidal/ocean energy tend to be location specific with fewer opportunities for global replication.

Table 1.1 draws out the diversity of different renewable energy sources and highlights some of the environmental aspects. There is a strong distinction to be made between bioenergy and other renewables such as wind and solar and these are therefore treated separately.

Renewables other than bioenergy

Renewables other than bioenergy tend to take the form of 'plug and play' installations that produce, most often, power, but also heat, for direct use or for input into energy networks. Non-bioenergy renewables are generally 'zero-carbon' in the sense that in normal operation they do not give rise to CO_2 emissions. This does not mean that life-cycle emissions are zero, as there are CO_2 emissions associated with equipment manufacture and maintenance. However, these emissions tend to be very low compared to the fossil fuel alternatives (Committee on Climate Change, 2013).

Most forms of renewable energy tend to have operating costs that are low in comparison to their initial capital costs. However, this

Table 1.1: Characteristics of different types of renewable energy

Type of renewable energy	Maturity	Energy vectors	Storage and dispatch	Capital intensity	Geographical scope	Climate change impacts	Other environmental impacts
Solar PV	Different technologies range from research and development (R&D) to maturity	Power	No	High	Widespread but more resource in low latitudes	'Zero' carbon	
Concentrated solar power (CSP)	Demonstration	Power	Can integrate storage	High	Low latitudes	'Zero' carbon	Water resources and pollution
Solar thermal	Mature	Heat	Yes	High	Widespread but more resource in low latitudes	'Zero' carbon	
Wind	Mature/early deployment offshore	Power	No	High	Widespread, but large variations	'Zero' carbon	Landscape, noise, bird life
Hydro	Mature	Power	Partly	High	Location specific	'Zero' carbon	Land use, hydrological, ecosystem impacts
Tidal barrage	Mature	Power	Partly	High	Location specific	'Zero' carbon	Marine, ecosystem impacts
Tidal stream	Demonstration	Power	No	High	Location specific	'Zero' carbon	Marine environment

Wave energy	Demonstration	Power	No	High	Location specific	'Zero' carbon	Marine environment
Other ocean	R&D	Power	No	High	Location specific	'Zero' carbon	Marine environment
Geothermal	Mature	Heat and power	Dispatchable, can integrate storage	High	Location specific	'Zero' carbon	Land use, ecosystem impacts, water resources and pollution
Traditional biomass	Mature	Heat and light	Yes	Low	Low income countries		Adverse human health effects
Biomass heat and power	Mature, but further development possible	Heat and power	Yes	Medium		Low if forests managed sustainably	Air pollution if not strictly regulated
Biofuels first generation	Mature in some countries	Liquid fuel	Storable	Medium	Widespread but the nature of the resource geographically dependent	Modest or even negative benefits compared to fossil	Food v fuel and indirect land use change
Biofuels second generation	Development and demonstration	Liquid fuel	Storable	Medium	Widespread	Greater benefits compared to fossil	Indirect land use change
Biogas	Demonstration, deployed small-scale	Gas	Storable	Medium	Widespread	Low if managed sustainably	Ecosystem impacts

is not to say that operating costs (which can range from replacing wind turbine blades through to removing dust from solar panels in desert environments), are negligible but simply that the balance between capital and operating costs is different from fossil fuels. This has implications for the deployment of renewable energy into systems that were designed for less capital-intensive forms of energy. For instance, many electricity systems are based on 'energy-only' markets with prices continuously varying. This volatility creates uncertainty about revenue streams and are better managed by operators of fossil plants who have a natural hedge since electricity prices tend to be correlated with the prices of input fossil fuels. The absolute cost of renewable energy *vis-à-vis* competing fossil fuel alternatives is discussed below.

The variability, or intermittency, of output from forms of renewable energy such as wind or solar poses challenges for large-scale integration into existing electricity networks where supply and demand must balance. Low levels of penetration (<20%) can be accommodated relatively easily (Gross and Heptonstall, 2006). The need to provide back-up capacity to cover periods of low output adds to the cost of integrating these forms of renewables. Other ways of dealing with, and potentially reducing the cost of, the integration of renewables include energy storage and greater interconnection between different energy networks. The development of smart grids that allow levels of demand to adjust to fluctuating levels of supply would also help to manage intermittency.

The wider environmental impacts of renewable energy are diverse, depending largely on whether they are deployed in urban, rural or marine environments. For sources other than bioenergy, environmental impacts are generally location specific and can be addressed through siting decisions and effective environmental management of projects.

Bioenergy

Bioenergy is a system concept, referring to numerous supply chains covering crop cultivation, harvesting, processing, transport, conversion and final use. Bioenergy involves tradable products which can be in solid form (biomass), liquid form (biofuels) or gaseous form (biogases). Operating costs are high relative to capital costs. Bioenergy can be stored, and installations relying on bioenergy fuels can be 'dispatched', in the sense that they can be called upon, or their output curtailed, when required. In a sense, the bioenergy system mirrors the fossil fuel system. One of the attractions of bioenergy is that it can readily be dropped into existing energy systems — for example by converting coal-fired power stations, blending biofuels with transport fuels or injecting biogas into existing networks.

Accounting for CO_2 emissions from bioenergy supply chains is complex and controversial (European Environment Agency Scientific Committee, 2011). In principle, bioenergy cycles can be carbon neutral because the CO_2 emitted during combustion is balanced by CO_2 sequestered from the atmosphere during crop growth. However, this depends on crops being cultivated sustainably and this condition is not met if, for example, mature forests are cut down. There are also emissions associated with cultivation, harvesting, processing and transport. Figure 1.4 compares greenhouse gas (GHG) emissions associated with a range of bioenergy chains and their fossil fuel alternatives.

The situation is further complicated because, under international rules, bioenergy emissions are accounted for under the agriculture, forestry and land use (AFOLU) sector rather than the energy sector, in which emissions at the point of combustion are assigned a zero value. This can incentivise countries whose emissions are capped (for example under the Kyoto Protocol or the EU Emissions Trading Scheme (ETS)), to import bioenergy from countries whose emissions are not capped. This results in emission reductions lower than they are given credit for and could, in the worst cases, result in increases in emissions. This problem is acknowledged (European Environment Agency Scientific Committee, 2011) and has resulted in the development of 'sustainability frameworks', or regulatory approaches designed to screen out unsustainable uses of bioenergy. These frameworks can themselves be controversial because of their interaction with World Trade Organization (WTO) rules.

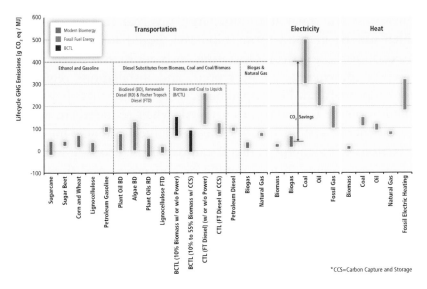

Fig. 1.4: GHG emissions per unit energy output (MJ) from major modern bioenergy chains (Source: Chum, Faaij and Moreira , 2011)

The use of traditional biomass can have severe adverse effects on human health through air pollution. Adopting improved combustion technologies and switching to electricity and modern commercial fuels is desirable. All forms of bioenergy production have land use implications and the displacement of land that would otherwise be used for food crops is a particular concern. The use of food crops such as corn or sugar for energy purposes can also put upward pressure on food prices. The development of second-generation bioenergy, based on processing the lignocellulosic (woody) portion of biomass from non-food crops such as miscanthus (switch grass) or willow/poplar trees, offers the opportunity to both reduce CO_2 emissions and better manage food-versus-fuel tensions.

Technology maturity and emerging markets

Individual renewable energy technologies vary greatly in their maturity and the degree to which they have been deployed, either on grounds of cost advantage or as a result of public subsidies. Traditional biomass has been used for millennia and is still used for cooking and lighting in many developing countries. In low income countries, it makes a major contribution to meeting energy demand. Biomass is also used for electricity and heat production using more advanced technologies in forested temperate countries, for example in Scandinavia and the Baltic states. Hydro-electricity is a mature technology which has been established since the 19th century and the capacity of the largest facilities is in thousands of megawatts. Solar and wind power are on the cusp of full commercial deployment and are cost competitive with fossil fuel alternatives in certain locations. However, some forms of renewable energy, notably advanced solar, wave, tidal stream and second generation biofuels are still at the demonstration stage and/or require further investment in research and development (R&D).

Renewable energy already meets almost 13% of global primary energy demand, a proportion that has not moved significantly since 1990 (Fig. 1.5). However, 70% of this is in the form of biomass (including traditional biomass) and waste, with most of the remainder accounted for by types of renewable energy that can only be delivered as electricity. Growth in renewables has proceeded at roughly the same pace as energy demand in general, around 2% per annum.

The contribution of renewables to electricity production globally was in decline from the mid-1990s but turned sharply upwards from 2003 to reach a 20% market share in 2011 (Fig. 1.6). Most of the growth of 3.6% per annum from 2003–2011 is accounted for by increased hydro output in absolute terms, but the fastest rates of growth were associated with wind and solar energy. Together, they grew at 29% per annum from 2001–2011 (Fig. 1.7) with wind in developed (OECD) countries accounting for most of the growth, but with wind in emerging economies (notably China) and solar energy in developed countries picking up from 2004 onwards. Wind and solar energy now meet about 4% of electricity demand in both developed and developing countries.

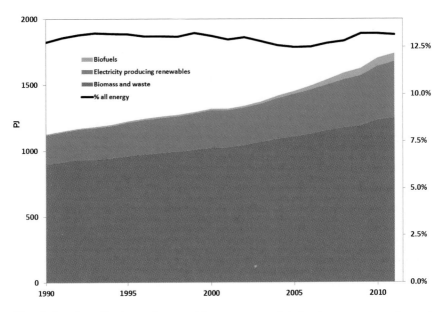

Fig. 1.5: Contribution of renewable energy to global primary energy demand (Source: International Energy Agency, 2013d)

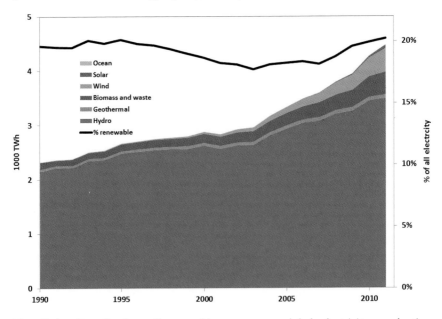

Fig. 1.6: Contribution of renewable energy to global electricity production (Source: International Energy Agency, 2013d)

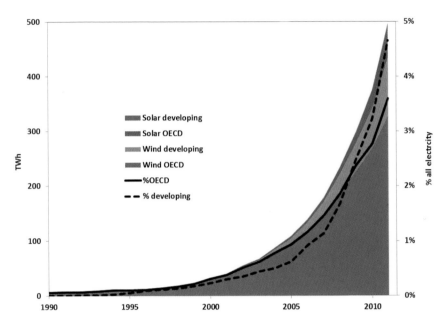

Fig. 1.7:　Growth of wind and solar energy output (Source: International Energy Agency, 2013a)

Figure 1.8 shows that global wind energy capacity has now reached over 300 GW, with six countries — China, Germany, India, Spain, the UK and the US — accounting for 75% of capacity. Capacity in China and the UK doubled between 2010 and 2013. There is a similar concentration of capacity in rapidly growing PV generation (Fig. 1.9). Again, six countries — China, Germany, Italy, Japan, Spain and the US — account for 75% of capacity.

Liquid biofuels for transport currently meet about 2% of transport fuel demand (Fig. 1.10). Supply grew at 21% per annum between 2001 and 2011 but growth slowed to 8% between 2010 and 2011. Two thirds of manufactured liquid biofuels are in the form of ethanol (which substitutes for gasoline/petrol) with the remainder made up by biodiesel. Brazil was the first country to have a major push on ethanol based on sugar cane but its ethanol use was overtaken by the US, using corn ethanol, in 2003. The use of ethanol is heavily concentrated in a small number of countries with China and Canada two other significant producers. Ethanol production has been motivated

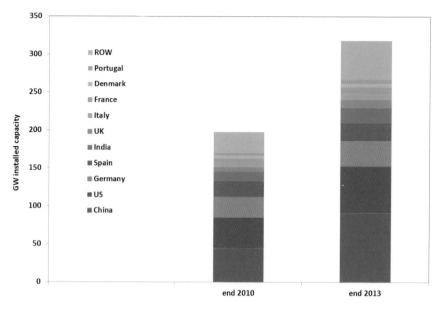

Fig. 1.8: Growth in wind capacity by country 2010–2013 (Source: Global Wind Energy Council, 2014)

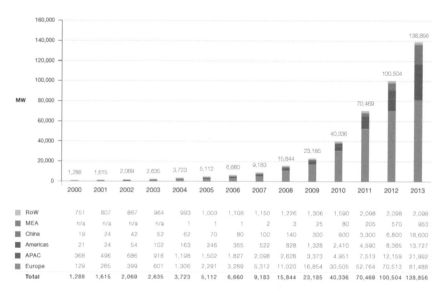

Fig. 1.9: Evolution of global PV cumulative installed capacity 2000–2013 (Source: European Photovoltaic Industry Association, 2014)

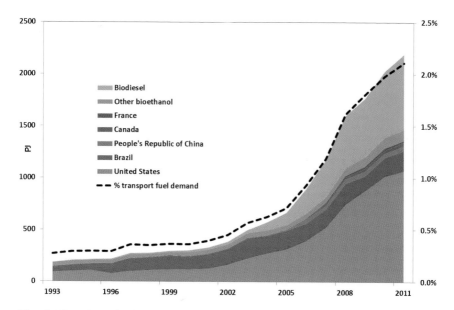

Fig. 1.10: Growth of transport biofuel production (Source: International Energy Agency, 2013b)

by the desire to exploit indigenous energy resources and displace imported fossil fuels, rather than to reduce CO_2 emissions.

The use of biodiesel is much more widely distributed than the use of ethanol, but EU countries account for about 45% of the global total as a result of a policy drive to increase the proportion of transport fuels sourced from bioenergy.

This brief review shows that the 'hotspots' for renewable energy development are wind energy, solar power and transport biofuels. These have significant global potential. This is not to say that other forms of renewable energy lack potential, but technologies that have yet to be deployed at scale, such as wave or tidal, are probably candidates for development in niche markets or in specific locations.

A Range of Futures for Renewable Energy

Only a few organisations that publish outlooks or scenarios for energy at the global level identify the role of specific types of renewable energy. It can be difficult to compare even aggregate projections of renewable energy because of different conventions for reporting primary energy and the inclusion or otherwise of traditional biomass. This section focuses on the three most important forms of 'new' renewable energy where markets have expanded rapidly — wind, solar and transport biofuels — looking at medium-term prospects up to 2030. The three bodies reporting their projections in sufficient detail to allow a meaningful comparison are: the US Energy Information Administration (EIA, 2013); the International Energy Agency (IEA, 2014); and Royal Dutch Shell (Shell, 2013).

The projections of these organisations follow different philosophies and this has implications for interpretation. The EIA generates an 'outlook' to 2040 involving an extrapolation of current trends based on foreseeable developments and assumptions about energy prices and economic growth. Sensitivities to prices and growth are explored, but otherwise it is a 'business-as-usual' scenario.

The IEA produces scenarios up to 2050 which depend on different assumptions about the strength of climate change policies. The IEA 6 °C Scenario (6DS) is essentially an extrapolation analogous to the EIA outlook. The 4 °C Scenario (4DS) assumes that countries fulfil the pledges that they made at the UNFCCC Conference of the Parties (the 'Cancun pledges') in 2010. This results in lower projected CO_2 emissions. The 2 °C Scenario (2DS) is normative in character. It assumes that the UNFCC goal of limiting temperature increases to 2 °C is attained, and develops the pathways and technology deployment patterns consistent with meeting that goal at least cost. The Shell New Lens scenarios (such as the Mountains scenario and Oceans scenario) like the IEA's 2DS, are not 'business-as-usual'. They explore alternative futures underpinned by qualitative storylines about broader social and economic trends.

In the Shell Mountains scenario, 'status quo power is locked in, resulting in rigidity within the system which dampens economic dynamism and stifles social mobility'. In the Oceans scenario, 'power is devolved, competing interests and economic productivity, while social cohesion is sometimes eroded and politics destabilised. Market forces have greater prominence'. The Shell scenarios challenge both company and outsiders to consider how robust their strategies are against a variety of outcomes for energy markets.

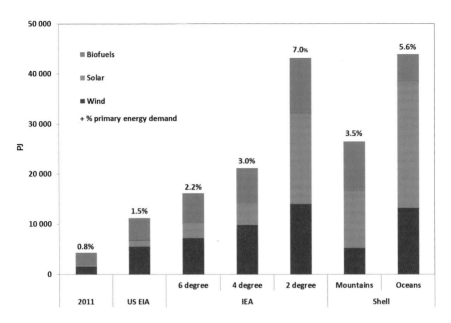

Fig. 1.11: 'New' renewable energy in 2030 in various scenarios (Source: IEA, 2014; Shell, 2013; EIA, 2013)

Figure 1.11 shows the market shares of wind, solar and transport biofuels in each of these scenarios compared with their shares in 2011. The contributions of the three forms of renewables rise in all scenarios and, given the variety in the underlying assumptions, this is a very robust conclusion. The EIA and the three IEA scenarios, with increasing levels of climate policy ambition, form a progression in terms of market share of primary energy demand. In the EIA outlook, the market share of the 'new' renewables doubles from 0.8% to 1.5%, while in the IEA 2DS scenario market share rises by an order of magnitude to 7.0%.

The contributions of the individual forms of renewable energy grow at very different rates. Wind surpasses transport biofuels in all scenarios. Solar energy makes the lowest contribution in all scenarios except IEA 2DS where it easily overtakes both wind and biofuels. The IEA 2DS, with its high level of ambition, is markedly different from the others in terms of renewable contributions. The average annual growth rates between 2011 and 2030 range from 2.6% (EIA outlook) to 8.2% (2DS) for biofuels, from 6.2% to 12.2% for wind, and from 8.0% to 25.2% for solar. Even against the conservative assumptions in the EIA outlook, these are impressive growth rates.

The Shell scenarios are intended to challenge, and deserve separate attention. Renewables make rapid progress in the bottom–up, market-driven Oceans scenario and their market share is comparable to that in the IEA 2DS. The one exception, however, is that transport biofuel demand is almost as low as in the EIA outlook. The Oceans scenario explicitly assumes a breakthrough for solar energy which grows at an annual average rate of rate of 28% from 2011 to 2030. In the top–down status quo-led Mountains scenario, renewables make much slower progress, with wind energy output following below the level in the EIA outlook. However, solar and biofuels are somewhere between the IEA 2DS and 4DS. In general, the Shell scenarios are more bullish about solar energy than they are about wind.

The key messages are that there are firm prospects for growth in all forms of 'new' energy, but that the level of growth is uncertain and is closely linked to the ambition of future climate policy. The balance of growth between different forms of energy is also uncertain.

Costs and Prices

The costs of many forms of renewable energy have fallen in the last few decades, allowing some projects to compete with conventional energy on cost grounds and reducing the need for subsidies for less cost-competitive projects. The investment costs associated with solar PV, for instance, have fallen by a factor of four to five over the last 20 years (Fig. 1.12) while those of onshore wind fell by about two thirds between the early 1980s and the year 2000, before starting to rise again (Fig. 1.13). The dramatic declines in PV costs can be attributed to 'learning-by-doing' as the industry has scaled up, and by the entry of low-cost producers, notably China. The initial decline in wind energy costs can be linked to learning-by-doing and by scale economies in individual turbines, whose individual capacities have risen from typically 75 kW in the 1980s to 2–5 MW at present (Turkenburg, 2012). The subsequent rise in costs can be attributed to a variety of

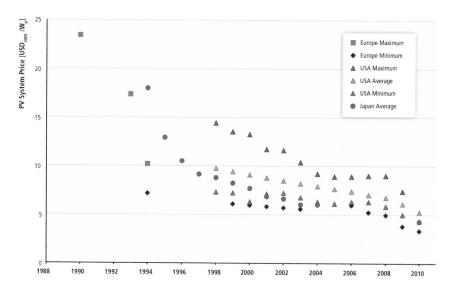

Fig. 1.12: Installed costs of PV systems smaller than 100 kW$_e$ in Europe, Japan and the US (Source: Arvizu and Balaya, 2011)

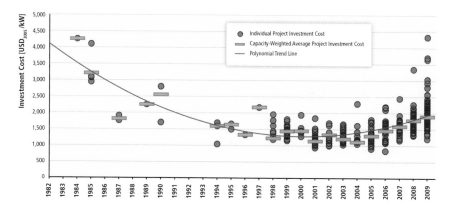

Fig. 1.13: Investment costs of onshore wind power plants in the US (Source: Wiser and Yang, 2011)

factors, including the cost of raw materials, the cost of constructing turbines with improved energy capture (which, however, drives down the cost of electricity generated) and congestion in supply chains as rising demand for new turbines has stretched supply capacity (Greenacre, Gross and Heptonstall, 2011; Wiser and Yang, 2011).

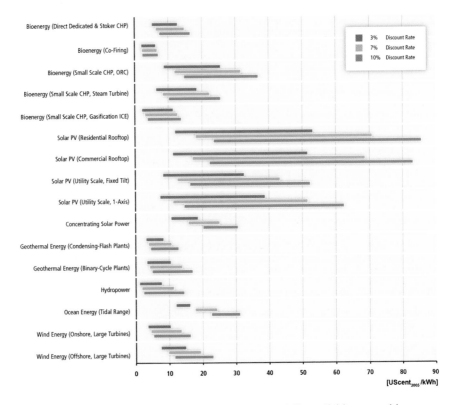

Fig. 1.14: Levelised costs of electricity for commercially available renewable energy technologies (Source: Fischedick and Schaeffer, 2011)

A key question for market development is whether the electricity generated from wind or solar, and the fuels derived from biomass, are cost competitive with incumbent fuels and technologies. There is no generic answer to that question because the cost of renewables is location specific and may vary quite widely.

Figure 1.14 shows the levelised cost of electricity from various forms of renewable energy computed at three different real discount rates — 3%, 5% and 7%. The higher discount rate would correspond better to rates of return required in a competitive generation market while 3% corresponds to a long-term social discount rate. For comparison, wholesale electricity prices in Europe in 2013 ranged from about 4.5 cents/kWh in Germany (European Power Exchange,

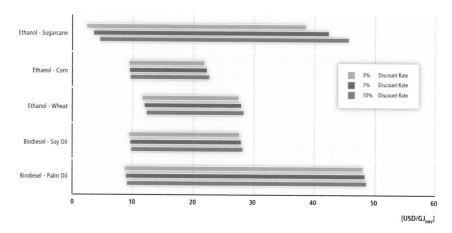

Fig. 1.15: Levelised costs of fuels for commercially available biomass conversion technologies (Source: Fischedick & Schaeffer, 2011)

2014) and Scandinavia (Nordpool, 2014) to around 7.5 cents/kWh in the UK (Energy–UK 2014)[1]. This suggests that many hydropower, geothermal and bioenergy projects could compete without subsidy in wholesale markets while some onshore wind projects have reached, or are approaching, that stage. It is unlikely that any solar or offshore wind projects could compete on that basis. The cost of solar power is very location specific depending strongly on the latitude and the degree of insolation.

However, small-scale solar energy, for example on residential roofs, would compete not with wholesale electricity prices but with retail. Within Europe, retail prices for household electricity range widely from 8.6–24.0 cents/kWh with an average of 16.3 cents (excluding taxes) while industrial prices range from 8.0–22.8 cents/kWh with an average of 11.0 cents/kWh (International Energy Agency, 2012). Prices tend to be higher in Southern Europe where insolation is greater. On that basis, many solar projects would be cost competitive.

The costs of transport fuels from biomass also vary greatly (Fig. 1.15). With the pre-tax price of motor spirit in the range

---

[1] These prices are converted to 2005 US$ for compatibility with Fig. 1.15.

US$20–25/GJ in most developed countries (International Energy Agency, 2012), it is apparent that a wide range of bioenergy chains can provide transportation fuels at competitive prices. Sugarcane ethanol, as produced in Brazil, appears to be particularly cost competitive.

The Role of Policy

While some renewable energy sources are — or are on their way — to being cost competitive, many still need policy support if projects are to come forward. There is now considerable experience with implementing policies to support renewable energy. Renewables will also benefit from cross-cutting policies that establish a price for carbon, and thus penalise fossil fuels. However, carbon prices, notably in the EU Emissions Trading Scheme (ETS), have been too low and too uncertain to stimulate investment in low-carbon technologies by themselves. Even where a carbon price has been in place, targeted support for renewable energy has provided the main incentive for investment. The rationale for targeted support is that the external costs associated with climate change represent only one of the market failures linked to renewable energy. Targeted support can, for example, also address the well-known market failure associated with under-investment in R&D, and innovation. It can bring down costs through learning-by-doing and innovation with a view to ultimately achieving cost competitiveness (Gross *et al.*, 2012). This provides an important rationale for policy support in many countries, though this view has been challenged by those who believe that a technology-neutral carbon price plus generic R&D support would be more appropriate (Helm, 2012).

Policy support for renewable energy has a long history in Europe and North America. Policies to support renewable energy are also developing rapidly in emerging economies, notably China and India. In the EU, renewables support is underpinned by the 2009 Renewable Energy Directive (RED) which requires 20% of all EU energy (including electricity, heat and transport energy) to be sourced from renewables (European Union, 2009a). The target for individual Member States varies depending on their 2005 starting point and the level of national income. A variety of policies is in place at the Member State level to meet the respective RED requirements.

The effect of policies in the electricity sector is generally to allow renewable energy projects to receive a higher price than they would in a competitive market and, in some cases to receive a guaranteed price that takes out the volatility which adds to the risk of capital-intensive projects, as discussed earlier in the chapter. It is beyond the scope of the chapter to review the effectiveness of different policies which have been comprehensively reviewed elsewhere, but they generally fall into one of two categories (Haas *et al.*, 2004).

Under quantity-based quota obligations, such as Renewable Portfolio Standards (RPS) that have been adopted in the United States, the amount of renewable energy which electricity suppliers are required to source is specified, and suppliers must offer generators a price sufficient to meet their quotas. It is also possible to allow suppliers to trade their obligations, allowing a market price to develop. A buy-out price may also be specified. The potential weakness of obligation systems is that there is still price volatility. Furthermore, only the lowest cost, most mature renewable technologies tend to be encouraged. The latter problem can be addressed by 'banding' support for different renewable technologies. Obligations have also been used in countries such as the UK and Sweden.

The most common form of support in Europe has been the feed-in tariff (FiT) which guarantees a price for generators thus overcoming the price volatility/capital intensity challenge. In principle, FiTs should be more costly than obligation-based policies as low-cost projects will face the same price as the most expensive projects. However, the price certainty provided by FiTs appears to reduce the cost of capital and, if anything, FiTS appear to have resulted in lower costs for consumers (Haas *et al.*, 2004).

Flagship policies such as FiTS/obligations need to be reinforced by other supporting policies. In the US, support for renewables in the electricity sector has developed bottom–up at the State level, mainly through RPSs. These are often bolstered by tax credits, not common in Europe, which reduce effective investment costs. In all countries, grid codes which set the rules for market access, for example by providing priority access for renewables, play a vital role.

The most important mechanism for promoting renewable transport fuels have been mandates that effectively specify the proportion of biofuels to be blended into transport fuels (Mitchell *et al.*, 2011). As with renewable electricity, these are usually reinforced by supporting policies which, in this case, take the form of fiscal incentives for biofuel producers or consumers, and financial support for production facilities. Brazil's promotion of biofuels began in the 1970s with a requirement that there should be a 20–25% blend of ethanol in petrol. A subsidised ethanol production programme drove down costs and in the 1990s the removal of subsidies began, and ethanol become cost competitive with petrol in 2004 (Goldemberg *et al.*, 2004). In the EU, the RED requires that by 2020, 10% of energy used for transport in each Member State should be from renewable sources (European Union, 2009a). This is reinforced by a Fuel Quality Directive, which requires that the life-cycle GHG emissions per unit of energy supplied from petrol and diesel fuels should fall by at least 6% by 2020 compared to fossil fuels in 2010 (European Union, 2009b).

Future Policy and Challenges

Policy support has played a major role in the rapid expansion of wind, solar and transport biofuels. An enhanced role for renewable energy is foreseen in all major world regions. The EU's proposed 2030 framework for climate and energy policies envisages the contribution of renewable energy rising from 20% in 2020 to 27% in 2030, although the current proposal is that targets would not be binding at the Member State level (European Commission, 2014). China's Twelfth Five-Year Plan 2011–2015 (Deutsche Bank Group, 2012) requires non-fossil fuel resources to meet 11.4% of primary energy consumption by 2015, with specific deployment targets for hydro (120 GW entering construction), wind (70 GW) and solar PV (5 GW). In November 2014, China announced its intention to increase the share of non-fossil fuels in primary energy consumption to around 20% by 2030.

Nevertheless, support for renewables is not unqualified. Concerns about the affordability of renewable subsidies have led the UK to introduce a Levy Control Framework which puts an annual cap on financial support (HM Treasury, 2011) while Spain retrospectively ended its FiT system in 2013, replacing it with guaranteed rates of return for renewable projects (CSP World, 2013). Both of these steps can be linked to the aftermath of the 2008 financial crisis. In the future, renewable electricity ambition is likely to be balanced by financial affordability concerns in a number of developed countries.

For transport biofuels, the environmental sustainability concerns described earlier may pose the greatest challenge to policy ambition. For example, the EU has proposed changes to the 2009 RED that constrain the way in which biofuels can contribute to renewables targets (European Commission, 2012). Proposals include: introducing a 5% limit on the contribution that biofuels from food crops could make to meeting the 10% transport renewable energy target by 2020; including emissions associated with indirect land use change in the calculation of life-cycle GHG emission savings; and raising the minimum GHG saving threshold for biofuels that count towards the RED targets.

Conclusions

Although market growth has been rapid, renewable energy's absolute contribution to the energy mix remains modest. There is a universal perception that markets will continue to expand and renewables will command an ever-increasing share of energy markets. However, there is less agreement about the rate of market growth and the balance between different forms of renewable energy in the medium to long term.

Although renewable energy costs have been falling, innovation support is needed if cost reductions are to continue. As renewable resources are location specific, renewable energy has become cost competitive in some specific markets but, broadly, still requires policy support to make it financially viable.

Renewable energy developers can be confident of expanding markets, but need to be cognisant of inherent uncertainties. They need to monitor technological, market and policy developments in order to direct their efforts most profitably. The key uncertainties relate to: progress in reducing costs and improving performance; wider trends in energy markets; the strength of policy commitment to high-level goals (notably on climate change); and the balancing of renewables ambition against wider goals such as energy affordability and wider sustainability.

References

Arvizu, D. and Balaya, P. (2011). 'Direct Solar Energy', in Edenhofer, O., Pichs-Madruga, R., Sokona, Y., Seyboth, K., Matschoss, P., Kadner, S., Zwickel, T., Eickemeier, P., Hansen, G., Schlömer, S. and von Stechow C. (eds), *IPCC Special Report on Renewable Energy Sources and Climate Change Mitigation*, Cambridge University Press, Cambridge, pp. 337–400.

BP (2014). 'BP Statistical Review of World Energy'. Available at: http://www.bp.com/content/dam/bp/pdf/statistical-review/statistical_review_of_world_energy_2013.pdf [accessed 9 March 2015].

Chum, H., Faaij, A. and Moreira, J. (2011). 'Bioenergy', in Edenhofer, O., Pichs-Madruga, R., Sokona, Y., Seyboth, K., Matschoss, P., Kadner, S., Zwickel, T., Eickemeier, P., Hansen, G., Schlömer, S. and von Stechow C. (eds), *IPCC Special Report on Renewable Energy Sources and Climate Change Mitigation*, Cambridge University Press, Cambridge, pp. 209–332.

Committee on Climate Change (2013). 'Reducing the UK's carbon footprint and managing competitiveness risks'. Available at: http://www.theccc.org.uk/wp-content/uploads/2013/04/CF-C-Summary-Rep-web1.pdf [accessed 9 March 2015].

CSP World (2013). 'Spain kills Feed-in Tariff for renewable energy'. Available at: http://www.csp-world.com/news/20130713/001121/spain-kills-feed-tariff-renewable-energy [accessed August 21 2014].

Deutsche Bank Group (2012). Scaling Wind and Solar Power in China, Available at: https://www.db.com/cr/en/docs/China_Wind_and_Solar-Feb2012.pdf [accessed 9 March 2015].

Energy–UK (2014). Wholesale Electricity Market Report, London. Available at: http://www.energy-uk.org.uk/publication/finish/5-research-and-reports/1069-wholesale-market-report-march-2014.html [accessed 15 April 2014].

European Commission (2012). 'Proposal for a DIRECTIVE OF THE EUROPEAN PARLIAMENT AND OF THE COUNCIL amending Directive 98/70/EC relating to the quality of petrol and diesel fuels and amending Directive 2009/28/EC on the promotion of the use of energy from renewable sources'.

European Commission (2014). *A Policy Framework for Climate and Energy in the Period from 2020 to 2030*, European Commission, Brussels, Belgium.

European Environment Agency Scientific Committee (2011). *Opinion of the EEA Scientific Committee on Greenhouse Gas Accounting in Relation to Bioenergy*, EEAS, Copenhagen.

European Photovoltaic Industry Association (2014). *Global Market Outlook for Photovoltaics 2014–18*, EPIA, Brussels.

European Power Exchange (2014). 'EPEX Spot'. Available at: http://www.epexspot.com/en/product-info/auction/germany-austria [accessed 21 August 2014].

European Union (2009a). 'DIRECTIVE 2009/28/EC OF THE EUROPEAN PARLIAMENT AND OF THE COUNCIL of 23 April 2009 on the promotion of the use of energy from renewable sources and amending and subsequently repealing Directives 2001/77/EC and 2003/30/EC. Official Journal of the European Union, L 140(16)'.

European Union (2009b). 'DIRECTIVE 2009/30/EC OF THE EUROPEAN PARLIAMENT AND OF THE COUNCIL of 23 April 2009 amending Directive 98/70/EC as regards the specification of petrol, diesel and gas-oil and introducing a mechanism to monitor and reduce greenhouse gas emissions and amend. Official Journal of the European Union, L 140(88)'.

Fischedick, M. and Schaeffer, R. (2011). 'Mitigation Potential and Costs', in Edenhofer, O., Pichs-Madruga, R., Sokona, Y., Seyboth, K., Matschoss, P., Kadner, S., Zwickel, T., Eickemeier, P., Hansen, G., Schlömer, S. and von Stechow C. (eds), *IPCC Special Report on Renewable Energy Sources and Climate Change Mitigation*, Cambridge University Press, Cambridge, pp.791–864.

Global Wind Energy Council (2014). 'Global Wind Report Annual Market Update 2013', Brussels. Available at: http://www.gwec.net/wp-content/uploads/2014/04/GWEC-Global-Wind-Report_9-April-2014.pdf [accessed 21 August 2014].

Goldemberg, J., Coehlo, S. T., Nastari, P. M. and Lucon, O. (2004). 'Ethanol learning curve — the Brazilian experience. Biomass and

Bioenergy'. Available at: http://linkinghub.elsevier.com/retrieve/pii/ S0961953403001259 [Accessed 21 August 2014].

Greenacre, P., Gross, R. and Heptonstall, P. (2011). 'Great Expectations: The cost of offshore wind in UK waters — understanding the past and projecting the future', London. Available at: https://spiral.imperial. ac.uk/bitstream/10044/1/12649/6/Great%20Expectations%20-%20 The%20cost%20of%20offshore%20wind%20in%20UK%20waters.pdf [accessed 9 March 2015].

Gross, R., Stern, J., Charles, C., Nicholls, J., Candelise, C., Heptonstall, P. and Greenacre, P. (2012). 'On picking winners: The need for targeted support for renewable energy', ICL, London.

Gross, R. and Heptonstall, P. (2006). 'The Costs and Impacts of Intermittency: An assessment of the evidence on the costs and impacts of intermittent generation on the British electricity network', London. Available at: http://www.ukerc.ac.uk/Downloads/PDF/06/0604Intermittency/06 04IntermittencyReport.pdf [accessed 12 August 2014].

Haas, R., Eichhammerb, W., Hubera, C., Langnissc, O., Lorenzonid, A., Madlenere, R., Menanteauf, P., Morthorstg, P. E., Martinsh, A., Oniszki, A., Schleichb, J., Smith, A. Vassk, Z. and Verbruggen, A. (2004). 'How to promote renewable energy systems successfully and effectively'. Available at: http://linkinghub.elsevier.com/retrieve/pii/ S0301421502003373 [accessed 21 August 2014].

Helm, D. (2012). *The Carbon Crunch: How We're Getting Climate Change Wrong — and How to Fix It*, Yale University Press, New Haven and London.

HM Treasury (2011). 'Control framework for DECC levy-funded spend-ing', London. Available at: http://webarchive.nationalarchives.gov. uk/20130129110402/http:/www.hm-treasury.gov.uk/d/control_ framework_decc250311.pdf [accessed 9 March 2015].

Intergovernmental Panel on Climate Change (2013). 'Summary for Policymakers', in Stocker, T. F., Qin, D., Plattner, G–K., Tignor, M., Allen, S., Boschung, J., Nauels, A., Xia, Y., Bex, V. and Midgley, P. (eds), *Climate Change 2013: The Physical Science Basis. Contribution of Working Group I to the Fifth Assessment Report of the Intergovernmental Panel on Climate Change*, Cambridge University Press, Cambridge.

Intergovernmental Panel on Climate Change (2014a). 'Summary for Policymakers', in *Climate Change 2014: Impacts, Adaptation, and Vulnerability. Part A: Global and Sectoral Aspects. Contribution of*

Working Group II to the Fifth Assessment Report of the Intergovernmental Panel on Climate Change, Cambridge University Press, Cambridge.

Intergovernmental Panel on Climate Change (2014b). 'Summary for Policymakers', in *Climate Change 2014, Mitigation of Climate Change. Contribution of Working Group III to the Fifth Assessment Report of the Intergovernmental Panel on Climate Change*, Cambridge University Press, Cambridge.

International Energy Agency (2012). 'Energy Prices and Taxes'. Available at: http://dx.doi.org/10.5257/iea/ept/2012q1 [accessed 9 March 2015].

International Energy Agency (2013a). 'Electricity information'. Available at: http://dx.doi.org/10.5257/iea/elec/2013 [accessed 9 March 2015].

International Energy Agency (2013b). 'Renewables Information'. Available at: http://dx.doi.org/10.5257/iea/ri/2013 [accessed 9 March 2015].

International Energy Agency (2013c). 'Resources to reserves 2013: Oil, Gas and Coal Technologies for the Energy Markets of the Future'. Available at: http://www.oecd-ilibrary.org/energy/resources-to-reserves-2013_9789264090705-en [accessed 9 March 2015].

International Energy Agency (2013d). 'World Energy Balances'. Available at: http://dx.doi.org/10.5257/iea/web/2013 [accessed 9 March 2015].

International Energy Agency (2014). 'Energy Technology Perspectives 2014: Harnessing Electrcity's Potential', International Energy Agency, Paris.

Mitchell, C., Sawin, J., Pokharel, G. Kammen, D. and Wang, Z. (2011). 'Policy, Financing and Implementation', in Edenhofer, O., Pichs-Madruga, R., Sokona, Y., Seyboth, K., Matschoss, P., Kadner, S., Zwickel, T., Eickemeier, P., Hansen, G., Schlömer, S. and von Stechow C. (eds), *IPCC Special Report on Renewable Energy Sources and Climate Change Mitigation*, Cambridge University Press, Cambridge, pp. 865–950.

Nordpool (2014). 'Nordpool Spot'. Available at: http://www.nordpoolspot.com/ [accessed 21 August 2014].

Royal Dutch Shell (2013). 'New Lens Scenarios'. Available at: http://www.shell.com/global/future-energy/scenarios/new-lens-scenarios.html [accessed 21 August 2014].

Turkenburg, W. C. (2012). 'Renewable Energy', in Johansson, T. B., Patwardhan, A., Nakicenovic, N., Gomez-Echeverri, L and Turkenburg, W. C. (eds), *Global Energy Assessment: Towards a Sustainable Future*, Cambridge University Press, Cambridge.

UN Data (2014). 'National Accounts Estimates of Main Aggregates'. Available at: http://data.un.org/Data.aspx?d=SNAAMA&f=grID:101;currID:USD;pcFlag:0 [accessed 21 August 2014].

US Energy Information Administration (2013). 'International Energy Outlook 2013'. Available at: http://www.eia.gov/forecasts/ieo/ [accessed 21 August 2014].

Victor, D. and Zhou D. (2014). 'Introductory Chapter', in *Climate Change 2014: Mitigation of Climate Change*, Cambridge University Press, Cambridge.

Wiser, R. and Yang, Z. (2011). 'Wind Energy', in *Intergovernmental Panel on Climate Change, ed. IPCC Special Report on Renewable Energy Sources and Climate Change Mitigation*, Cambridge University Press, Cambridge.

Chapter Two

How Much Renewable Energy Will the Global Economy Need?

Guy Turner, Independent Economist and Author[†]

Introduction

The purpose of this chapter is to set out the context of the need and demand for renewable energy. The amount of renewable energy demanded by the world depends on two key factors: how much energy is needed (or at least desired depending on your point of view); and the share of that energy that can usefully be provided by renewable sources.

How Much Energy Does the World Need?

The ability of fossil fuels to provide a reliable, abundant and relatively low-cost source of energy is often cited as having been the single most important driver of economic growth since the start of the industrial revolution. For the vast part of the 19th and 20th centuries standards of living have been improved by consuming greater quantities of

---

[†]Former Chief Economist, Bloomberg New Energy Finance.

energy. Energy heats and cools our buildings, enabling us to live comfortably throughout the year anywhere in the world; powers industrial processes that manufacture the goods we crave; and enables us to travel quickly and comfortably virtually anywhere on the planet within the time it takes for the Earth to make one rotation on its axis.

Although in some developed countries energy needs are nearing saturation point, and economic value is increasingly being created through ingenuity and creativity rather than consumption of more raw materials and energy, the welfare of the majority of the world's population would still be increased by consuming more energy. Many people in the world still need better homes with reliable access to heating, cooling, sanitation and communications. Most people would probably also desire their own car, a computer and mobile for everyone in the family, a wide range of clean and fresh food, foreign holidays, access to sport, cultural and leisure facilities — essentially all the trappings of a modern affluent society.

These needs and desires all require energy. Technology has come a long way in terms of energy efficiency, enabling more functionality and value to be provided with less energy, but the rate of growth in demand for goods and services on a global scale is out-pacing these improvements. The net result is globally increasing demand for energy.

Figure 2.1 shows the change in energy intensity of four key economic sectors in Europe: crude steel, cement, car fleet and total household energy consumption. In each sector, energy intensity is measured in terms of energy consumption per unit of physical output (tonnes of oil equivalent (toe) per tonne of steel and cement; litres of fuel per 100 km for the car fleet; and toe per dwelling for households). Between 2000 and 2011 energy intensity has reduced by between 10 and 20% across the four sectors. The greatest improvement is in cement production, which in 2011 took 20% less energy to produce the same quantity of output it did in 2000. The least improvement has been in the car fleet which has reduced specific fuel consumption by 12% over the period. This is partly due to relatively slow turnover of the vehicle stock. In 2011 the average fuel efficiency of new cars sold in Europe was 25% better than in 2000.

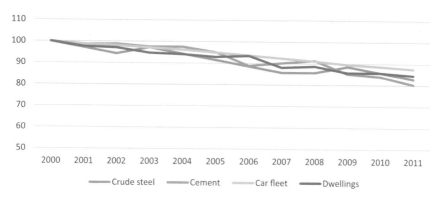

Fig. 2.1: Change in energy intensity of selected economic sectors (EU only) (Source: Odyssee-Mure, 2014)

Although the data in Fig. 2.1 are for Europe, they are likely to be echoed in most other countries as many of the changes are part of global technical trends. These apply in developing as well as developed countries.

In spite of these improvements, world energy consumption continues to increase and is projected to do so up to 2030 and beyond. Table 2.1 shows recent projections of world primary energy demand from four global modelling organaisations; MIT, the IEA, Shell and BP. All sources project world primary energy demand increasing by between 30% and 40% from 2010 to 2030, between 47% and 70% from 2010 to 2050.

How Much *Renewable* Energy does the World Need?

It is not an exaggeration to say that in the fullness of time the world will need to acquire all its energy from renewable sources. Fossil fuels and nuclear power are finite. The challenge for predicting the rate of growth in renewable energy use is that the date of their expiration is a long way off, and still very uncertain.

Although, according to the World Energy Council, at a global level coal reserves have been depleted by around 10% since the early

Table 2.1: World primary energy consumption projections

Year of publication	Source	Title	Scenario	Units	2010	2030	2050	2010–2030	2010–2050
2014	MIT	2014 Energy and Climate Outlook	Central (only)	EJ	500	700	850	40%	70%
2014	IEA	World Energy Outlook	Central (new policies)	mtoe	12,797	16,600	n/a	30%	–
2014	Shell	Shell energy scenarios to 2050	Scramble	EJ	531	734	880	38%	66%
			Blueprints	EJ	524	692	769	32%	47%
2015	BP	Energy Outlook 2035	Central	mtoe	11,956	16,619	n/a	39%	–

Source: IEA (2014), MIT (2014), Shell (2014), BP (2015).
Note: n/a means not available.

1990s, the currently proven reserves of coal will last the world for over a 100 years at current rates of consumption. These lifetime figures exclude the potential to find and develop new reserves of coal which would extend these deadlines. The US for example, was recorded as having 168 billion tonnes of coal reserves in 1993 and in spite of an extraction rate of around 1 billion tonnes a year, the reserves had increased to 237 billion by 2011. Similarly, China reported a nearly 50% increase in its coal reserves between 1993 and 2011 (World Energy Council, 2013).

Estimating how many years of oil and gas consumption are left is similarly tricky. Based on World Energy Council data, in 1993 the world had 44 years left of crude oil at the consumption rates of that time. By 2011, in spite of world oil consumption increasing by 25%, the life of known oil reserves had been extended to 56 years. The stated reserves of crude oil had increased by over 50% during this period, largely due to the reclassification of Canadian oil sands, and reserve revisions in the major OPEC countries Iran, Venezuela and Qatar.

In terms of natural gas, the world has been depleting its known reserves of conventional sources, albeit at a relatively slow rate. In 1993 the World Energy Council estimated there were 65 years of consumption left from these sources. By 2011 this had reduced to 60 years. Production had increased by 61% but reserves by only 48%.

These figures, however, do not include the vast reserves of unconventional gas now being exploited, notably in the US. The World Energy Council puts these resources at 456 trillion cubic metres. This is twice the current reserves of conventional sources of natural gas.

Already renewable energy contributes between 9% and 17% of world primary energy consumption. This range may seem surprising given the resources devoted to tracking energy statistics. The difference depends on what types of renewable are included and how the energy use is measured. In terms of the types of renewable energy, the main distinction relates to the inclusion of 'traditional biomass'. This covers the use of animal manure, woody biomass and charcoal as a fuel for inefficient open fires and stoves for heating and cooking — in developing countries this is a major source of energy in homes.

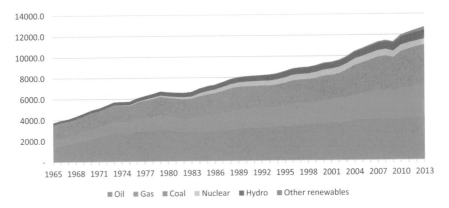

Fig. 2.2: World primary energy consumption by fuel type (mtoe) (Source: BP, 2014)

According to the IEA, traditional biomass represented around 70% of the global biomass used for energy purposes in 2010 (IEA, 2012).

Excluding traditional biomass, the largest contributor to renewable energy sources is hydro power. According to BP's 'Statistical Review of World Energy', in 2013 three quarters of world renewable energy production came from hydro power. China dominates this share accounting for 25% of world hydro output, with US, Canada and Brazil combined producing another 25%. Somewhat surprisingly given the policy attention and media coverage, the three well-known forms of renewable energy — wind, solar and (new) biomass — currently make up only 2.2% of the world primary energy consumption[1], as shown in Fig. 2.2.

The Importance of Prices

The need to replace fossil fuels with renewables, however, is not driven by capacity shortages but by prices. If world demand for energy continues to increase and fossil reserves become scarcer or more difficult and costly to access, then the prices of these commodities will rise. If these price rises are sustained and predictable then there will be a

---

[1] These figures use the substitution method of energy accounting which assumes an average conversion efficiency into a primary energy equivalent of 38%.

gradual shift away from fossil fuels to lower-cost alternatives. At the same time the cost of renewable technologies should continue to fall making them more competitive.

The other driving force for renewable energy is policy intervention. Virtually all of the recent growth in wind, solar and biofuels capacity in the last decade has been as a result of subsidies to promote renewable energy. The justification for this is founded on three principles: environmental protection to reduce emissions of greenhouse gases and improve local air quality; energy security; and industrial competitiveness.

The rest of this chapter explores in more detail the economics of renewable energy and the related landscape.

Cost Competitiveness of Renewable Energy Technologies

Any analysis of the competitiveness of renewable energy technologies needs to take into account the costs of both fossil and renewable technologies. Fossil fuels are the incumbent source of energy in most countries, and renewable technologies need to show they can deliver the same utility at equal cost in order to displace them.

Fossil fuel prices, however, are not static. In a world with a limited resource base, increasing demand should lead to higher prices. This has certainly been observed in the last two decades, with the prices of coal, oil and gas increasing markedly in nominal and real terms, especially during the period 2000–2008. Since 2008, however, prices of different fuels have followed very difference paths depending on the fuel and geography.

Figure 2.3 shows prices for domestic US coal, and the seaborne market, exported from Australia. There is a significant difference in prices, with the former insulated from internationally traded prices by the cost advantages of localised production and the cheap transport links in the US. Seaborne coal traded up to US$140/short ton in 2008, whereas the US price peaked at just under US$70 in 2010. Seaborne prices from Newcastle in Australia are broadly regarded as representative of a global coal price.

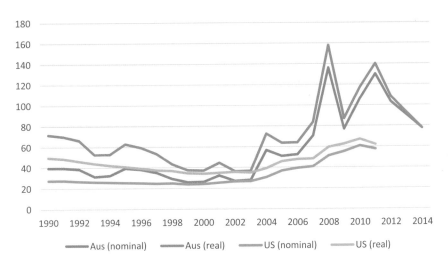

Fig. 2.3:   Coal price history 1990–2014 (bituminous coal, $/short ton) (Source: U.S. EIA, 2014a; Index Mundi, 2014a)

Note: Real prices in US$2014 deflated from nominal prices based on average 2.5% US$ inflation rate 1990–2014. Historic data on US coal prices from EIA only available up to 2011. Australia thermal coal based on FOB Newcastle/Port Kembla.

Gas prices in Fig. 2.4 are shown for the US (Henry Hub spot prices) and the UK (National Balancing Point — NBP). This chart also illustrates the build-up in prices from 2000, and their collapse following the 2008 financial crisis. It also highlights the divergence in gas prices now seen across the Atlantic. The price of gas traded on the British NBP has rebounded noticeably since 2008, influenced strongly by the cost of importing liquefied natural gas (LNG) and averaging around US$10/million British thermal units (MMBtu). This is in contrast to the US where, as a result of rapid exploration of shale oil and gas reserves, natural gas trades at around US$4/MMBtu. The difference is even greater in Asia where the costs of shipping LNG longer distances means the market has traded at around US$17/MMBtu for the past few years.

Figure 2.5 shows prices for crude oil, West Texas Intermediate — often used as the benchmark for global oil prices. Again this shows the strong build-up in price since 2000 and the post 2008 collapse. Note that the annual averaging here smoothes out intra-year fluctuations;

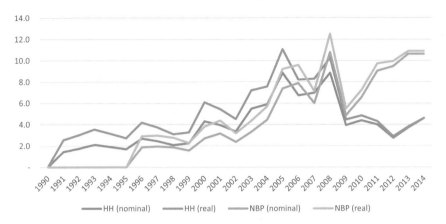

Fig. 2.4: US (Henry Hub) and UK (NBP) gas prices ($/MMBtu) (Source: BP, 2014; Index Mundi, 2014b)

Note: Henry Hub natural gas futures end of day settlement price. GB Prices NBP. Real prices in US$2014 deflated from nominal prices based on average 2.5% US$ inflation rate 1990–2014.

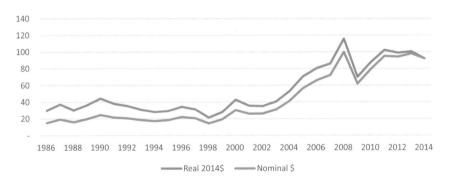

Fig. 2.5: Oil price history 1986–2014 (WTI spot, $/barrel) (Source: U.S. EIA, 2014b)

Note: Real prices in US$2014 deflated from nominal prices based on average 2.5% US$ inflation rate 1990–2014. 2014 prices show average of year to date (1 Jan–10 November 2014).

the oil market actually peaked on 7 July 2008 at US$141/barrel (bl) and then dived to US$37/bl on the 18 December the same year.

The commodity boom and price peaks in 2008 were, however, exceptional, and the prices of all three fossil fuels have not since reached these levels. The US gas price has shown the greatest reduction, falling by 70%, followed by coal, which in late 2014 was half its 2008 peak (in real terms). Although not shown on the chart, the oil price is at the time of writing (January 2015) at US$60/bl, down 40% from the 2008 average. Of these fuels, only the seaborne LNG market has recovered — supplying the UK, the rest of Europe and Asia. Previously in the UK, gas demand could be met by cheaper domestic sources in the North Sea.

Acknowledging that the commodity boom was exactly that — a 'boom' rather than a reflection of the long-term costs of extracting fossil fuels — it is useful to understand the causes of the price movements since 2008 in terms of making longer-term projections. Certainly, the overly bullish build-up of prices during the boom years, driven by a surge in demand from developing countries, China in particular, and amplified by traders' fears of pending shortages, meant that prices for all fuels had further to fall when the crisis hit. The coal, and to some degree oil, markets have also been suppressed by an overhang of production capacity that was started during the 2000s. These effects however are relatively short term. Capacity will be removed from the market if prices are consistently below the costs of production.

The important issue, in the context of the need for future energy resources, is the long-term cost of extraction and processing of these fuels at future levels of demand. In the coal sector the supply curve appears relatively flat. There is no shortage of the fuel on a global basis, and new mines are able to be exploited efficiently, often in developing countries, such as Indonesia, South Africa and Mongolia, with low land and labour costs. Some of the downward pressure in the last few years is most likely caused by producers selling at prices close to, or even below, variable production costs as available capacity outstrips demand — a predictable phenomenon of commodity cycles. But even as unprofitable mines are closed and prices recover to long-run average costs of production, few analysts are predicting a sustained increase in the global coal price. Simply, coal is cheap to produce and is likely to remain so for many years.

As noted above, gas prices are very much regionally determined, but the prospect of shale exploitation is likely to cap the long-term price of this fuel. North America has proven it can extract shale gas in large volumes, and on paper Europe and China also possess significant shale resources, although it is not clear that they could be developed to the same extent as North America. According to the EIA, China possesses some 1,115 trillion cubic feet of technically recoverable shale gas. This is twice the EIA's estimate of shale gas resources in the US.

The cost at which this gas can be recovered is, however, highly uncertain. The US has pioneered hydraulic fracturing, and aided by supportive planning policies and a technically advanced oil and gas services industry, has been able to exploit the shale reserves cheaply. Although the price fell as low as US\$2/MMBtu during 2012, the long-run marginal cost of extraction is likely to lie in the US\$5–6/MMBtu range. The current Henry Hub futures curve rises to US\$5.5/MMBtu in 2025, and fundamental modelling suggests US\$5/MMBtu by 2025 (Bloomberg New Energy Finance, 2014a).

Over the next 10 or 20 years then, there is little to suggest that the price of coal and gas will increase significantly despite resources dwindling and undiminished demand. A longer-term timeframe may well see prices rise in real terms again as the known reserves become harder to exploit, but, as noted earlier in this chapter, predicting when this will occur and the extent of the price rise is extremely difficult to predict.

Oil is arguably the fuel where supply side constraints are most likely to be felt in the medium to long term. As conventional resources run dry, international oil companies have started to explore ever more ambitious and costly projects to maintain reserves and production. This new frontier now includes deep and ultra-deep water projects in the Gulf of Mexico and off the coast of Brazil, oil sands in the US and Canada, and arctic drilling. The US's experience with shale oil and gas has provided breathing space for the world's largest consumer of oil with net oil imports in 2013 half their peak in 2006 (U.S. EIA, 2014c), but on a global basis new, more costly resources are likely to be needed to meet growing world demand.

Apart from slight downturns after the oil crises of 1974 and 1979, and the recession of 2009, world oil consumption has risen steadily each year for the last half century. In 2013 world crude oil consumption reached a new record, just shy of 90 million barrels per day. While theories of peak oil continue to circulate, the major fore-casting centres still foresee long-term growth in oil demand with a gradual decline in developed country markets being more than offset by growth in the developing world. The EIA's 2013 International Energy Outlook reference case forecasts world oil demand growing by 40% between 2015 and 2040.

Work for the Carbon Tracker Initiative by Rystad Energy presents a global supply curve for the oil industry in 2020 (Carbon Tracker Initiative, 2014). This shows that at current consumption levels of 90 million barrels per day (mbpd) the marginal cost of production from known resources is likely to be US$80–90/bl, driven by these new projects in particular ultra-deep water. Beyond this, if demand reaches 100 mbpd or more, the marginal cost of production could well exceed US$150/bl.

The conclusion is that in spite of world energy demand continu-ing to grow, the real price of fossil fuels, especially gas and coal that are used to produce power, are unlikely to provide much support to the renewable technologies. If renewable technologies are to make headway they will need to prove that they can compete with the utility and price fossil fuels at today's levels. The exception is the transport sector where there is more scope for long-term oil price increases which could open the door for the new technologies of plug-in hybrids, fully electric vehicles, hydrogen and compressed natural gas power vehicles.

Renewable Technologies

The decline in the cost of renewable technologies over the past dec-ade, in particular solar power, has been widely documented. Prices of solar photovoltaic (PV) modules declined by around 95% in nominal terms between 1990 and 2014. Modules themselves account for around half of the total installed cost of PV plant with the remainder comprising auxiliary electrical systems, such as inverters, balance of plant and general construction. Costs of these elements has also fallen, although not by quite the same extent as modules, with the result that the cost of solar PV systems are also a fraction of their 1990 prices.

As well as cost reductions, the performance of solar PV modules has also improved although not by the same extent. The efficiency of solar cells (crystalline silicon) to turn sunlight into electricity has increased by about 50% from around 12% in 1990 to 18% today (EPRI, 2009). Taking into account both the improvements in efficiency and capital cost reductions the levelised cost of electricity (LCOE) of PV plants has also reduced dramatically, again by around 96%, producing power at around $140/MWh (see Fig. 2.6). This figure assumes a conversion efficiency of 18% which is typical in a good, sunny location, such as southern Europe or US. Of course, at higher latitudes or locations with more cloud cover, efficiencies fall and LCOEs rise.

In the wind sector, over the past three decades costs have also come down and efficiencies have improved. The dollar cost per kW of onshore wind turbines has fallen from around US$2,000–$3,000 in 1980 to just over US$800–$900 in 2014 (BNEF 2014c; IEA, 2012b). Capacity factors have improved as larger and more efficient turbines are able to convert more of the wind energy into electricity.

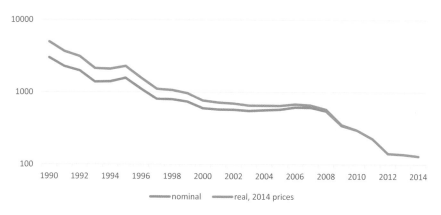

Fig. 2.6: LCOE from solar PV (utility scale, crystalline silicon, $/MWh Log) (Source: BNEF, 2014b; IRENA, 2012; US DoE, 2012)

Note: Calculations assume 2.5% annual inflation rate for US$, average life of 20 years and 10% weighted average cost of capital.

In the US the fleet-wide capacity factor of new installations improved from around 25% in 1999 to 32% in 2010, while that in Denmark increased from 25% in 2002 to 35% in 2009 (IEA, 2012b).

Figure 2.7 shows estimates for LCOEs for onshore wind turbines since 1990 in nominal terms. It should be noted that these figures represent averages and site-specific factors, in particular load factors, which can significantly change the LCOEs. For example in the US, the cost of generating power (unsubsidised) from wind plants can be as low as US$58/MWh in Texas, whereas it can be as high as US$108/MWh in less windy areas such as Alabama and Georgia.

National Renewable Energy Laboratory (NREL) figures are for the US and the Danish Energy Agency (DEA) for Denmark. The Bloomberg New Energy Finance (BNEF) figures from 2010 to 2014 represent global average of turbines installed in each year. Although there are differences between the three datasets, there is a pattern. Towards the end of the 1990s in Denmark and 2004 in the US, LCOEs stopped falling and, in the case of the US, started increasing. Other studies of prices showed the same effect in other countries (IEA, 2012b). The more recent data from BNEF, showing LCOEs since 2010, are broadly consistent with the last reported data from the NREL study in the same year. Since 2010 there has been relatively little change in the LCOE from onshore wind, at around US$80/MWh.

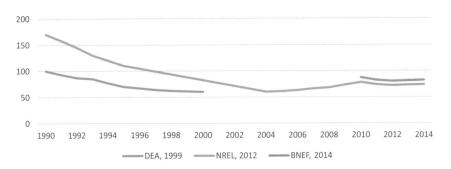

Fig. 2.7: LCOE for onshore wind ($/MWh, nominal) (Source: BNEF, 2014d; DEA, 1999; IEA, 2012b)

Note: Calculations assume average life of 20 years and 10% weighted average cost of capital.

One of the main factors causing the increase in costs from 2004 to 2010 was the rise in the price of raw materials to make turbines, notably steel and copper. European steel, for example, increased from an average of US$300–$400/tonne between 2000 and 2002, to over US$1,200/tonne in the summer of 2008. After the financial crisis in 2008 and 2009, prices plunged to US$500/tonne but have since stabilised at around US$700/tonne (Steelbenchmarker, 2014). The other factor behind the increase in costs was simply the imbalance of demand over supply during that period. Between 2005 and 2009 annual global demand for wind turbines increased three-fold from 11,000 MW to 38,000 MW (GWEC, 2015). The turbine industry was simply able to increase prices as demand exceeded supply.

Since 2010 LCOEs have remained stable, particularly in Europe and the US, as good sites become harder to find. With limited land availability developers have sought to extract more power from the available sites by deploying larger turbines. The improvements in efficiency from larger turbines have been largely offset by higher capital costs.

Figure 2.8 compares the cost of generating power from the four main technologies, coal, gas, wind and solar PV in Europe. Europe is used here as representative of a 'global average' as both coal and gas prices are governed by internationally traded markets. In the US coal

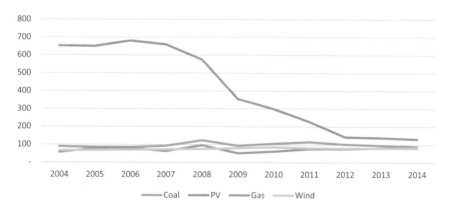

Fig. 2.8: Comparison of LCOE in Europe 2004–2014 ($/MWh, utility scale projects, real 2014 prices)

Note: Calculations assumed average life of 20 years, 10% weighted average cost of capital, 2.5% US$ inflation.

and gas prices are lower than in Europe due to export limitations. In Asia, and in particular China, coal prices are determined by local production, while, gas prices are the highest in the world due to the reliance on seaborne LNG.

When comparing LCOEs inevitably many assumptions need to be made. For renewable technologies capacity factors are critical — average wind speeds can vary by a factor of two or three depending on site location, which can alter the LCOE by a similar proportion. The efficiency of solar PV plants tends to vary less than wind as sunshine is more predictable, but can still vary by a factor of two across Europe. Northern latitude countries such as the UK make do with capacity factors of around 9% whereas Spain and Turkey enjoy factors around 18% (BNEF, 2014e). In spite of these assumptions one can draw a general conclusion: at good sites the LCOE of onshore wind without any subsidies is now competitive with the cost of new power generation from coal or natural gas at around US$80/MWh. PV however is still more expensive at the best sites around US$140/MWh.

The costs in Fig. 2.8 are just for Europe. Outside Europe one can find more favourable conditions for renewable technologies. For example, capacity factors for solar PV in Latin America and southern US states can regularly achieve 19–20%, translating into LCOEs of around US$110–120/MWh and US$150/MWh respectively. These figures could be even lower if it were not for the relatively high cost of finance in these countries (BNEF, 2014e). Latin America also has some of the best sites for onshore wind in the world with capacity factors reaching 50% in some parts of Brazil. At these wind speeds LCOEs can be as low as US$60–70/MWh and can bid into capacity auctions without any further subsidies to compete with fossil power stations in the form of natural gas combined-cycle turbines (BNEF, 2014d).

The greatest opportunity for solar PV, however, is not as a source of centralised power connected to the grid, but as a decentralised generation source supplying local electricity loads. Often these are roof-mounted systems fitted in residential or commercial applications. When used in this way, PV systems compete with the price of delivered

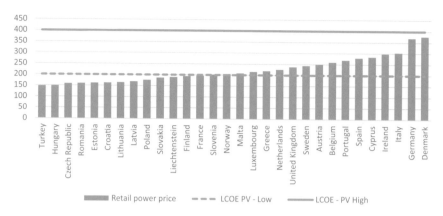

Fig. 2.9: Comparison of domestic PV LCOE and retail power prices in Europe 2014 (US$/MWh) (Source: Bazilian, 2013; EC, 2014a)

Note: Retail power price includes all costs, charges and taxes.

electricity after the addition of charges for transmission, distribution and other taxes.

Across Europe, network costs and other taxes and charges make up over half of the final retail price of electricity. In 2014 domestic electricity prices ranged from €119/MWh (US$147) in Turkey to €300/MWh (US$377) in Germany and Denmark inclusive of all costs, charges and taxes (EC, 2014a). Installing PV systems in a domestic application is not comparable with utility scale projects as the surveying and installation costs are higher on a per kW basis for domestic projects. These extra costs can raise the LCOEs for domestic PV installations in Europe to around $200–400/MWh (Bazilian, 2013; EC, 2014a). Even at these costs however domestic PV installations are cost competitive with retail power in some countries, particularly those with higher retail prices (>£200/MWh) and good solar resources. This includes Spain, southern Germany and Italy (see Fig. 2.9).

Looking forward, the costs of both wind and solar are likely to continue to fall, although by lesser degrees than seen over the last few decades. As noted above, the LCOE from onshore wind appears to have stabilised since 2010, although unit costs of the turbines themselves have declined by around 3% in the last three years. Long-term projections presented in the IEA's 2012 Cost of Wind study show a range of scenarios. Taking the 20th and 80th percentiles, the range of LCOE projections is narrowed to roughly a 20%–30% reduction in LCOE between 2010 and 2030.

In the solar sector, IRENA presents cost projections for utility scale solar PV systems from the IEA and EPIA (European Photovoltaic Industry Association). These show LCOEs coming down from US$150–200 in 2015 to US$100–200 by 2020 and US$50–150 by 2030 (IRENA, 2012).

For countries that are able to achieve these LCOEs by combining the right sites with the appropriate technology and financing structures, then wind and solar could well compete on a per kWh basis at both the utility and retail level by as early as 2020.

While these figures appear compelling for the renewables story, it is important to sound a note of caution. LCOE comparisons are not all that they seem, in that they treat every kWh of power equally. In practice, the ability to dispatch power when needed is critical to the functioning of a modern energy system. Fuels that are stored in solid or liquid form have a distinct advantage in this regard. This certainly applies to coal, oil, gas and hydro, but also to biofuels in the form of liquid or solid biomass.

Policy Intervention

Nearly every country in the world now has some form of policy target and support mechanism for renewable energy (Ren 21, 2014)[2]. These support mechanisms can either be to incentivise renewable energy directly or to disadvantage fossil fuels in the form of a carbon tax, emissions trading schemes or direct legislation, such as emissions limits or planning controls. In some regions these schemes are material to the size and shape of the energy system. In Europe, for example, in 2012 renewable energy and energy efficiency subsidies represented nearly €50 bn of public expenditure accounting for around 10% of wholesale energy expenditures, and nearly 20% of aggregate

---

[2] According to Ren 21 (2014), 144 out of a total of 196 countries in the world had renewable energy policy targets.

Table 2.2: Support for renewable energy and
energy efficiency measures in the EU in 2012
(Source: EC, 2014a, 2014b)

Technology	€ Millions
Solar	14,730
Wind	11,480
Biomass	8,340
Hydro	5,180
Geothermal	70
RE other	1,020
Total Renewable Energy	**40,820**
Support for energy savings	8,590
Total clean energy	**49,410**
Total wholesale energy expenditure	**500,000**

consumer electricity expenditure across the continent (EC, 2014a, 2014b; see Table 2.2).

The European Commission report behind Table 2.2 suggests that 2012 is likely to be a peak in expenditure on renewable energy subsidies in Europe as governments scale back these policies and the cost of renewables becomes closer to grid parity. Nevertheless it illustrates the extent to which some governments are willing to support the expansion of renewable energy.

Publically funded support for renewable energy also creates one further benefit — it accelerates the reduction in costs of the technology. The costs of rapidly advancing technologies like solar PV, offshore wind turbines, cellulosic ethanol and advanced batteries, are reduced not only by research and development (R&D) innovation to design better devices, but through economies of scale and improvements in manufacturing processes which are driven by the need to meet increasing demand. In the PV sector, research shows a causal relationship between market creation policies and price reductions (Candelise *et al.*, 2013). This was most evident over the period 2008–2012 where PV module prices more than halved from US$4.50/Wp to around US$2.00/Wp at the same time as global demand increased five-fold from 6 GW to 30 GW (EPIA, 2014). Much of the growth in demand over this period came from Europe, and in particular Germany, in line with the block's legislation on renewable energy targets. Europe therefore, while benefiting itself from the cost reductions, also allowed the rest of the world to benefit from its expenditure.

What does the Future Hold?

The future growth of renewable energy deployment is ultimately driven by two factors: natural demand where the economics of renewable energy technologies are compelling without the need for subsidies, and the extent of future policy support. The former will be determined by continued cost reductions of renewable technologies alongside any increase in the cost of fossil fuels. Over time the number of situations where renewables are cost-effective without subsidy will increase as costs come down even further. Currently these opportunities are limited to countries with good solar resources and high electricity prices for PV (e.g., Italy, Spain), good wind resources for onshore wind (e.g., northwest Europe, Brazil), and power networks that use oil-based fuels as the main fuel source (e.g., small islands).

To date the vast majority of renewable capacity has been built with the help of subsidies, and if this were to continue at the current rate, the penetration of renewables into the world energy mix would certainly increase. But how far future policy efforts will go to maintaining this support is difficult to predict. Recent history shows a wide range of willingness to support renewables across the world and over time. In some countries policy targets for renewable energy are structured in relation to total energy consumption, while others may have capacity growth targets for specific technologies. For example, Europe has ambitious targets for the share of renewable energy in total energy consumption for 2020, and more recently 2030, while the US has no federal-level target for renewable energy, preferring instead to leave energy policies decisions to state governments. In the developing world China has targets for 'non-fossil' energy sources up to 2020 but these include nuclear power, whereas India has a target for renewables share of electricity consumption only up to 2015, but a specific solar capacity target by 2022.

The policy position of countries also changes over time. In Europe the economic drag of higher retail energy prices caused by the cost of renewable subsidies is now a major political issue. Spain and the Czech Republic have already implemented retroactive reductions in tariff support for renewable energy projects, while Germany and the UK have scaled back the level of support offered to certain types of technologies, notably solar PV. These concerns have also affected the shape of future energy policies. For example, Europe's recent 2030 energy policy is framed primarily around carbon emission reductions rather than targets for renewable energy. Europe intends to reduce carbon emissions by 40% by 2030 from 1990 levels and has put in place the principles and mechanisms to enforce these targets at Member State level. And while there is also a target for renewable energy of 27% of EU energy consumption by 2030, this is only binding at the EU level and lacks legal enforcement within Member States (European Council, 2014). The direction of policymaking in Europe therefore appears to be towards more flexibility, moving away from prescriptive renewable energy targets for countries and technologies.

As noted above there are multiple reasons why governments have supported renewable energy to date, reflecting different national circumstances and priorities. Over time though these drivers are likely to converge around the major themes and governments become wiser in the use of public money in this sector. Table 2.3 summarises a change in policy drivers that might be expected to 2020 and beyond.

The justification for policy intervention based on national interests such as job creation will be deemed short-sighted as it becomes apparent that this is a futile exercise for most governments in the long run — given the scale economies required in the supply chains to manufacture wind turbines, solar modules, etc., governments will realise it is impossible for all countries to be world leaders in these markets. Some local content rules may be applied but these will also diminish over time.

Worries about energy independence will also evolve. Currently these concerns are felt most acutely in Europe with the heavy reliance on gas piped from Russia — a country with whom Europe has strained political relations — and while renewables provide a useful way of reducing this dependence, there are other solutions. Expansion

Table 2.3: Possible evolution of policy drivers for renewable energy

Policy driver	Rationale	Up to 2020	2020 onwards
Employment	Create domestic employment in the renewables sector	Weak	Weak
Energy independence	Protection from high and volatile international fossil fuel prices, and reliance of imports particularly from ideologically different countries	Moderate	Moderate
Air quality	Improve local air quality by reducing use of coal and oil	Moderate	Weak
Long-term cost reduction of renewables	Accelerate long-term reductions in cost of renewable technologies	Weak	Weak
Nuclear phase out	Avoid risks associated with nuclear power	Moderate	Weak
Climate change	Reduce emissions of fossil-based CO_2	Moderate	Strong

of LNG capacity and completion of gas pipelines from other parts of Africa and central Asia will go a long way to mitigating this risk, as would a return to greater use of coal, although this clearly has other drawbacks. In other parts of the world the importing of fossil fuels is more of an economic burden than a political one, with serious implications for trade deficits and economic instability. But to replace the imported fuel with more expensive domestic energy sources would be illogical. Only if the price of imported fuels is expected to increase sufficiently over time to cover the cost of the domestic energy sources would such a rationale be justified. But where this is the case the government's role is again questionable, as the private sector will also see the opportunities and may well make the necessary investments without the need for government support.

Concerns about the risks of nuclear power will also diminish over time as the lessons from Fukushima are learned, and security and maintenance procedures around nuclear facilities are improved. As the risks of climate change become more apparent, nuclear power will be seen as an important part of the energy mix. Air quality will remain an issue for many cities and regions, and renewable technologies will be supported as part of the solution. The worst of the pollution and the effects it causes, however, will be solved by improving the combustion processes of existing facilities, switching out of the dirtiest fuels, notably coal and oil, to cleaner-burning natural gas, and relocating major polluting factories out of urban areas. In Europe and North America, where coal still comprises a significant part of the energy mix, the retrofitting of emissions control technologies on factories and power stations has gone a long way to improving air quality. Residual air quality problems in these regions are largely caused by road transport, but solving this is less a case for renewable energy, more one of implementing low-emission vehicle technologies. These may still rely on fossil fuels of some sort, including petrol, diesel or natural gas, or involve a complete switch to electric vehicles.

Ultimately the principle justification for long-term policy intervention to support renewables over and above the direct incentive provided by developing a cheaper source of energy than fossil fuels, is the need to tackle climate change. The risks of climate change are now accepted by virtually all countries as a serious danger, and the solutions can only be addressed at the scale required through government action. And while reducing the demand for energy is undoubtedly a key part of the solution, this has its limits, as does nuclear power. If emissions of CO_2 are to be reduced, there is little alternative to significantly expanding the use of renewable energy to displace fossil fuels.

The question then arises about what level of support should be applied. The latest report from the IPCC reiterates the need for a rapid turnaround in emissions if the worst effects of climate change are to be avoided. This would mean global greenhouse gas emissions being lowered by 40–70% by 2050 compared with 2010, and then to near zero levels by the end of the century (IPCC, 2014). If one assumes nuclear power is unlikely to be a major part of the solution, which is not an unreasonable assumption given current sentiment towards the technology, then renewables would need to contribute to the bulk of this transition.

A large uncertainty on the implications for renewables is the role of carbon capture and storage (CCS). Although much talked about, to date there is only one large-scale use of CCS technology which started operation in Canada in October 2014 (*The Guardian*, 2014). But even if this plant proves to work effectively, a global roll out of CCS is by no means assured. Estimates of the costs of the technology range widely from US$50/tCO2 for a pulverised coal plant to US$80/tCO2 for a combined-cycle gas turbine (IEA, 2011), and to US$150 to US$230/tCO2 for industrial processes (Element Energy, 2013). The technology is also limited in the number of locations where it can be used as there needs to be a suitable underground repository. The waste CO_2 can be piped to suitable geological sites, but this adds to the cost.

The IPPC AR5 report shows that if emissions of greenhouse gases are to be reduced to keep the world within the 2 °C warming limit, the share of low-carbon energy sources, including renewables, nuclear energy and fossil fuels with CCS, in the energy mix would need to grow from 17% in 2010 to 60% in 2050, and to 90% by 2100. Under less ambitious targets where the 2 °C threshold would be missed but the extreme effects of climate change avoided (equivalent to CO_2 concentrations in 2100 of 580–720 ppm), renewables would still make up 40% of the energy mix in 2050 and 75% in 2100.

The report claims that the economic costs of pursuing even the most ambitious emissions reduction targets would be small. Economic output would be lowered by 1% to 4% relative to world output in 2100 which would grow by 300% to 900% over the century. Lord Stern's work of a few years earlier proposed that unabated climate change would cost the world between 5% and 20% of its GDP in perpetuity, whereas the costs of mitigation would only require a cost of 1% of GDP (Stern, 2006).

An alternative way of expressing the costs and benefits of reducing greenhouse gas emissions is to look at the economic cost climate change per unit of CO_2 emitted — referred to as the social cost of carbon (SCC). In this way it is possible to create climate policies that can be compared internationally and achieve fair distribution of the costs.

The Stern Review in 2006 calculated SCC values equivalent to €25, €30 and €85/tCO2e (updated to 2012 prices) depending on the climate scenario, and a paper by Dietz and Stern (2014) recommended the use of US$32–103/tCO2e, or US$25–80/tCO2e (2012 prices). In 2010 the US government produced an estimate of the SCC of US$5–65/tCO2e (2007 prices). The work was updated in 2013 and the values increased to US$11–90/tCO2e (2007 prices) in 2010, with a central estimate of US$33/tCO2e, rising to US$43/tCO2e in 2020 (EC, 2014b).

The ranges in these estimates are wide, but necessarily reflect the uncertainties in this kind of analysis. Taking 2020 as a reference year, central estimates from the various studies range from US$43 to US$70/tCO2e, with a midpoint of around US$50/tCO2e.

One can therefore use this figure of US$50/tCO2e as a guide to the long-term level of support that governments would be willing to provide to renewable energy. Of course, this ignores the other attributes of renewable energy which governments seem intent on using as a rationale for high levels of subsidies, but as noted above some of these may not stand the test of time.

Figure 2.10 shows the effect on the competitiveness of selected energy technologies by adding a US$50/tCO2 tax. Note that the central values are not precise as the ranges in costs of electricity production are so large, encompassing examples from around the world[3]. They do, however, illustrate the relative effect of adding the carbon tax onto coal and gas. As can be seen, a US$50/tCO2 of tax is sufficient to materially change the choice of core power generation technologies in a number of locations where the decision is purely based on the cost of MWh produced. The central value of the cost of new coal fired generation increases to just under US$150/MWh, while CCGT increases to around US$130/MWh. At these levels of support the cost of wind power is likely to be cheaper at around the half the locations

---

[3] Note: the central values for renewable technologies are broadly weighted according to capacity of installations at different locations. They appear near the bottom of the range as there are a small number of examples of renewable plants, such as wind and solar, being installed in inappropriate and very costly locations. The central values for gas and coal are simple averages of the low and high ranges.

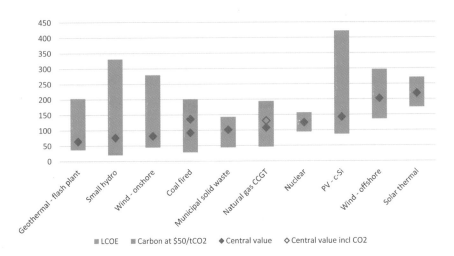

Fig. 2.10: LCOE (utility scale) with and without a carbon tax ($/MWh, 2014 prices) (figures extracted from BNEF, 2014f)

Note: US$50/tCO2 calculations assume carbon intensity of power generation from coal and CCGT of 0.88t/MWh and 0.45t/MWh respectively.

in the world. Geothermal power, small hydro and energy from municipal solid waste are all competitive in many situations without the need for the carbon price support, but are limited by resource availability. Solar PV and offshore wind, by contrast, still appear expensive, even with the carbon price support at US$50/tCO2.

This comparison assumes that each MWh delivered is the same, ignoring the reliability of supply, and there is certainly a premium attached to dispatchable technologies over the intermittent sources, such as wind and solar, that is not captured in this analysis. There are ways of better managing this variability, for example, through better interconnection and power storage, but this additional infrastructure comes at a cost.

How much renewable energy the world needs, or even wants, therefore will depend on society's willingness to fund the core renewable energy infrastructure, including the need to manage intermittency. A global carbon price of around US$50/tCO2 will help but is likely to be insufficient to lead to a complete transformation of the energy sector from fossil to renewable. Recent research has shown that current subsidies for wind and solar in Germany amount to around US\$75/tCO2 and US\$700/tCO2 respectively. Over time, as the damage, or risks of damage, from climate change grows then the US\$50/tCO2 may need to be increased. But it questionable whether the calculations of external costs would ever reach the subsidy levels seen in Germany.

In the meantime renewable technologies, for power generation at least, are unlikely to be supported by higher fossil fuel prices for the foreseeable future. Of course, in the fullness of time as resources are depleted fossil fuel prices will rise, but for coal and gas this is unlikely to happen for a generation or so. Oil is different, and one can see oil prices rising as the rate of depletion starts to overtake the rate of new discoveries. A large and sustained increase in oil prices would transform the transport sector in favour of alternative-fuelled vehicles, but would not greatly affect the power and industrial sectors which rely on coal and natural gas in many countries.

This therefore creates a challenge where the costs of renewable energy relative to fossil fuels, are higher than the estimates external costs. The net result will be a gradual evolution of the global energy mix, with an increasing share of renewables but with fossil fuels, and nuclear, continuing to provide significant share. Renewable technologies will not be implemented equally everywhere, but where it is most cost-effective to do so. This will see solar technology being developed in sunny parts of the world, wind technology being implemented where it is windy, and biomass production concentrating on highly productive agricultural regions. Alongside this, individual countries will have their own energy and political priorities that will drive them to develop indigenous renewable energy sources, even if they are more costly than the fossil alternatives.

References

Bazilian, M., Liebreich, M., MacGill, I., Chase, J., Shah, J., Gielen, D., Arent, D., Landfear, D. and Zhengrong, S. (2013). 'Re-considering the Economics of Photovoltaic Power', *Renewable Energy*, 53, May 2013, pp 329–338.

Bloomberg New Energy Finance (2014a). 'Q3 2014 North American Gas Outlook'.

Bloomberg New Energy Finance (2014b). 'Q2 2014, Global PV Market Outlook'.

Bloomberg New Energy Finance (2014c). 'Wind Turbine Price Index'.

Bloomberg New Energy Finance (2014d). 'H2 Wind Levelised Cost of Electricity Update'.

Bloomberg New Energy Finance (2014e). 'H2 PV Levelised Cost of Electricity Update'.

Bloomberg New Energy Finance (2014f). 'H2 2014 Levelised Cost of Electricity Update'.

BP (2014). 'Statistical Review of World Energy'. Available at: http://www.bp.com/en/global/corporate/about-bp/energy-economics/statistical-review-of-world-energy.html [accessed 9 March 2015].

BP (2015). 'Energy Outlook 2035'. Available at: http://www.bp.com/en/global/corporate/about-bp/energy-economics/energy-outlook.html [accessed 21 April 2015].

Candelise, C., Winksel, M., Gross, R. (2013). 'The Dynamics of Solar PV Costs and Prices as a Challenge for Technology Forecasting', *Renewable and Sustainable Energy Reviews*, **26**, 96–107.

Carbon Tracker Initiative (2014). 'Carbon Supply Cost Curves: Evaluating Financial Risk to Oil Capital Expenditures'. Available at: http://www.carbontracker.org/report/carbon-supply-cost-curves-evaluating-financial-risk-to-oil-capital-expenditures/ [accessed 9 March 2015].

Dietz, S. and Stern, N. (2014). 'Endogenous growth, convexity of damages and climate risk: how Nordhaus' framework supports deep cuts in carbon emissions', LSE Working Paper. Available at: http://www.lse.ac.uk/GranthamInstitute/wp-content/uploads/2014/06/Working-Paper-159-Dietz-and-Stern-20141.pdf [accessed 9 March 2015].

EC (European Commission) (2014a). 'Staff Working Document, Energy prices and costs in Europe COM(2014)21 Final'. Available at: http://eur-lex.europa.eu/legal-content/EN/TXT/?uri=CELEX:52014DC0021 [accessed 9 March 2015].

EC (European Commission) (2014b). 'Subsidies and Costs of EU Energy — An Interim Report (a report by Ecofys)'. Available at: https://ec.europa.eu/energy/sites/ener/files/documents/ECOFYS%202014%20Subsidies%20and%20costs%20of%20EU%20energy_11_Nov.pdf [accessed 9 March 2015].

Element Energy (2013). 'The Costs of Carbon Capture and Storage (CCS) for UK Industry — A High Level Review (report for BIS)'. Available at: https://www.gov.uk/government/uploads/system/uploads/attachment_data/file/181161/bis-13-745-the-costs-of-carbon-capture-and-storage-for-uk-industry-a-high-level-review.pdf [accessed 9 March 2015].

EPIA (European Photovoltaic Industry Association) (2014). 'Global Market Outlook for Photovoltaics 2014-2018'. Available at: http://www.epia. org/index.php?eID=tx_nawsecuredl&u=0&file=/uploads/tx_epiapubli-cations/44_epia_gmo_report_ver_17_mr.pdf&t=1426102104&hash=45 f565e4809447e35cbc39ed0bfc5a3e067a784f [accessed 9 March 2015].

EPRI (Electricity Power Research Institute) (2009). *Solar Photovoltaics: Status, Costs and Trends*, EPRI, Palo Alto, CA.

European Council (2014). EUCO 169/14 Conclusions 23/24 October 2014.

GWEC (Global Wind Energy Council) (2015). 'Global Wind Statistics 2014'. Available at: http://www.gwec.net/global-figures/graphs/ [accessed 9 March 2015].

IEA (International Energy Agency) (2011). 'Cost and Performance of Carbon Dioxide Capture from Power Stations'. Available at: http:// www.iea.org/publications/freepublications/publication/costperf_ccs_powergen.pdf [accessed 9 March 2015].

IEA (International Energy Agency) (2012a). 'World Energy Outlook 2012'. Available at: http://www.iea.org/publications/ [accessed 9 March 2015].

IEA (International Energy Agency) (2012b). 'Wind Task 26: The Past and Future Cost of Wind Energy'. Available at: http://www.ieawind.org/ task_26_public/PDF/WP2_task26.pdf [accessed 9 March 2015].

IEA (International Energy Agency) (2013). 'World Energy Outlook 2013'. Available at: http://www.iea.org/publications/ [accessed 9 March 2015].

IEA (International Energy Agency) (2014). "World Energy Outlook". Available at: http://www.iea.org/newsroomandevents/pressreleases/ 2014/november/signs-of-stress-must-not-be-ignored-iea-warns-in-its-new-world-energy-outlook.html [accessed 21 April 2015].

Index Mundi (2014a). 'Coal, Australian Thermal Coal Monthly Price, quoting World Bank data'. Available at: http://www.indexmundi.com/commodities/ ?commodity=coal-australian&months=300 [accessed 9 March 2015].

Index Mundi (2014b). 'Natural Gas Monthly Price quoting IMF data'. Available at: http://www.indexmundi.com/commodities/?commodity= natural-gas&months=300 [accessed 9 March 2015].

IPCC (Intergovernmental Panel on Climate Change) (2014). 'Mitigation of Climate Change', IPCC Working Group III Contribution to AR5. Available at: http://www.ipcc.ch/report/ar5/wg3/ [accessed 9 March 2015].

IRENA (International Renewable Energy Agency) (2012). 'Renewable Energy Technologies: Cost Analysis'. Available at: http://www.irena. org/DocumentDownloads/Publications/RE_Technologies_Cost_Analysis-SOLAR_PV.pdf [accessed 9 March 2015].

MIT (Massachusetts Institute of Technology) (2014). '2014 Energy and Climate Outlook'. Available at: http://globalchange.mit.edu/files/2014% 20Energy%20%26%20Climate%20Outlook.pdf [accessed 21 April 2015].

Odyssee-Mure (2014). 'Key Indicators, Industry/Transport/Households'. Available at: http://www.indicators.odyssee-mure.eu/online-indicators. html [accessed 9 March 2015].

Ren 21 (2014). 'Renewables 2014 Global Status Report'. Available at: http://www.ren21.net/ren21activities/globalstatusreport.aspx [accessed 9 March 2015].

Shell (2014) 'Shell Energy Scenarios to 2050'. Available at: https://s00. static-shell.com/content/dam/shell/static/future-energy/downloads/ shell-scenarios/shell-energy-scenarios2050.pdf [accessed 21 April 2015].

Steelbenchmarker (2014). 'Price History, tables and charts'. Available at: http://steelbenchmarker.com/files/history.pdf [accessed 9 March 2015].

Stern, N. (2006). 'Stern Review on the Economics of Climate Change'. Available at: http://webarchive.nationalarchives.gov.uk/+/http:/www. hm-treasury.gov.uk/stern_review_report.htm [accessed 9 March 2015].

The Guardian (2014). 'Canada switches on world's first carbon capture power plant'. Available at: http://www.theguardian.com/environment/ 2014/oct/01/canada-switches-on-worlds-first-carbon-capture-power-plant [accessed 9 March 2015].

U.S. EIA (Energy Information Administration) (2013). 'International Energy Outlook 2013'. Available at: http://www.eia.gov/oiaf/aeo/tablebrowser/ #release=IEO2013&subject=1-IEO2013&table=1-IEO2013&region=0-0&cases=Reference-d041117 [accessed 9 March 2015].

U.S. EIA (Energy Information Administration) (2014a). 'Coal price data'. Available at: http://www.eia.gov/coal/data.cfm#prices [accessed 9 March 2015].

U.S. EIA (Energy Information Administration) (2014b). 'Oil price data'. Available at: http://www.eia.gov/dnav/pet/pet_pri_spt_s1_d.htm [accessed 9 March 2015].

U.S. EIA (Energy Information Administration) (2014c). 'Petroleum & Other Liquids, US Net Imports by Country'. Available at: http://www. eia.gov/dnav/pet/pet_move_neti_a_ep00_IMN_mbblpd_a.htm [accessed 9 March 2015].

US DoE (Department of Energy) (2012). 'Photovoltaic (PV) System Pricing Trends: Historical, Recent and Near Term Projections'. Available at: http://www.nrel.gov/docs/fy13osti/56776.pdf [accessed 9 March 2015].

World Energy Council (2013). 'World Energy Resources 2013 Survey'.

Chapter Three

Investor-Specific Cost of Capital and Renewable Energy Investment Decisions

Thorsten Helms, Research Associate, University of St. Gallen
Sarah Salm, Research Associate, University of St. Gallen
Rolf Wüstenhagen, Good Energies Professor for Management
of Renewable Energies, University of St. Gallen

Introduction

Incumbents versus new investors in the renewable energy sector

The diffusion of renewables in Germany and other European countries has fundamentally changed the energy investor landscape. For several decades, investment in power generation infrastructure in Germany was largely dominated by four utility incumbents, often termed the 'Big Four'[1], which controlled 76% of the conventional generation capacities in 2012 (Bundesnetzagentur, 2013). In the emerging renewable energy segment, however, 90% of German wind power capacity and 96% of distributed solar capacity was owned by

---

[1] Energie Baden-Württemberg (EnBW); E.ON; Rheinisch-Westfälisches Elektrizitätswerk (RWE) and Vattenfall.

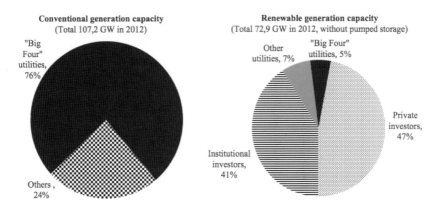

Fig. 3.1: Shares of ownership of investor groups for conventional and renewable energy generation capacities in Germany in 2012 (Source: Own illustration; Data: Bundesnetzagentur, 2013; Trendresearch and Leuphana, 2013)

non-utilities in 2012 (see Fig. 3.1). Private investors, such as home-owners, farmers and cooperatives, account for 47% of German renewable energy capacity. Moreover, institutional investors[2], such as pension and investment funds and insurance companies, play a significant role in financing renewables and own 42% of installed capacities (Trendresearch and Leuphana, 2013).

We propose that differences in the cost of capital among investor groups, common techniques of investment valuation, along with the financial characteristics of renewable and fossil technologies, explain the aforementioned shift in investment behavior. More specifically, we conjecture that electric utilities have traditionally invested in high-risk/high-return power generation projects, implying high costs of capital. Using the same metrics to assess lower-risk/lower-return projects in the field of renewables, such as wind parks or PV projects with guaranteed feed-in tariffs, has led to a systematic underestimation of their attractiveness, resulting in a loss of market

---

[2] In Trendresearch and Leuphana (2013) this category is termed 'institutional & strategic investors' and includes project developers, industrial and trade firms. However for reasons of simplification we decided to term this group 'institutional investors' and focus in the following on financial-oriented institutional investors, such as funds and insurances.

share of utilities *vis-à-vis* other investors with lower cost of capital. Our findings complement existing views, which consider primarily technological and regulatory risks as a major barrier to investment in renewable energies.

Conceptual Model

Our conceptual model, illustrated in Fig. 3.2, provides an explanation for investor heterogeneity in renewable energy investments. The propositions and underlying assumptions are explained in detail in the following sections. First, we introduce and define the term 'cost of capital', its role and influence for valuation methods, and the major determinants of investor-specific cost of capital. We argue that the cost of capital is influenced by the risk and return profile of past investments (Proposition 1a) and the returns of accessible investment opportunities, resulting in opportunity cost of capital (Proposition 1b). Subsequently, we discuss differences in the cost of capital of three major renewable energy investor groups, namely (large) utilities, institutional investors and private investors. Next, we illustrate the specific financial characteristics of renewable energies in comparison to fossil technologies, particularly in terms of risk and life-cycle cost composition. Then, we illustrate how the use of a uniform company-wide cost of capital in the valuation favors high-risk/high-return investment

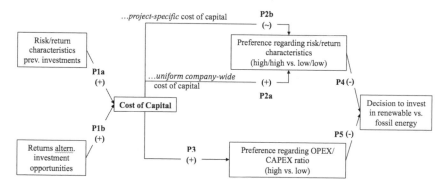

Fig. 3.2:   Conceptual model, illustrating the influence of cost of capital on the valuation of renewable energy investments

opportunities (Proposition 2a), whereas a project-specific cost of capital should sufficiently account for the specific risk characteristics of an investment. Low-risk/low-return investments should be valued equally, leading to an indifference of investors regarding high-risk/high-return and low-risk/low-return projects (Proposition 2b). Moreover, we show that a high cost of capital may lead to the selection of operating expense (OPEX)-intensive fossil energy projects and the rejection of capital-intensive projects (Proposition 3). Our model suggests that utilities' preference for high-risk/high-return (Proposition 4), and less capital-intensive projects (Proposition 5) results in negative renewable energy investment decisions and finally lower investment levels for investors with higher cost of capital, and vice versa. Finally, implications for practice and theory and conclusions are discussed.

The Cost of Capital in Valuation Methods and its Determinants

To explain the heterogeneity of renewable energy investors on the German energy market with regard to the cost of capital, it is necessary to understand what the 'cost of capital' is, and what major factors influence investor-specific cost of capital.

What is the cost of capital? A differentiated view and a definition

The definition of the 'cost of capital' varies. Further adding confusion, the term is often used interchangeably with terms such as 'discount rate', 'hurdle rate' or 'weighted average cost of capital' (WACC) (Pratt and Grabowski, 2010). One underlying reason may be the different motivations one has when speaking about 'cost of capital', and the fact that the cost of capital can be viewed from different perspectives, reflecting both sides of a balance sheet (see also Fig. 3.3):

First, from a *liability perspective*[3], the cost of capital is the supposed economic cost for a firm to obtain capital from its equity

---

[3] The liability side indicates where the firm's capital comes from, e.g. debt and equity.

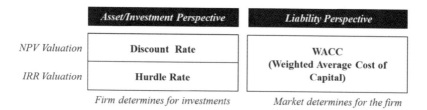

	Asset/Investment Perspective	Liability Perspective
NPV Valuation	**Discount Rate**	**WACC** (Weighted Average Cost of Capital)
IRR Valuation	**Hurdle Rate**	
	Firm determines for investments	*Market determines for the firm*

Fig. 3.3: Asset/investment and liability perspectives on the cost of capital

holders and creditors. The firm's average overall cost of capital, including the cost of equity and debt, is commonly termed WACC (e.g., Pratt and Grabowski, 2010). The firm though cannot set its WACC by itself; it is the market that determines this input factor, representing the return that the firm's shareholders and creditors demand as appropriate return. Moreover, this investor-specific cost of capital is an *expected* and *forward-looking* measure (Pratt and Grabowski, 2010). In reality though, shareholders' and creditors' expectations are often shaped by analysis of historical data (Pratt and Grabowski, 2010) and hence strongly influenced by past activities of the firm. This is an important aspect, as it implies that previous activities resulting in the current cost of capital have an impact on the choice of future investment projects.

Second, from an *asset perspective* of a firm's balance sheet, the cost of capital is the rate at which future cash flows from investments that the firm aims to conduct should be discounted to present values (Pratt and Grabowski, 2010). Discounted cash flow techniques, such as the calculation of the 'net present value' (NPV) and the 'internal rate of return' (IRR), are common standard tools to evaluate investments (Graham and Harvey, 2001; Titman and Martin, 2008). In the former case, the cost of capital enters in the valuation as 'discount factor' and converts anticipated future incomes or cash flows into a present value. The NPV represents the time value of anticipated future cash flows and risks (Pratt and Grabowski, 2010; Titman and Martin, 2008).

$$NPV = \sum_{t=1}^{N} \frac{PFCF_t}{(1+i)^t} - Investment_0$$

Investment decision rule: if NPV >0 → invest!

PFCF = project free cash flows (available for distribution to project creditors and equity holders)

i = discount factor

Source: Titman and Martin (2008)

In the latter case, the IRR[4] is obtained by solving the previous equation for i and assuming an NPV of 0. The IRR is then the discount factor which equals the present value of future cash flows with the initial investment. Some investors apply a 'hurdle rate' for investment valuation which is the minimum return that an investor expects from investing into a certain project, and that the IRR has to exceed:

$$Investment_0 = \sum_{t=1}^{N} \frac{PFCF_t}{(1 + IRR)^t}$$

Investment decision rule: if IRR > hurdle rate → invest!

Source: Titman and Martin (2008)

A project with an IRR above the cost of its capital is commonly assumed to create value (Fama and French, 1999; Pratt and Grabowski, 2010; Titman and Martin, 2008). Some investors may apply the investor-specific WACC as a hurdle, but often choose substantially different rates, for reasons explained in the following section. Hence, the hurdle rate can be regarded as a cost of capital the investment return must exceed (Pratt and Grabowski, 2010; Titman and Martin, 2008).

In conclusion, as we apply an asset or investment perspective, we use the term 'cost of capital' as the investors 'pricing' of the risk of an investment, and as a threshold return that potential investments have to meet to be viewed positively.

The cost of capital is commonly regarded as a function of the particular investment and its risk, but also an opportunity cost to returns of investment with similar risk levels that could have been

---

[4]The IRR of an investment is a relative measure for the profitability (Dinica, 2006) and is independent of the size and financing structure of the project. It is therefore well suited for the comparison of mutually exclusive investment opportunities.

earned instead (Pratt and Grabowski, 2010, Titman and Martin, 2008). The following section briefly illustrates the major determinants of the cost of capital in corporate practice.

Major determinants of investor-specific cost of capital

The 'capital asset pricing model' (CAPM) proposes that the cost of capital of every capital asset should apply to the specific risks[5] of the investment projects. The cost of capital is a linear combination of the risk-free interest rate plus a market risk premium (Bruner *et al.*, 1998; Copeland *et al.*, 2005; Graham and Harvey, 2001; Lintner, 1965; Markowitz, 1952; Sharpe, 1964). However, corporate practice shows that many firms or investors apply an *investor*-specific, instead of a *project*-specific, cost of capital (Bierman, 1993; Brounen *et al.*, 2004; Graham and Harvey, 2001; Titman and Martin, 2008). One explanation for this is the tendency for firms to simplify corporate valuation processes, and to reduce 'influence costs', resulting, for instance, from excessive lobbying of project sponsors for low cost of capital for particular projects (Martin and Titman, 2008; Milgrom and Roberts, 1990).

The WACC, with its components 'cost of debt' and 'cost of equity', has gained major practical relevance for the valuation of investments and as discount rate (Brounen *et al.*, 2004; Gitman and Forrester, 1977; Graham and Harvey, 2001). The relationship between risk and cost of capital for specific investment also implies that the firm itself is subject to risk valuations, and its WACC is set by those investing in the firm's equity and debt. As mentioned above the shareholders' and creditors' assessment of the firm's risk often results from the analysis of historical data and past activities of the firm (Pratt and Grabowski, 2010). Therefore, past risky activities will result in a higher WACC. Hence we propose that past activities and the 'risk and return' profile of previous investments shapes the costs a firm has to pay for its capital in the market, and, as a result, impacts the cost of capital for its proper investments (Proposition 1a).

---

[5]This applies only for the *systemic* risk correlated with the market development. The *unsystemic* risk is specific to a certain investment, and can be minimized by diversifying portfolios and contribute little to the variability of a portfolio (Titman and Martin, 2008).

When using only a single investor-specific discount factor, and from a value creation perspective, companies should realize all possible investment opportunities until the firm's cost of capital equals the marginal return of the last investment project (Driver and Temple, 2010; Pratt and Grabowski, 2010). In reality, firms or investors often apply hurdle rates (and hence cost of capital) above their own WACC, or involve an 'NPV cushion'. Hurdle premiums of 5% or more above the firm's estimated cost of capital are not unusual (Driver and Temple, 2010; Meier and Tarhan, 2007; Titman and Martin, 2008). Reasons for the application of such elevated hurdle premiums may include the objective to offset optimistic cash flow expectations from project sponsors, or to provide incentives for management to optimize the bargain process with externals (Titman and Martin, 2008). However, the most crucial explanation in the energy context is that the capability to invest may be constrained by access to capital and human resources. Different investment opportunities may become mutually exclusive, requiring firms to filter the most profitable projects. If the number of realizable investment projects is constrained, the WACC does not represent the real 'opportunity cost'. The 'opportunity cost of capital' should reflect the returns of the 'next best project' that has to be rejected in favor of the evaluated project (Titman and Martin, 2008).

Such theoretical assumptions are confirmed by empirical evidence: Meier and Tarhan (2007) analyzed the influence of the economic success of industries and the existence of growth opportunities on applied hurdle rates. Indeed, they found evidence that the applied hurdle rate premiums were positively correlated with the existence of growth opportunities, and the financial performance of firms and industries[6]. Firms subsequently behave in a more discriminating manner when approving projects compared with firms that had experienced more mediocre performance in the recent past (Meier and Tarhan, 2007). Hence, financially successful firms with a range of attractive investment opportunities applied higher hurdle rates. In the energy context, the previous high profitability of conventional power generation may

---

[6] Past performance of industries was thereby considered as a proxy for the existence of growth opportunities.

have led to high hurdle rates for new generation projects. We propose that the 'opportunity cost of capital' for investments (for instance, in the form of hurdle rates) is higher when other attractive investment opportunities with high returns are accessible, and results in higher cost of capital for the investment valuation (Proposition 1b).

Based on these foundations, the next section discusses the cost of capital levels for three central energy investor groups.

Cost of Capital Levels for Three Different Investor Groups

We propose different investor-specific costs of capital as a major determinant for the participation in renewable energy investment. Table 3.1 summarizes our conjectures on the cost of capital for three different investor groups, namely utilities, institutional and private investors.

The cost of capital and historic returns of utilities

Compared to other industries, utilities generally operate with mid-range WACCs due to their operations within a partly regulated sector. Eurelectric (2013) estimated an average WACC of 8.2% for leading European utility companies in 2012; Figure 3.4 illustrates their

Table 3.1: Cost of capital assumptions for different investor groups

	Cost of capital level	Rationale
Utilities	High single-digit to double-digit range	• Previous activities in high-risk/ high-return fossil generation result in medium to high WACCs • Access to high-return investments, high opportunity cost of capital
Institutional Investors	Medium single-digit range	• Preference for low-risk investments and stable long-term cash flows
Private Investors	Medium to low single-digit range	• Alternative investments with low return (e.g. consumption, savings account), low opportunity cost of capital

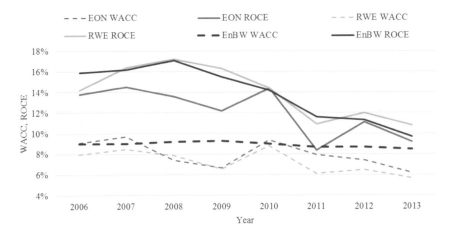

Fig. 3.4: Historical development of ROCE and WACC of leading utilities RWE and E.ON in Germany (Source: Own illustration; Data from Bloomberg; company reports)

WACC and 'return on capital employed' (ROCE) [7], showing that WACCs in recent years hovered around 8%. Hence the *real* investor-specific cost of capital remained in the upper single-digit area. If we consider an additional hurdle premium of 5% or more on the WACC, as is common in many industries, renewables such as PV with moderate IRRs will struggle to meet such valuation hurdles.

The ROCE can be regarded as a performance measure of the firm's operations related to the capital employed, and as a proxy for the 'opportunity cost of capital', as previously introduced. Moreover, most utilities operate in two fundamentally distinct markets, *regulated* markets like grid operations, which are 'natural monopolies', and *liberalized* markets, such as trading, retail and particularly power generation. Liberalized activities are related to higher risks due to competition and market volatility, but also provide more upside potential, especially in times of rising power prices as in the years before the financial crisis. By contrast, in regulated markets, moderate returns are practically guaranteed, but growth or increase of profitability can be

---

[7] The data for the fourth of the 'Big Four' utility companies in Germany, Vattenfall, is only partially publicly available, and has therefore not been considered in the figure.

difficult to achieve. Furthermore, many utilities are organized along the value chain; thus when renewable energy activities are organizationally situated in the generation division, it is likely that they have to compete for capital resources with fossil power generation, and corresponding returns accounting for the higher risks involved. It is difficult to estimate previous expected returns for fossil power generation at this point, but studies provide evidence that expected return rates were clearly above the IRRs for PV (e.g. Fraunhofer ISE, 2013).

Overall, utilities are characterized by medium WACCs, and high opportunity cost of capital due to the high profitability of fossil generation, at the beginning of the major growth of renewable energy and PV in 2009 in Germany. Therefore we assume a single-digit to double-digit cost of capital level for the valuation of renewables.

The cost of capital of institutional investors

Institutional investors, such as pension funds, insurance companies or investment funds, can become a major financing source for renewable energy diffusion, owing to their impressive amount of assets under management — US$71 trillion worldwide (Kaminker and Stewart, 2012). Pension funds and insurance companies tend to prefer long-term investments with limited risks, limited operational interaction and stable cash flows, matching their long-term liabilities (DECC, 2013; Kaminker and Stewart, 2012; Milford *et al.*, 2011). Additionally, institutional investors actively look for portfolio diversification, which can be achieved by investing in different asset classes with little systematic correlation (Kaminker and Stewart, 2012). Such preferences appear to match well with renewable energy characteristics. Typical capital costs for institutional investors would often take other low-risk, long-term investment opportunities as a benchmark, such as government bonds, and therefore may range in the medium to low single-digit range.

The cost of capital of private investors

Determination of the cost of capital for non-professional private investors is a non-trivial task. These investors may not, for instance, be explicitly aware of opportunity costs, and many of them will have no prior experience of investing in (renewable) energy projects. According to our model presented in Fig. 3.2, the other relevant factor determining cost of capital is the return of alternative investment opportunities. This raises the question against which other uses of capital a private investor will benchmark his or her renewable energy investment.

A recent survey in Germany provides some empirical insights (Hübner *et al.*, 2012). Households were asked what the purchase of a rooftop PV system would be compared to. Whereas most respondents compared the PV system with an investment in building insulation (43%), a significant share compared it to investing in long-term consumables such as 'a new kitchen' (23%) or 'a new car' (9%). From a financial perspective these items are 'investments' with highly negative returns; there is no positive cash flow associated with owning a private car or a kitchen. This translates into low opportunity cost of capital.

Another accessible benchmark for private investors might be financial deposits and assets with low-risk characteristics such as savings accounts or life insurance. Institutions such as the German state promotional bank KfW[8] provide loans for renewable energy projects to private and institutional investors with interest rates of 2% or less. We would therefore argue that the cost of capital for private investors in rooftop PV systems is likely to be in the low single-digit range, particularly due to the limited access to high-return investments and resulting low opportunity costs of capital.

After discussing characteristics of different investor types, we now need to take a closer look at the financial characteristics of renewable energies.

Comparison of Investment Profiles of Renewable and Fossil Energy Projects

From a financial perspective, renewables differ from fossil energy, particularly in terms of risk. As Awerbuch (2000) summarized,

---

[8] Kreditanstalt für Wiederaufbau.

renewables such as PV come 'as close as a real asset can to providing the systematically risk-free (zero-beta) characteristics of a US Treasury bill' (Awerbuch, 2000: 1030; Awerbuch, 1995). These financial differences, summarized in Table 3.2, root in the fundamental technological and regulatory differences between renewables and fossil energies, particularly in terms of risks.

First, renewable energy projects like solar and wind are free of fuel price risks whereas fossil fuel prices expose significant volatility (Awerbuch, 2000; Blanco, 2009). *Second*, in Germany and several other countries, feed-in tariffs shield renewable energy generators from revenue risks resulting from electricity price fluctuations. In contrast, fossil power plants have to compete on the liberalized energy market and are exposed to volatile electricity wholesale prices (Blanco, 2009; Bürer and Wüstenhagen, 2009; Couture and Gagnon, 2009; Lüthi and Wüstenhagen, 2008; Menanteau *et al.*, 2003; Wüstenhagen and Bilharz, 2006). *Third*, renewable energies are not exposed to carbon risk, whereas fossil fuels may face increasing exposure to policies aimed at limiting greenhouse gas emissions, such as carbon taxes or emissions trading (Green, 2008). *Fourth*, solar PV requires very little maintenance due to the absence of moving parts, and is therefore characterized by extremely low operational risk (Schleicher-Tappeser, 2012). Wind turbines are relatively more maintenance intensive, but with 225,000 turbines operating worldwide at the end of 2012 (GWEC, 2015), they represent a mature technology, too. *Fifth*, different studies have identified 'unsystematic' project risks as reasons why companies chose higher discount rates for projects than proposed by theory (Driver and Temple 2010; Meier and Tarhan, 2007; Oxera, 2011). Distributed renewable energy projects are an order of magnitude smaller than most fossil power plants. Conducting a larger number of small investments will allow investors to diversify and reduce such unsystematic risks of investment portfolios, compared to large bulk generation plants. Moreover, the modularity and scalability of PV projects compared to fossil power plants reduces the risk of creating excess capacities (Awerbuch, 2000), which may take up to a decade between investment decision and operation. We summarize these risks as 'bulk risk', and conclude that they are substantially lower for distributed

Table 3.2: Investment profiles of renewable and fossil power generation projects

		Fuel-free renewable energy project (e.g. wind or solar)	Fossil fuel power project (e.g. gas or coal)
Risks	Fuel price risk (input price volatility)	*No*	*Yes*
	Revenue risk (output price volatility)	*No* (if remunerated under secure feed-in tariff. Yes otherwise)	*Yes*
	Carbon risk	*Low*	*High* (gas) to *Very High* (coal)
	Operational risk	*Low* in case of PV *Medium* in case of wind	*Medium*
	Bulk risk (project scale)	*Low* (Medium for wind parks)	*High*
Cost Composition	Ratio OPEX/ CAPEX	*Low*	*High*

renewables than for large-scale fossil generation. *Sixth*, we have to consider the different composition of life-cycle costs for both renewable and fossil technologies. Renewable energies are very *capital intensive.* They require high upfront payments and capital expenditures (CAPEX), but entail very low OPEX (Awerbuch, 2000; Blanco, 2009; Känzig and Wüstenhagen, 2010). Whereas the upfront investment in a wind farm makes up 80% and for PV an even higher share of the total life-cycle costs, capital expenditures account for only about 40% of life-cycle costs of a gas power plant, with the remainder being related to fuel costs, operation and maintenance (Blanco, 2009). With the investment profile skewed towards the early part of the life-cycle of a project, renewables therefore represent a more challenging proposition to high capital cost investors than fossil power generation.

The low risk of PV projects is reflected in moderate returns. Spertino *et al.* (2013) conducted an economic analysis of historic PV

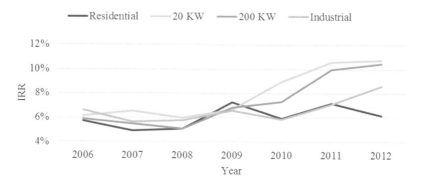

Fig. 3.5: Historic IRRs for PV systems in Germany (Source: Own illustration; Data: Spertino *et al.*, 2013)

system returns in Germany. Figure 3.5 shows the IRR over the life-time[9] for different years of commissioning and different system sizes. IRRs ranged in the medium single-digit range initially and then climbed up to 8–11% for larger installations[10]. The rising returns from 2009 onwards can be explained by a divergence between system costs and feed-in tariffs. While feed-in tariffs were reduced by 5–10 % annually, PV systems prices declined by 30% per annum in the same period (e.g. Spertino *et al.*, 2013). Comparing returns from investing in solar PVs with historic ROCEs of the big German utilities shows that, at least in the 2006–2009 period, they seemed to have other more profitable investment opportunities (see 'The cost of capital and historic returns of utilities' and Fig. 3.4).

We can conclude that renewable energies are, in many regards, less exposed to risks; a source of stable and moderate returns; and that life-cycle costs are largely determined by the investment and CAPEX, whereas OPEX play a relatively smaller role. These characteristics

---

[9]These returns are guaranteed through the feed-in tariff for a period of 20 years. The variance of IRRs is hence not the variance of IRRs of a single plant, but for different plants commissioned in different years.

[10]A high *gearing* — the share of debt for financing — improves the return on equity for the investor, when debt can be obtained at low interest rates (Fraunhofer ISE; 2013). The *return on equity* of the project might then range clearly above the IRR. Gearing issues are not further considered.

influence the outcome of investment valuations. Utilities previously engaged in fossil energies may possess higher costs of capital, accounting for the numerous market risks of fossil power generation. For those investors, not appreciating the lower risk exposure of renewable energies and applying a uniform company-wide cost of capital will lead to rejecting renewable energy investments in favor of riskier assets with higher expected returns, such as fossil power generation projects.

DCF and Cost-Based Valuation and How Capital Costs Impact the Outcome

Rejection of low-risk projects in case of high cost of capital

Finance theory is explicit about the appropriate discount rates for projects, and proposes the application of *project-specific* discount factors for the valuation of investments, reflecting specific opportunity costs and risks of the project (Bierman, 1993; Brealey *et al.*, 2008; Brounen *et al.*, 2004; Graham and Harvey, 2001; Titman and Martin, 2008). In the previous sections, however, we argued that in corporate practice many companies apply, instead, *investor-specific* discount factors. Most firms do not even vary the discount rate between their different divisions (Meier and Tarhan, 2007), which appears to be a source of systematic bias in the case of utilities, considering the different characteristics of the businesses they are involved in. The project-specific cost of capital considers the specific risk inherent in the project, and hence is a positive linear relationship between risk and return of a specific project, as proposed by CAPM theory.

The simplification of applying the same investor-specific capital cost in the valuation process may lead to systematic undervaluation and rejection of safer projects, and, on the other side, to the acceptance of riskier projects to cope with their investor's cost of capital, as demonstrated in Fig. 3.6. Technically 'good' projects are those on or above the dashed line, as they possess a low risk-to-return ratio. The horizontal line represents the investor-specific capital cost. Applying this as a discount rate on all corporate investments implies

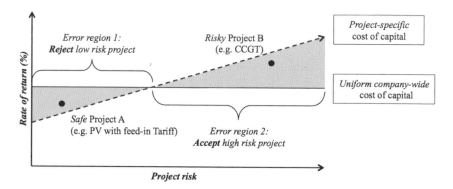

Fig. 3.6: Investment errors through the application of a uniform company-wide cost of capital (Source: Adapted from Titman and Martin, 2008)

the ignorance of specific project risks. Investors with higher capital costs will then tend to invest in riskier projects that meet their higher return expectations (Titman and Martin, 2008). If a firm or an investor with high investor-specific capital costs compares a low-risk project, with a risk and return profile below the horizontal line, the valuation outcome will possibly be negative, although the relationship between risk and return of the project suggests a positive valuation outcome. In Fig. 3.6, this concerns projects falling within *Error region 1*. On the other hand, higher capital costs will lead to the acceptance of projects with disproportionately high risks, illustrated by *Error region 2*.

Thus, when applying single *investor*-specific cost of capital, investors with high cost of capital tend to favor investments with high-risk/high-return characteristics (Proposition 2a). Projects that would also reduce the overall portfolio risk are systematically rejected. One underlying reasoning of this model is that companies will probably find it much easier to measure, compare and communicate *returns* for past and present investments, and to determine expected returns for future projects than determining and comparing *risks* of these projects. The use of a project-specific cost of capital would result in an equal valuation for high-risk/high-return and low-risk/low-return projects, and the selection of projects with an optimal risk/return ratio. Investors would then be indifferent regarding the choice between high/high and low/low projects (Proposition 2b).

Undervaluation of capital-intensive investments in case of high cost of capital

We previously described that a major difference between renewable and fossil power generation is that the former is dominated by CAPEX whereas the latter is dominated by OPEX. We will illustrate that CAPEX (the annual costs for amortization and interests) are a function of the cost of capital. This in turn may explain the preference of investors with high cost of capital for OPEX-intensive and less capital-intensive projects such as fossil power generation.

In his forward-thinking paper, 'Investing in photovoltaics: risk, accounting and the value of new technology', Awerbuch (2000) criticized the widespread application of 'engineering-economic' methods for the comparative calculation of PV against other technologies. These methods would not adjust project valuation for risk, a central principle of modern finance. Indeed, costing models estimating the lifetime cost per kilowatt-hour have played a dominating role for planning and investment valuation in the energy industry (Bergek *et al.*, 2013). But in addition to the different risk specificities for the technologies in combination with investor-specific cost of capital (discussed in the previous section), it is also the different cost composition of renewable and fossil energies that influences the valuation outcome in favor of the former or the latter technology, depending on the applied cost of capital. A common approach, the 'levelized lifetime cost of electricity' (LCOE) analysis, is well suited to demonstrate this effect. The least 'cost investment opportunity' is found by discounting the cumulated capital and operational costs and dividing them by the economic output of the power plant (Awerbuch, 2000; Awerbuch, 2003; Bergek *et al.*, 2013; Bhattacharya and Kojima, 2012; Söderholm *et al.*, 2007; Söderholm and Pettersson, 2011). So what is the impact of the cost of capital when comparing fossil generation technologies and renewables with a cost-based valuation approach? Let us illustrate this with a simple example. The following equation is our starting point. The LCOE multiplied with the annual produced energy equals the overall cost of the plant (Branker *et al.*, 2011):

$$\sum_{t=0}^{n} \frac{LCOE_t}{(1+i)^t} \times M_{t,el} = \sum_{t=0}^{n} \frac{C_t}{(1+i)^t}$$

When solved for LCOE, assuming a constant value, and by splitting overall costs into annual operational costs and the initial investment, one obtains the LCOE with the following formula (Branker *et al.*, 2011; Fraunhofer ISE, 2013; Konstantin, 2007)

$$LCOE = \frac{I_0 + \sum_{t=1}^{n} \frac{A_t}{(1+i)^t}}{\sum_{t=1}^{n} \frac{M_{t,el}}{(1+i)^t}}$$

I_0 = Initial investment in year 0
C_t = annual net costs in year t
A_t = Annual operational costs in year t
(Fixed and variable operational costs, disposal asset)
$M_{t, el}$ = produced electricity in kWh year t
i = cost of capital, real
n = economic plant lifetime
t = year
Sources: (Branker *et al.*, 2011; Fraunhofer ISE, 2013;
Konstantin, 2007)

We do not want to provide a full comparative calculation between fossil and renewable investments based on a 'real' figure, because the result for fossil investments is highly sensitive to the selection of the input variables. Instead, we split the equation. In the first case, we only consider the investment and capital expenditures and no operational costs (a simplified assumption for a PV plant). Moreover, we know from financial mathematics that an annuity can be transformed, as follows:

$$\sum_{t=1}^{n} \frac{1}{(1+i)^t} = \frac{1 - (1+i)^{-n}}{i}$$

Assuming that the power generation (and in the following also the operational costs) remains constant throughout its lifetime, the equation for the LCOE in the first case simplifies to:

$$LCOE_{CAPEX} = \frac{I_o}{\sum_{t=1}^{n} \dfrac{M_{t,el}}{(1+i)^t}} = \frac{I_o \times i}{M_{el} \times \left(1 - (1+i)^{-n}\right)}$$

In the second case, we only consider operational expenditures, such as fuel costs, and investments I_0 is zero. The equation for the LCOE then simplifies to:

$$LCOE_{OPEX} = \frac{A}{M_{el}}$$

We obtain that the LCOE in the latter case is independent from the magnitude of cost of capital i and remains constant, whereas the graph for the $LCOE_{CAPEX}$ increases with rising cost of capital (see Fig. 3.7). The rationale behind this is that an investment needs to be financed, which results in CAPEX such as amortization and interests, a function of the considered cost of capital. The OPEX instead can be covered annually by the operational cash flows, and is independent from the cost of capital. If we now assume two extreme cases, a renewable energy investment with very high CAPEX, and a fossil energy project with very high OPEX, it is likely that the two graphs cross each other at a certain cost of capital[11]. To the left of this point, the investors with lower capital cost prefer the renewable energy investment due to the lower LCOE, whereas to the right the investors with higher capital costs prefer the fossil energy investment. Thus, this example demonstrates that investors with higher capital costs obtain more favorable LCOEs for investments with lower CAPEX when using a cost-based approach, and favor OPEX-intensive over capital-intensive investment opportunities, and vice versa (Proposition 3).

---

[11] In case of an investment with both CAPEX and OPEX, the resulting graph is a combination of capital expenditures that rise with increasing capital costs, and operational costs not affected by the capital costs.

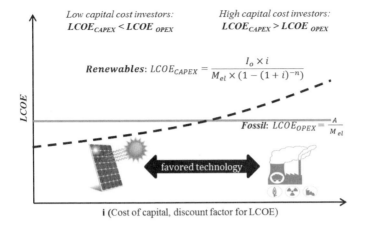

Fig. 3.7: Effects of cost of capital and OPEX/CAPEX on LCOE for renewable and fossil energies

Conclusion: Renewable Energy Investment Decisions as a Function of Cost of Capital

This chapter contributes to the discussion about financing the energy transition by taking a closer look at the drivers of the observed investor heterogeneity in renewable energy markets. We propose differences in cost of capital between incumbent utilities and new, non-utility investors as a previously under-researched aspect. We have developed a conceptual model which illustrates how previous investment activities and alternative investment opportunities shape investors' cost of capital, and how the higher cost of capital of incumbent utilities may serve as an explanatory factor for their lack of renewable energy investments compared to new low capital cost investors, such as private or institutional investors. Renewable energies are characterized by a different investment profile than fossil fuel power generation projects — they tend to avoid a number of risks of conventional power plants, and they have a low OPEX-to-CAPEX ratio. Combining these characteristics with differences in investor-specific cost of capital may provide a new explanation for the investor heterogeneity observed in the renewable energy market. Furthermore, firms or investors previously engaged in high-risk/high-return projects might find it difficult to shift attention and resources towards investments with lower risk and returns, such as shifting from fossil to renewable energy projects.

Our observations have important managerial and policy implications. Electric utilities who want to increase the share of renewables in their asset portfolio are well advised to rethink their capital allocation practices. Applying project-specific cost of capital rather than using a uniform company-wide hurdle rate may be a way to account for systematically lower risks in fuel-free, scalable renewable energy projects with low operating expenses. As for policymakers, our analysis shows that electric utilities tend to require high returns in order to invest in any project, including renewables. An alternative to designing renewable energy policies aimed at providing these high returns, however, might be for policymakers to either convey to utility investment professionals that renewables have systematically lower risks, or target institutional investors who tend to have a preference for a different end of the risk-return spectrum, in that they may accept lower returns as long as they can expect stable long-term cash flows with limited risk.

References

Awerbuch, S. (1995). 'New economic cost perspectives for valuing renewables', in Boer, K. (ed.), *Advances in Solar Energy*, American Solar Energy Society, Colorado.

Awerbuch, S. (2000). 'Investing in Photovoltaics: Risk, Accounting and the Value of New Technology', *Energy Policy*, **28**(14), 1023–1035.

Awerbuch, S. (2003). 'Determining the Real Cost: Why Renewable Power is More Cost-Competitive than Previously Believed', *Renewable Energy World*, **6**(2), 52–61.

Bergek, A., Mignon, I. and Sundberg, G. (2013). 'Who Invests in Renewable Electricity Production? Empirical Evidence and Suggestions for Further Research', *Energy Policy*, **56**, 568–581.

Bhattacharya, A. and Kojima, S. (2012). 'Power Sector Investment Risk and Renewable Energy: A Japanese Case Study Using Portfolio Risk Optimization Method', *Energy Policy*, **40**, 69–80.

Bierman, H. (1993). 'Capital Budgeting in 1992: A Survey', *Financial Management*, **24**.

Blanco, M. I. (2009). 'The Economics of Wind Energy', *Renewable and Sustainable Energy Reviews*, **13**(6), 1372–1382.

Branker, K., Pathak, M. J. M. and Pearce, J. M. (2011). 'A Review of Solar Photovoltaic Levelized Cost of Electricity', *Renewable and Sustainable Energy Reviews*, **15**(9), 4470–4482.

Brealey, R. A., Myers, S. C. Allen, F. (2008). *Principles of Corporate Finance*, McGraw-Hill Education, New York.

Brounen, D., de Jong, A. and Koedijk, K. (2004). 'Corporate Finance in Europe: Confronting Theory with Practice', *Financial Management*, 33(4), 71–101.

Bruner, R. F., Eades, K. M., Harris, R. S., and Higgins, R. C. (1998). 'Best Practices in Estimating the Cost Of Capital: Survey And Synthesis', *Financial Practice and Education*, **8**, 13–28.

Bundesnetzagentur (2013). 'Monitoringbericht 2013'. Available at: http://www.bundesnetzagentur.de/SharedDocs/Downloads/DE/Allgemeines/Bundesnetzagentur/Publikationen/Berichte/2013/131217_Monitoringbericht2013.pdf [accessed 8 September 2014].

Bürer, M. J. and Wüstenhagen, R. (2009). 'Which Renewable Energy Policy is a Venture Capitalist's Best Friend? Empirical Evidence from A Survey of International Cleantech Investors', *Energy Policy*, **37**(12), 4997–5006.

Copeland, T., Weston, J. and Shastri, K. (2005). 'Changes in Hurdle Rates for Low Carbon Generation Technologies due to the Shift from the UK Renewables Obligation to a Contracts for Difference Regime'. Available at: https://www.gov.uk/government/publications/nera-economic-consulting-report-changes-in-hurdle-rates-for-low-carbon-generation-technologies [accessed 8 September 2014].

Dinica, V. (2006). 'Support Systems for the Diffusion of Renewable Energy Technologies—An Investor Perspective', *Energy Policy*, **34**(4), 461–480.

Driver, C. and Temple, P. (2010). 'Why Do Hurdle Rates Differ From The Cost of Capital?', *Cambridge Journal of Economics*, **34**(3), 501–523.

Eurelectric (2013). 'The financial situation of the Electricity Industry — Economic and financial update'. Available at: http://www.eurelectric.org/media/81890/fg_fe_paper__final-2013-540-0004-01-e.pdf [accessed 6 December 2013].

Fraunhofer ISE. (2013). 'Stromgestehungskosten Erneuerbare Energien'. Available at: http://www.ise.fraunhofer.de/de/veroeffentlichungen/veroeffentlichungen-pdf-dateien/studien-und-konzeptpapiere/

studie-stromgestehungskosten-erneuerbare-energien.pdf [Accessed 8 September 2014].

Fraunhofer ISE. (2014). 'Photovoltaics report 2014'. Available at: http://www.ise.fraunhofer.de/de/downloads/pdf-files/aktuelles/photovoltaics-report-in-englischer-sprache.pdf [accessed 8 September 2014].

Gitman, L. J. and Forrester Jr, J. R. (1977). 'A Survey of Capital Budgeting Techniques Used by Major US Firms', *Financial Management*, **6**(3), 66–71.

Graham, J. R. and Harvey, C. R. (2001). 'The Theory and Practice of Corporate Finance: Evidence From the Field', *Journal of Financial Economics*, **60**(2), 187–243.

Green, R. (2008). 'Carbon Tax or Carbon Permits: The Impact on Generators' Risks', *The Energy Journal*, **29**, 67–89.

GWEC (2015). 'Wind in numbers'. Available at: http://www.gwec.net/global-figures/wind-in-numbers/ [accessed 9 March 2015].

Hübner, G., Müller, M., Röhr, U., Vinz, D., Kösters, J., Simon, A., Wüstenhagen, R., Chassot, S., Roser, A., Gruber, E., Gebhardt, T., Frahm, B.-J. and Alber, G. (2012). 'Erneuerbare Energien und Ökostrom — Zielgruppenspezifische Kommunikationsstrategien', *Abschlussbericht zum BMU Verbundprojekt* (FKZ: 0325107/8), Halle/Berlin.

Kaminker, C. and Stewart, F. (2012). 'The role of institutional investors in financing clean energy', OECD Working Papers on Finance.

Känzig, J. and Wüstenhagen, R. (2010). 'The Effect of Life Cycle Cost Information on Consumer Investment Decisions Regarding Eco Innovation', *Journal of Industrial Ecology*, **14**(1), 121–136.

Koller, T., Goedhart, M. and Wessels, D. (2010). *Valuation: Measuring and Managing The Value of Companies*, John Wiley and Sons, New York.

Konstantin, P. (2007). 'The Valuation of Risk Assets and the Selection of Risky Investments in Stock Portfolios and Capital Budgets', *The Review of Economics and Statistics*, 13–37.

Lüthi, S. and Wüstenhagen, R. (2012). 'The Price of Policy Risk — Empirical Insights From Choice Experiments With European Photovoltaic Project Developers', *Energy Economics*, **34**(4), 1001–1011.

Markowitz, H. (1952). 'Portfolio Selection', *The Journal of Finance*, 7(1), 77–91.

Martin, J. and Titman, S. (2008). 'Single vs. Multiple Discount Rates: How to Limit 'Influence Costs' in the Capital Allocation Process', *Journal of Applied Corporate Finance*, **20**(2), 79–83.

Masini, A. and Menichetti, E. (2012). 'The Impact of Behavioural Factors in the Renewable Energy Investment Decision Making Process: Conceptual Framework and Empirical Findings', *Energy Policy*, **40**, 28–38.

Meier, I. and Tarhan, V. (2007). 'Corporate investment decision practices and the hurdle rate premium puzzle'. Available at SSRN 960161.

Menanteau, P., Finon, D. and Lamy, M. L. (2003). 'Prices versus Quantities: Choosing Policies for Promoting The Development of Renewable Energy', *Energy Policy*, 31(8), 799–812.

Milford, L., Tyler, R. and Morey, J. (2011). 'Strategies to finance large-scale deployment of renewable energy projects: an economic development and infrastructure approach', Montpelier: Clean Energy Group.

Milgrom, P. and Roberts, J. (1990). 'Bargaining Costs, Influence Costs, and the Organization of Economic Activity', *Perspectives on Positive Political Economy*, 57, 60.

Oxera (2011). 'Discount rates for low carbon and renewable generation technologies'. Available at: http://www.oxera.com/Oxera/media/Oxera/downloads/reports/Oxera-report-on-low-carbon-discount-rates.pdf?ext=.pdf [accessed 8 September 2014].

Pratt, S. P. and Grabowski, R. J. (2008). *Cost of Capital*, John Wiley and Sons, New York

Schleicher-Tappeser, R. (2012). 'How Renewables will Change Electricity Markets in the Next Five Years', *Energy Policy*, 48, 64–75.

Sharpe, W. F. (1964). 'Capital Asset Prices: A Theory of Market Equilibrium under Conditions of Risk', *The Journal of Finance*, 19(3), 425–442.

Söderholm, P. and Pettersson, M. (2011). 'Offshore Wind Power Policy and Planning In Sweden', *Energy Policy*, 39(2), 518–525.

Söderholm, P., Ek, K. and Pettersson, M. (2007). 'Wind Power Development in Sweden: Global Policies and Local Obstacles', *Renewable and Sustainable Energy Reviews*, 11(3), 365–400.

Spertino, F., Di Leo, P. and Cocina, V. (2013). 'Economic Analysis of Investment in the Rooftop Photovoltaic Systems: A Long-Term Research in the Two Main Markets', *Renewable and Sustainable Energy Reviews*, 28, 531–540.

Titman, S. and Martin, J. D. (2008). *Valuation: The Art and Science of Corporate Investment Decisions*, Addison-Wesley, New York.

Trendresearch GmbH and Leuphana Universität Lüneburg (2013). 'Definition und Marktanalyse von Bürgerenergie in Deutschland'. Available at: http://www.die-buergerenergiewende.de/wp-content/uploads/2013/10/definition-und-marktanalyse-von-buergerenergie-in-deutschland_akt_2.pdf [accessed 8 September 2014].

Wüstenhagen, R. and Bilharz, M. (2006). 'Green Energy Market Development in Germany: Effective Public Policy and Emerging Customer Demand', *Energy Policy*, 34(13), 1681–1696.

Section II

Chapter Four

Markets, Governments and Renewable Electricity

Richard Green, Alan and Sabine Howard Professor of
Sustainable Energy Business, Imperial College Business School

Introduction

The starting point of this chapter is that renewable electricity projects produce a valuable commodity which is traded on many markets around the world, but that they do so at a cost which is generally higher than the prices in those markets. Such projects can only be financially viable with some kind of support from a government, but will continue to interact with the market, even if they no longer rely on it for revenues. This chapter discusses those interactions and the main ways in which governments support renewable energy. It does not say much about carbon pricing, which could support renewable generation indirectly by raising the cost of competing technologies and hence the price that renewables have to beat. At present, most of the carbon prices seen around the world, whether in the form of taxes or from tradable emissions permits, are low relative to central estimates of the social cost of carbon and they are too low to make most renewable generators competitive without additional support.

As described in the book's Introduction, that support can be justified as a way of overcoming market failures in research and development (R&D) and in innovation, as well as in terms of the failure to price carbon properly.

When discussing renewable electricity generation, it is important to remember the key physical characteristics of electricity. These include the facts that it is hard to store, so demand and generation must balance at every moment in time, and that flows through the power grid are hard to control, so that the system must be operated as a coordinated unit. The traditional response to these facts, as described in the next section, was vertical integration and economic regulation; once some countries started to introduce electricity markets, they had to take these constraints into account. The choice between a fully regulated electricity industry and one with markets has significant consequences for renewable generators. It is relatively straightforward to instruct a regulated firm to introduce renewable power, but much harder to secure it in a market-based industry. Next, the chapter discusses the main ways in which governments provide additional revenue to renewable projects, in terms of their advantages and disadvantages for the project's investors, and its interactions with the wider market. Those interactions are further considered in the following section, thinking about both the short-term impact on market prices and the longer-term effect on other generators. The section also asks whether present market designs can provide the right incentives for the transition to a low-carbon energy system, or whether a return to regulation offers better prospects. Brief conclusions also touch on this point, but in the context of the need to engage consumers and adopt new business models; something which a regulated system is unlikely to excel at.

How the Physical Nature of Electricity Shapes its Markets

For reasons that will be explored shortly, electricity generators must be operated as an integrated system. Traditionally, this meant that the industry was operated as a monopoly: sometimes nationwide but sometimes on a more local basis. The monopoly might be vertically integrated from the power station to the customer's meter, but in many countries a large generation and transmission organisation would sell bulk supplies of power to local distribution companies. Large industrial firms were often allowed to run their own generators, and the electricity supply industry would accept their surplus output, but the underlying principle was that the electricity system should be organised in a way that reflected the tight central control required. If the industry was a natural monopoly, then it would be necessary to control its behaviour, either by public ownership or by government regulation.

Over time, however, it has been recognised that central control of how generators are operated need not mean unified ownership. In many countries, new generating plants have been built as independent power producers (IPPs), running the station and selling its output to the grid as the main focus of their business, rather than as the by-product from an industrial process. The US Public Utility Regulatory Policies Act of 1978 allowed this, in order to encourage renewable generation and combined heat and power; in other countries, IPPs have access to capital markets that are not available to the incumbents and can be seen as a way of increasing capacity without breaching limits on public borrowing. International institutions such as the World Bank have encouraged many middle- and low-income countries to introduce IPPs as an alternative to state-owned monopoly generation.

The other model that combined central coordination without unified ownership was the power pool, through which a number of companies ran their power stations in ways intended to minimise the cost of the whole. Chile introduced a market based on a power pool in 1978 (although most financial flows were based on regulated prices and contracts) and the UK made a pool-based market the centrepiece of the electricity industry's privatisation in 1990. The following year, Norway expanded the scope of its power pool to create a fully fledged market that grew into the world's first international power market, Nord Pool. The success of these early markets encouraged many other countries to follow suit, with the EU adopting its first Electricity Directive in 1996, starting a process of liberalisation with the aim of creating a Single Electricity Market. In the US, several regional markets were created in the late 1990s, although the implosion of California's badly designed restructuring was a significant set-back. The market designs have since been improved, and ten regional transmission organisations manage about 60% of the power delivered to US consumers. In the west and south-east of the country, however, the traditional model based around integrated and regulated utilities still dominates, albeit with some IPPs in every state.

While the electricity industry's organisational forms differ around the world, the laws of physics do not. At the moment, electricity cannot economically be stored on a large scale, except where the local landscape allows a pumped storage hydro-electric station to pump water uphill when power is in surplus and therefore cheap, running it downhill through the turbines later to generate when the electricity will be scarcer and hence more valuable. If consumers try to take more (or less) energy out of the power system than generators are putting into it, the frequency with which every generator is turning will slow (or rise). A small deviation from the design frequency (50 cycles a second (Hz) in Europe, 60 Hz in North America) can be tolerated, but a large imbalance in either direction will cause the system to fail. Because power stations take time to start, the system operator must always maintain a spinning reserve of stations currently running at less than their full capacity and hence able to increase output very quickly. Other stations are contracted to start up and provide power at short notice, should demand be higher than expected or another generator fail. Some (typically large) customers are also able to reduce their demand on request and are paid for doing so, but the electricity market is complicated by the fact that the balance between demand and supply can change far more quickly than the prices which most customers see. The market for oil is kept in balance by producers and consumers autonomously changing their behaviour in response to price changes, and by adjustments to stocks; an electricity system requires a system operator that can quickly issue direct commands. Where there is an electricity market, these commands will need to be accompanied by appropriate payments, but they must be issued more quickly than a contract can be negotiated.

A second key fact about electricity is that current flows through all the lines on an interconnected system, in inverse proportion to the resistance (or strictly speaking, impedance) on each line. If one element fails, whether a power station or a transmission line, the flows will immediately reallocate themselves to reflect the new situation, even though this might mean that a line or transformer somewhere is overloaded. If it is, a circuit-breaker will be triggered to protect that asset, and the flows will change once more. If the new pattern of flows risks an overload elsewhere, it is possible for a series of failures to cascade through the grid, blacking out a large area. Recent examples include Ontario and New York State in August 2003, Italy in September 2003, much of Germany and its neighbours in 2006 and Denmark and southern Sweden, also in September 2003. The latter blackout is unusual in that it occurred as a result of two separate faults in quick succession. The system should always be run in 'N minus one' mode, so that it remains stable after any single problem (something that was not achieved before the other examples mentioned); even so, troubles do sometimes come in pairs[1].

These facts mean that the value of electricity depends upon when, and where, it is generated. Two popular measures of the relative cost of different technologies ignore this. The levelised cost of electricity (LCOE) simply divides the net present value of the power that a station might be expected to generate (running with a high load factor) by the net present value of its costs. It is inappropriate for comparing the cost of stations that would be expected to run for different times during the year. The second measure, grid parity, identifies the point when the cost per kWh of a technology, such as a solar PV panel, is equal to the price per kWh paid by the consumer thinking of installing it. This is the relevant calculation for that consumer, but ignores the fact that electricity prices also cover the fixed cost of the transmission and distribution grids, and those costs have to be paid by someone. Utilities may face a vicious circle if they try to cover those fixed costs

---

[1]When building the power system, it is best to aim for 'N minus 2', so that it can still be operated to the 'N minus 1' standard with any single element out of action for maintenance. 'N minus 3' is more secure, but more expensive.

from a declining sales volume, thus raising their prices and making it more attractive to install PV.

Electricity markets ought to reflect the differing value of power at different times. Electricity generated when demand is high is normally more valuable than at times of low demand — indeed, the market price of power at those times can even be negative. This is because many power stations cannot generate at low levels for sustained periods, but if they are switched off instead, they will then have to incur the fuel cost and the wear and tear of starting up again once demand has risen. Their owners are willing to pay to avoid a restart, and the market price of power can reflect this. Similarly, electricity which cannot be transmitted to distant customers without risking an overload on the grid is less valuable than power from a station close to the load, which can charge a premium price.

Electricity markets in the US (and some other countries) reflect these facts with a system known as locational marginal pricing, or nodal pricing. In the so-called day-ahead market, every generator in the market submits offers to sell power, or bids to buy back electricity that it has already committed to produce through a bilateral contract. Similarly, the load-serving entities responsible for meeting customer demands bid to buy power, or offer to sell it back if they had over-contracted for their needs through bilateral trading. The independent system operator (ISO) for the market combines these offers and bids, and its knowledge of the transmission system's characteristics, to produce the least-cost schedule for the following day that would balance generation and demand while observing transmission constraints. The ISO calculates the marginal cost of increasing demand in each hour by a small amount at each node on the system in turn; this is the price for that node in that hour. Other prices are also calculated and paid for stations which provide reserve. Once the trades in this market have been published, generators are committed to provide the scheduled amount of power and receive the relevant prices, but they are also invited to submit adjustment bids (and offers) for which they would be willing to produce a different amount. When events on the day turn out differently to the previous day's expectation, as is inevitable, the ISO will use these adjustment bids as the basis for its redispatch, when it acquires more power to cope with an increased level of demand, for example. New prices will be calculated for this real-time market, and are used to settle all the differences between the amounts actually generated and consumed and those assumed in the day-ahead schedule.

Generators do not have to actively trade in the real-time market — they can submit prohibitively high offers and low bids, and the ISO will generally not ask them to adjust their output. Similarly, generators can trade all their power in advance through a bilateral contract, and simply fulfil that contract's terms without reference to what is actually happening around them. In general, however, it can be economically advantageous to react to changing conditions on the power system, and the ISO's organised markets provide the forum for doing so.

Electricity markets in Europe are typically less sophisticated. As with the US markets, a large proportion of the power is traded in advance through bilateral contracts, and there is an organised day-ahead market in most European countries (or groups of countries). The key difference is that the day-ahead markets are generally organised by power exchanges which are distinct from the transmission system operator, and are not used to procure reserves or to ensure that all transmission constraints are respected. Instead, the transmission operators must make separate trades for reserve and to adjust the location of generation if they are to be confident that the overall result will be electrically stable. There is also an imbalance process to ensure that generators are paid for everything they produce, and consumers pay for all their consumption, either through vertical integration, bilateral contracts, the day-ahead auction or this imbalance settlement.

The power exchanges increasingly collaborate through a process known as 'market coupling' to ensure that neighbouring countries will have the same electricity prices unless the transmission lines between them are congested. The power exchanges calculate the flow from, say, France to Belgium needed to ensure that the prices are equalised, given supply and demand in the two countries, and take this flow into account when setting the prices and quantities in each place. If the flow exceeds the capacity of the lines between them, however, then France (the exporter) will have a lower price and Belgium a higher one, reflecting the relative scarcity of power. Market coupling is replacing a less efficient system in which interconnector capacity was traded separately from the power exchanges, and electricity was sometimes scheduled to flow from a high-price region to a low-price one. If there is congestion inside a country, however, most power exchanges ignore it[2], and the transmission system operator has to buy and sell power to resolve the problem.

What does this imply for renewable generation projects? Despite the sophistication of electricity markets in the US and the EU, many countries do retain largely integrated utilities and selling power to these on a long-term contract may offer an easier environment in which to finance a project. Some countries with power markets also offer simple long-term contracts which allow generators (particularly smaller ones) to ignore market prices. If the generator does face market prices, however, it needs to be conscious that the price of power can vary significantly over the day, so that the timing of its output matters. Its predictability is also important — if a generator sells power in advance and then does not generate it, it may have to pay a very high price in the real-time market or through imbalance settlement. Generators located in an area with a structural surplus of generation relative to demand must be aware of the risk that they will face relatively lower prices than generators closer to the loads. At present, however, the key fact is that many renewable generators have costs that are higher than the market value of the power they can produce, and so it is unlikely that many would be viable in the absence of direct government support.

How Governments Support Renewable Power

As described in the Introduction, many governments see renewable energy as desirable, and therefore support it. The two broad ways of doing this at present are to ensure that the electricity industry (and

---

[2]The Nordic market is an honourable exception, for Norway can be divided into as many as five zones with different prices, and Sweden into four.

hence its customers) buys renewable power, even if it costs more than alternatives, or to give money to renewable generators to reduce their costs to the point where they are competitive with conventional power. Table 4.1, adapted from REN21 (2014), describes many of these policies and lists the number of countries using them. It is important to add that many individual national policies may not fit neatly into these boxes and that some of the categories used are very similar. For example, an energy production payment that gives a generator a payment from the public purse for each kWh generated will not be very different from a production tax credit that allows the generator to reduce its payments *into* the public purse by the same amount.

This kind of production tax credit is one of the main mechanisms used by the Federal Government in the US, which allows them to reduce corporation taxes by US2.3 cents per kWh generated over the first ten years of a wind or energy crop project's life. Other technologies get the credit for five years, or a lower credit (US1.1 cents per kWh) or both. One problem with the way that this system has been implemented is that the credit has been allowed to expire (or nearly so) several times, and this has been reflected in a stop–start pattern of project development. Until recently, eligibility depended on the date when the station was placed in service; the consequences of a completion delayed until after the credit had expired would thus be severe. In 2013, this was changed so that projects were eligible for ten years of support if they started construction when the credit was available, reducing the risk to developers. However, at the time of writing (January 2015) the credit appears to have expired once again.

Governments can frequently offer lower tax rates on renewable generation equipment (or the inputs it needs); its owners can also benefit from accelerated or enhanced depreciation when calculating taxes on corporate profits. Enhanced depreciation reduces the taxable profits from a project; accelerated depreciation does not change the project's lifetime profits but gives a cash flow benefit by delaying the payment of taxes. The cost of investing in renewable generation may be reduced by subsidies or other grants and the government may offer equity or loan finance. If the government commits itself to buy the

Renewable Energy Finance

Table 4.1: Renewable energy support policies

Policy	Description	High-income (45)	Upper-middle (41)	Lower-mid and low-income (54)	All (140)
			Number of countries adopting		
Tax reductions	Lower tax rates for renewable generators	28	24	39	91
Feed-in tariff	Guaranteed price (or premium to market price) for each kWh produced over a period, which the electricity industry has to buy	28	21	21	70
Public loans or grants	Government invests in the project or subsidises its upfront cost	26	21	21	68
Capital subsidy	One-off payment from government to reduce the initial cost of the generator	29	13	17	59
Tenders	Government (or industry body) runs auctions for contracts to build and run new capacity	21	18	16	55
Net metering	Customers can offset all their generation against (high-priced) purchases from the grid, rather than having to sell for a low price in periods when their generation exceeds their consumption	17	13	13	43

Quantity requirement	Electricity industry has to buy a proportion of its power from renewable generators — includes renewable portfolio standards and tradable green certificate schemes	26	7	8	41
Tax credit	Generator receives a tax rebate for each kWh produced, or on its investment costs	17	11	11	39
Energy production payment	Direct payment from government for each kWh produced	9	5	8	22
Non-electricity sector policies					
Biofuels obligation	Transport fuel companies have to blend a proportion of biofuel into their products	29	18	16	63
Heat obligation	Support for renewable sources of heat (various policies)	10	5	4	19

project's output for several years, this can help to unlock commercial finance. For example, in 2013 Air Products was helped to get financing for a 49 MW energy from waste plant (at Billingham on Teesside) when the UK government signed a 20-year deal to buy its output at a long-term fixed price (*Financial Times*, 2014).

One regulatory measure used to assist small-scale renewable generators is to allow for so-called net metering. This means that all the output produced by, for example, a PV panel is subtracted from its owner's household consumption (or vice versa), even if there are hours in which the house is exporting power because the panel's output is high and consumption is low. This matters because the tariffs that consumers pay for buying power need to cover the costs of the networks, and are therefore higher than the wholesale value of electricity. Net metering means that as much of the output as possible is valued at the higher retail price rather than the lower wholesale value. Electricity rates in California have an increasing block structure, where the marginal rate rises as monthly consumption crosses various thresholds, and solar companies there have become adept at installing panels sized so that their output replaces most of the higher-priced units, but are small enough not to replace many low-priced units (Borenstein, 2014). Maximising the consumer's savings also maximises the amount of revenue lost by the incumbent utilities from a given amount of solar output, and the utilities are pressing to be allowed to restructure their tariffs and recoup the losses. Even a notionally self-sufficient household receives valuable services from being connected to the distribution grid, and should pay for them through a tariff that reflects the true costs they impose on the industry.

There are three main ways in which governments arrange for the electricity industry to buy the output from renewable generators: tenders for specific projects, a quantity requirement (often organised as a renewables portfolio standard or tradable green certificate scheme) or a feed-in tariff (FiT). Under the first scheme, the responsible body decides on the kind of renewables that it would like to buy and issues a tender. This body might be a government department, an agency set up by the government or the transmission (or distribution) operator. The winning bidder will be determined by price, or by a mixture of price and other characteristics. Contrasting experiences in Denmark and the UK offer lessons for how such tenders should be conducted. In the 1990s, the UK government ran a series of tenders under the Non-Fossil Fuel Obligation, which contracted for 3271 MW of renewable capacity in England and Wales; however, only 1202 MW was ever delivered (Pollitt, 2010). One problem was that the bidders specified the project that they wished to build, and in order to reduce the cost of taking part in the auction, offers could be submitted before all the necessary consents were in place. In many cases, developers were later unable to obtain planning permission and had to abandon their project. There was no requirement to post any kind of completion bond when taking part in the tender, either, and a number of low-bidding developers may have suffered from the winners' curse, submitting a price that turned out to be lower than the cost of building their station. With no completion bond, it would be better for them to simply walk away, and many did so (Mitchell and Connor, 2004).

In contrast, when the Danish government organised a tender for the Anholt offshore wind project, it had already decided on the broad scope of the project and commissioned environmental impact studies, while the transmission company was able to specify the kind of connection to the grid that would be needed. This preparatory work greatly reduced the risks involved in the later stages of development, although the developer still had to bear construction risks and complete the station within a tight timetable. While a report to the Danish Ministry of Climate and Energy (Deloitte, 2011) suggested that greater flexibility in these conditions could have reduced the price paid, the cost of DKK 1.051 per kWh (£110 per MWh) already compares very favourably to the price to be paid in the UK (£155 per MWh in 2014/15).

Under the second approach, that of a renewable portfolio standard, the policymaker specifies an amount of renewable power that the industry should procure, often in terms of a percentage of demand. In a regulated system, it is then the responsibility of the utility to arrange this, and regulated prices can rise to cover the cost. In a market system, the duty is likely to fall on electricity retailers, which have to ensure that they buy this amount of qualifying power, or pay a buy-out charge to cover any shortfall. Generators are given certificates for each unit of electricity they produce, and it is these certificates that the retailers must surrender to show that they have met their obligation — in Europe, this is known as the tradable green certificate approach. The price of the certificate reflects the buy-out charge that the retailer can avoid by acquiring it. The generator may sell power and certificate together, minimising transactions costs, or separately.

The advantage of this approach is that the government can specify the amount of renewable energy that it wishes to have developed, and a high enough buy-out price can provide a good incentive to the industry to achieve this. If all generators are treated equally, then there will be a tendency to develop the lowest-cost resources first. This has obvious economic advantages, but risks ignoring other technologies with longer-term potential that currently have high costs. Some schemes give these technologies more certificates per MWh generated, bringing in more additional revenue to offset their higher costs. The main disadvantage of a tradable green certificate scheme for a project developer is that the generator is still responsible for selling its power in the electricity market, and the risk in this may affect its cost of capital, compared to schemes that offer a guaranteed overall revenue stream.

The third approach, the FiT, does offer this guarantee. The policymaker specifies the prices that will be paid for all qualifying electricity over a fixed period, and any project that meets the conditions will receive the relevant prices in exchange for its power. The prices may be based on the policymaker's assessment of technology costs, or on the results of earlier auctions for similar projects, as in China (IRENA, 2014). In Germany, the payments are made by the local distribution operator; in the UK, this is done by a retailer (supplier, in the UK's terminology). In each case, however, there is a mechanism for smearing the cost across all customers (Germany gives rebates to electricity-intensive firms facing international competition). The prices received by a given project should be determined when it is commissioned, and attempting to change these during the contract's term is a quick way of destroying confidence in the market, as the Spanish government discovered in 2012 when it introduced retroactive cuts to its FiTs; 1110 MW of wind capacity were installed in 2012 but just 175 MW in 2013. Pre-determined prices for a given project may still decline over time, however. Front-loading the support received by the generator allows it to pay down its debt rapidly and minimises financing costs. In reducing the amount at stake in the later years of the contract, it may also reduce political risks.

While the prices for a given project should be pre-determined at the date the scheme is commissioned, it is generally good practice for the prices for projects commissioned each year to be lower than those for previous years, in line with the expected decline in renewable costs. The rate at which prices decline should be known far in enough in advance for developers to plan, however; the UK government imposed significant losses on some solar developers when it cut the value of their FiTs in August 2011 with just six months' notice. A number of schemes were financially committed to go ahead but had insufficient time to commission before the deadline, thus losing at least a third of their expected revenue.

The tariff received by a renewable generator should reflect its costs and hence depend upon its characteristics. These obviously include its technology type, allowing higher-cost technologies a chance to prove themselves, but can also include the project size, when smaller projects can expect to have higher costs. This is particularly relevant for solar power, when individual householders can install a small panel on their roofs and receive government support for it, but at a much higher cost per kWh than larger installations in fields or on large buildings. The German government offers a lower average payment per MWh from wind farms in the windiest places than for energy generated at less fortunate sites. This might sound illogical, but is in fact a way of ensuring that the less-favoured farms receive enough revenue to cover their costs. If farms at good sites received the same average revenue, they would be over-compensated, and so they are paid less. Two features of the scheme are important, however. The payments are calibrated so that good sites will normally be more profitable and will be developed in preference to less-favoured places. Furthermore, no payments are made to farms at sites where the wind speed is too low to allow for sensible development.

The great advantages of a FiT for a project developer should be its simplicity and stability. The simplicity does not just extend to the fact that the developer will receive a single stream of payments to cover all of its costs, but because there is no need to actively market its power. The purchaser is required to take the electricity produced; the developer just has to meet the technical standards for connection to the grid and then start generating. If the developer can be confident of a predictable revenue stream, its cost of capital should be low.

The disadvantage of a FiT is that the government has little control over the amount of electricity that will be produced under it. If the level is set too high, then installing renewable capacity will be very profitable and a large amount will be developed; this effect has been seen with solar power in several countries where the tariffs failed to decline as fast as the cost of PV panels. The Spanish renewable energy law stated that its tariff would be reduced one year after the installed capacity reached a particular milestone; this created a window which was long enough for many developers to react to in the predictable manner, with 2,575 MW of new capacity added before the payments fell, compared to 555 MW in the previous year (Mitchell *et al.*, 2011). A far better alternative, used in Germany, is to make the decline in the tariff contingent on the amount of capacity actually installed but with a very short lag (if any), thus minimising the risk of the kind of rush to beat a deadline seen in Spain.

A variant on the FiT is known as the premium FiT approach. Under this, the generator is responsible for selling its power in the market, but will receive an additional income stream with a pre-set payment per MWh generated. This is, in effect, a straightforward subsidy to renewable generation; the costs could be recovered from electricity customers or from taxpayers (as in the Netherlands, for example (Couture *et al.*, 2010)). From the point of view of the developer, this is a halfway house between a renewable portfolio standard and a FiT, since the project faces a market price risk for its energy sales but not for the support scheme[3]. The advantage for the policymaker is that since the generator depends on the energy market for a significant part of its income, it should respond to the price signals sent by that market. The importance of this should become clear when we think about how large amounts of renewable generation can affect the electricity market.

How Renewable Power Affects the Electricity Market

It is important to distinguish between renewable generators that are dispatchable and can be turned on and off at will (such as biomass and hydro-electric generators with reservoirs) and those that have intermittent availability, notably wind and solar generators. System operators can schedule output from the former to rise and fall with the level of electricity demand; indeed, hydro-electric plants are among the most flexible, able to respond at short notice and reach full output quickly. In contrast, output from wind generators and solar PV panels is only available when conditions are right and must either be used at once or spilled, unless electricity storage is available. Concentrating solar thermal plants are a half-way house, in that many can store the fluid heated by the sun for a few hours before generation, giving more flexibility (and sometimes the ability to generate at times when prices are higher than when the sun was shining).

System operators thus have to predict the amount of intermittent renewable generation that will be available and adjust the output of other plants to offset this. To the extent that renewable outputs are less predictable than those of thermal stations, this requires more plant to be held in reserve, ready to generate. It need not mean that those stations are actually burning fuel, provided that scheduling decisions can be made late enough to have high-quality wind forecasts — the earlier the unit commitment is decided, the more likely that large

---

[3] The UK is adopting Contracts for Difference under which the payments to generators will vary inversely with the wholesale power price; if this variation exactly offset changes in the generator's market revenues, then it would be equivalent to (but more complex than) a FiT.

stations will be started and then not needed (Müsgens and Neuhoff, 2006). Some capacity may have to be part-loaded to cope with the risk of a rapid change in wind speeds across a wide area of the country and hence generation, although reserves already have to be sufficient to cope with the sudden loss of the largest single unit on the system, and those will often be able to cope with changes in the wind. Nonetheless, there will usually be changes between the close of day-ahead trading and real time, and these will have to be paid for.

It may also be necessary to constrain off (and compensate) some renewable generators if the system cannot accept their output, either because transmission lines from distant generators would be over-loaded or because the thermal generators they would replace cannot be turned off[4]. Trading power with neighbouring countries can prevent this, if the links are strong enough, and it can be possible to put surplus energy into storage, with pumped hydro stations or as heat. Combined heat and power plants in Denmark now face market prices that give them an incentive to use electric heating rather than conventional boilers to provide hot water at times when electricity prices are low.

This example shows the importance of market rules; as the proportion of renewable generation increases, the US market design is likely to out-perform the European one. In US markets, the independent system operator creates price signals from a simultaneous optimisation of energy production, reserves and transmission constraints, thus taking full account of the impacts of variable renewables. In Europe, most energy trading is separated from the task of managing reserves and constraints, and generators receive less accurate price signals. This is particularly true with regard to the value of power at different points on the grid; renewable electricity that is generated far from the loads may never reach consumers and distant generators should receive lower prices to reflect this. It may still be appropriate to build renewables in distant locations with good resources, rather than close to loads

---

[4]Thermal power stations cannot be turned off for short periods because of the stress involved in cooling and reheating their turbines. Ireland sometimes has to reduce the output of wind generators to ensure that it has enough turbines connected to the grid that their weight can provide inertia, slowing the speed at which the system frequency would fall after a fault.

but with low wind speeds or solar insolation; however, the price signal should be sent to ensure that the decision is an informed one. FiTs typically ignore differences in the value of the power produced; the European Commission (2014) has unveiled rules that require new renewable generators to sell their output in the market and thus to receive price signals. They must be responsible for paying for imbalances between contracted sales and actual outputs, and must not have an incentive to generate when prices are negative.

The relationship between renewable generation and wholesale power prices is complex. First, the average timing of renewable output may coincide with times when electricity prices have traditionally been high, as with solar generation in summer-peaking systems with large air conditioning loads. Wind speeds in northern Europe are higher in winter than summer, as are electricity demands. The highest demands in these countries occur in the dark winter evenings, however, when solar PV panels will produce nothing; some renewable generators systematically produce at times when the local demands are below average.

Second, whatever the broad pattern of renewable output and electricity demand, times of above-average output (such as particularly windy days) are likely to be correlated with below-average demand on the remaining plants and thus lower prices than would be normal for that time of day and year (Twomey and Neuhoff, 2010). Green and Vasilakos (2012) estimate that this effect reduced the average value of wind generation by 4.1% in eastern Denmark and by 8% in western Denmark. The effect was larger in the west because the share of wind output was greater; it would have been larger still if Denmark had not been able to export surplus wind generation (and import similar amounts of power at other times).

The third interaction between renewable generators and electricity prices is currently damaging the share prices of many utilities. Wholesale prices tend to be inversely correlated with the amount of spare capacity on the system. With little spare capacity, there is less competition and price-cost margins are typically higher; high-cost plants that might not be needed when there is surplus plant will also have to be used more. With perfect foresight, this is the market mechanism that should adjust supply to meet demand, but power markets have proved vulnerable to periods of optimistic over-investment that subsequently drive prices below costs: examples include both England and New England at the turn of the millennium. In those cases, profits suffered because of poor commercial decisions, but the rapid expansion of renewable capacity that is now having a similar effect is due to government policies. This phenomenon was first noticed in Germany, where it is called the merit order effect (Sensfuß *et al.*, 2008). It does offset the cost of renewable generation to consumers, but the lower wholesale prices are coming at the cost of existing conventional generators. Germany has so much solar generation that average day-time power prices can be lower than those at night, and the load factors of conventional generators have fallen dramatically. Australia adopted renewable targets that implied new generators would be meeting a significant part of the projected demand growth, but when demand actually fell, so did prices (AER, 2014).

This may just be a disequilibrium phenomenon; Green and Vasilakos (2011) have shown that in a long-run equilibrium, the amount and mix of capacity will adjust in response to the growth of renewable generation so that each type of power station can still expect to recover its costs. The problem, however, is that companies who have recently lost significant amounts of money may be reluctant (and indeed unable) to invest when new capacity is required. Furthermore, year-to-year profits may well become more volatile if the effects of fluctuations in renewable output are combined with those in demand. A higher proportion of capacity will need to be peaking stations that depend on a small number of running hours in which to recover their costs. If there is enough renewable capacity, there may be many hours in which it is marginal and drives the wholesale price down to zero. If the renewable generators stand to lose output-related subsidies, their marginal cost is negative[5]: can any market cope with large numbers of negative prices?

The UK government is adopting a set of policies known as Electricity Market Reform which will significantly reduce the role of

---

[5] The change to EU rules described above is intended to remove this incentive to create negative prices.

the market. Long-term contracts for low-carbon generators (nuclear, renewable and fossil with carbon capture and storage) will be allocated by tenders or negotiations and will largely insulate those generators from short-run fluctuations in market prices, although they will still have to sell their output into the wholesale market. To provide an incentive to keep enough additional capacity on the system, a capacity market has just started to operate, offering an additional income stream as long as the stations are available when needed (and penalties if not). The government fixes the demand curve in this market, and thus has a big influence on the amount of capacity that will be built (the market runs several years in advance so that it can support new stations) and the attractiveness of keeping older stations open. The actual operation of power stations will still be governed by the wholesale markets, but when the capacity mix is so heavily dependent on government support schemes, is this a true market? It is a long way from the 1990s, when some generators were building stations expecting to sell their output at most a year in advance.

There should be little doubt that it is easier to increase the amount of renewable generation when the electricity industry is still regulated — utilities can simply be ordered to build an appropriate mix of plants (or buy the output of independent generators) and allowed to pass the cost on in their prices. Would this be more efficient? A competitive system creates greater incentives to operate efficiently, and ensures that investors, rather than consumers, pay the cost of investment mistakes. Whether this ultimately reduces costs to consumers depends on two effects. The first is that a market generally involves greater incentives for efficiency, although these should be offset against the transactions costs of running it. The second effect comes about because a company in a competitive market faces greater risks and hence a higher cost of capital than a regulated firm[6]. If the competitive firm makes better investment decisions, the benefits of

---

[6] If this is simply because the firm now faces risks (e.g. of bad investments) that it would have passed on to the consumer in a regulated system, then there is a transfer but no change in welfare. In an electricity market, however, prices that go up and down with the cost of the marginal fuel may be riskier for both company and consumer than prices based on average costs in a regulated system.

these may outweigh its higher cost of capital, but this is not inevitable. The move to a low-carbon energy system increases the ratio of capital costs to operating costs, and thus the balance between the need to operate efficiently and to invest cost-effectively. Of itself, this need not change the balance of advantage between competition and regulation — it raises the impact of the cost of capital on overall costs, but also the importance of making the right investment decisions. At present, however, governments have such a large role in setting the mix of low-carbon plant that giving companies the right incentives over the remaining decisions seems secondary.

Pretending that there is a market when the government makes most of the decisions may simply raise the cost of capital, and it would be better to move to a regulated system in which lower returns were predictable and acceptable to investors. It is certainly the case that EU countries adopting a FiT for wind generators were able to develop a higher proportion of their resources — and for lower prices, relative to costs — than the countries that adopted the more market-based approach of quota or tradable green certificate schemes (Ragwitz *et al.*, 2007). The role of governments could fall in future, if carbon prices rise to a level where they are sufficient to drive investment in low-carbon electricity and governments do not need additional schemes to change the mix of technologies. Until this happens, however, we are unlikely to have a truly effective market for low-carbon power.

Conclusions

This chapter has discussed the interactions between technology, governments and electricity markets. Governments can choose whether they want a liberalised or a regulated industry, but the design of an electricity market has to take the laws of physics into account, and there are many engineering constraints on the move towards a low-carbon power system. There is also a financial constraint — at present, the price of carbon is not high enough to make most renewable generators economic, and so specific policies are needed to encourage investment in them. This requires governments to choose which technologies to support, for even a policy of paying the same to all renewable generators is effectively a policy of supporting those with the lowest costs at the present time, regardless of the benefits of developing those with the potential for lower costs in future. It seems that the policies which have been most successful in developing renewable generation are those which are furthest from the idea of a market: FiTs that offer a fixed price to all generators of a given type and force power companies to absorb their output. The need for decarbonisation is urgent, but as large amounts of new capacity depress prices, incumbents complain about their resulting losses.

This does not necessarily mean that a regulated industry is the answer. This chapter, like too much of the discussion of decarbonisation, has focused on the supply side — what can be done to make it profitable to invest in providing low-carbon power. The demand side also has a big role. Improving energy efficiency should lead to big reductions in carbon emissions — greater efficiency accounts for almost two fifths of the difference between business-as-usual and the International Energy Agency's '2 degrees scenario' (2DS), according to its *Energy Technology Perspectives.* Accommodating renewable energy in a cost-effective manner also requires a flexible demand side. If variations in renewable output can be met by postponing demand for loads that are not time-sensitive (such as water heating or laundry), fewer generators need to be kept on expensive standby, and less capacity is needed overall. Electric vehicles will lead to a big increase in the demand for electricity, but if their charging can be accomplished at times of otherwise low demand or high renewable output, it need not require a large addition to generation capacity. The new information and communications technologies behind the smart grid offer the means to achieve this flexibility, but there is no guarantee that their potential will be used.

Someone needs to come up with innovative business models that persuade large numbers of consumers to change the way in which they demand electricity. Incumbent utilities are not obvious candidates to do this, and keeping the industry open to competition makes it possible that we will get at least 'one smart agent' (Sutton, 1997) who can. A new business model may also change the way in which consumers buy their electricity. Samuel Insull drove the widespread adoption of metering and payment for kilowatt-hours, but the first electricity sales were based on the number of light bulbs a consumer had installed — in other words, consumers paid for capacity. Could this be a more appropriate way to buy power from renewable generators whose capital costs are much higher than their variable costs? Governments have a vital role to play in setting policies that support R&D and mandate decarbonisation, but when it comes to developing innovative business models, the best environment is sure to be a market with freedom of entry.

References

Australian Energy Regulator (2014). 'State of the Energy Market 2014', Australian Energy Regulator, Melbourne.

Borenstein, S. (2014) 'Rationalizing California's Electricity Rates'. Available at http://energyathaas.wordpress.com/2014/09/29/rationalizing-californias-residential-electricity-rates/ [accessed 19 October 2014].

Couture, T. D., Cory, K., Kreycik, C. and Williams, E. (2010). 'A Policymaker's Guide to Feed-in Tariff Policy Design, Technical Report NREL/TP-6A2-44849'. Available at www.nrel.gov/docs/fy10osti/44849.pdf [accessed 7 January 2015].

Deloitte (2011). *Analysis on the furthering of competition in relation to the establishment of large off-shore wind farms in Denmark*, Ministry of Climate and Energy, Deloitte, Copenhagen.

European Commission (2014). *Guidelines on State Aid for Environmental Protection and Energy 2014–2020 (2014/C 200/01)*, Commission of the European Communities, Brussels.

Financial Times (2014). 'Coalition seeks long-term energy deal worth about £300m'. Available at http://www.ft.com/cms/s/0/b6b80406-cbbc-11e3-8ccf-00144feabdc0.html#axzz3O8ZLz9rx. [accessed 7 January 2015].

Green, R. J. and Vasilakos, N. (2011). 'The Long-term impact of wind power on electricity prices and generating capacity CCP Working Paper 11-4', Centre for Competition Policy, University of East Anglia.

Green, R. J. and Vasilakos, N. (2012). 'Storing Wind for a Rainy Day: What Kind of Electricity Does Denmark Export?', *The Energy Journal*, **33**, 1–22.

IRENA (2014), 'Renewable Energy Prospects: China, REmap 2030 Analysis', IRENA, Abu Dhabi.

Mitchell, C. and Connor, P. (2004). 'Renewable Energy Policy in the UK 1990–2003', *Energy Policy*, **32**, 1935–1947.

Mitchell, C., Sawin, J., Pokharel, G. Kammen, D. and Wang, Z. (2011). 'Policy, Financing and Implementation', in Edenhofer, O., Pichs-Madruga, R., Sokona, Y., Seyboth, K., Matschoss, P., Kadner, S., Zwickel, T., Eickemeier, P., Hansen, G., Schlömer, S. and von Stechow C. (eds), *IPCC Special Report on Renewable Energy Sources and Climate Change Mitigation*, Cambridge University Press, Cambridge, pp. 865–950.

Müsgens, F. and Neuhoff, K. (2006). 'Modelling Dynamic Constraints in Electricity Markets and the Costs of Uncertain Wind Output', Electricity Policy Research Group Working Paper CWPE 06010 and EPRG 0514, University of Cambridge.

Pollitt, M.G. (2010). 'UK Renewable Energy Policy Since Privatisation', in Moselle, B., Padilla J. and Schmalensee R. (eds), *Harnessing Renewable Energy*, RFF Press and Earthscan, Washington DC, pp. 253–282.

Ragwitz, M., Held, A., Resch, G., Faber, T., Haas, R., Huber, C., Coeanraads, R., Voogt, M., Reece, G., Morthorst, P. E., Jensen, S. G., Konstantinaviciute I. and Heyder, B. (2007). 'Assessment and Optimisation of Renewable Energy Support Schemes in the European Electricity Market', *OPTRES Final Report*, Fraunhofer IRB Verlag, Karlsruhe.

REN21 (2014). 'Renewables 2014 Global Status Report', *Renewable Energy Policy Network for the Twenty First Century*, United Nations Environment Programme, Paris.

Sensfuß, F., Ragwitz M. and Genoese M. (2008). 'The Merit-Order Effect: A Detailed Analysis of The Price Effect of Renewable Electricity Generation on Spot Market Prices in Germany', *Energy Policy*, **36**, 3076–3084.

Sutton, (1997). 'One Smart Agent', *The RAND Journal of Economics*, **28**, 605–628.

Twomey, P. and Neuhoff K., (2010). 'Wind Power And Market Power In Competitive Markets', *Energy Policy*, **37**, 3198–3210.

Chapter Five

The Impact of Government Policies on Renewable Energy Investment

Gireesh Shrimali, Assistant Professor,
Monterey Institute of International Studies

Renewable energy is attractive to policymakers for a variety of reasons. First, renewable energy, due to its low emission profile, addresses the issue of climate change directly. Second, renewable energy, due to its non-reliance on imported fossil fuels, has positive implications for energy security. Finally, renewable energy has implications for increased jobs, especially in *manufacturing*, as well as project development.

Renewable energy policy may seek to achieve a number of objectives, such as increasing deployment of renewable energy, driving innovation, and reducing the cost of new technologies. An effective policy would achieve its objectives cost-effectively, equitably, and without introducing significant risks. Given limited government budgets, cost-effectiveness of policies becomes at least as important as other criteria.

In most economies, the private sector is the main source of funding for meeting renewable energy policy objectives. In such cases, financing and, therefore, financing costs lie at the heart of the investors' decision-making process. This has a crucial impact on the amount, cost, and associated risks of the renewable energy investments. In other words, financing is a key determinant of the effectiveness of renewable energy policy[1].

However, renewable projects, their investors, and the policy environments in which they operate are diverse and heterogeneous. Thus, there is no single prescription to design policy such that renewable projects are financed effectively. That is, it is not clear *ex-ante* how policies can influence financing costs in order to achieve their targets cost-effectively.

In this chapter, we identify some general principles of how policy influences investment decisions, with a view toward building tools to help policymakers design policies that can effectively and efficiently leverage investment in the renewable space. To do so, our analysis and discussion has several parts:

- First, we set out the specific mechanisms, or pathways, through which policy can impact the financing of renewable projects.
- Next, we study a series of cases based on real-world renewable energy projects in the US, Europe, and India (Varadrajan *et al.*, 2011). Applying this framework of policy impacts on potential investor types, we attempt to understand how policy has affected — or could have affected — the investment decision, costs, and risks of each project. In particular, we address two basic questions:
  - o How did policy affect project costs, revenues, and returns?
  - o How can policy impact the cost of financing these projects?
- Finally, we bring the findings from these case studies together to identify where there may be common lessons, and the circumstances under which these lessons could be applicable.

---

[1] In Climate Policy Initiative (CPI)'s 'Renewable Energy Financing and Climate Policy Effectiveness' Working Paper (2011), we explored how financing can be used to diagnose policy effectiveness outcomes, focusing on deployment of renewable energy, cost-effectiveness, distribution of risks, costs and benefits, innovation outcomes, and policy stability as key policy effectiveness criteria.

Policy Impacts Cost of Capital, and Therefore the Cost of Electricity, Through a Number of Pathways: Case Studies from the Developed World

Policy support may be provided in many forms. An example of a popular policy support mechanism is a grant from the government, to meet a part of the project's capital requirement. The structure of this policy support varies — for example, this support may be provided as a one-time grant at the beginning of the project, or in a phased manner spread over many years.

Policy influences the investment environment in many ways. It could affect the sharing of risks between the public and private sector, drive the choice of technology for generating power and impact the business practices of market participants. In this section, we explain various policy impact pathways on the basis of the six case studies.

Figure 5.1 depicts the indirect impacts of policies through the pathways described below in different scenarios. It shows that, in the US and the EU, the most important pathways are duration of revenue support, revenue certainty, and risk perception (Varadrajan *et al.*, 2011).

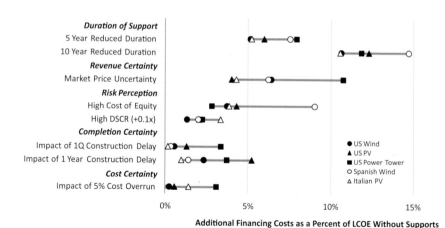

Fig. 5.1: Range of potential impacts on financing costs by pathway observed in projects (Varadrajan *et al.*, 2011)

Duration of revenue support

The duration of revenue support often directly affects the term of a project's financing. For example, loans may be provided for a longer duration if the policy support is provided throughout the project's lifetime. The project's financing term, in turn, strongly influences investment decisions by different classes of investors.

There is a strong correlation between the duration of revenue support and the duration of long-term debt financing that the project was able to secure [2]. The revenue support could take the form of feed-in tariff (FiT), feed-in premium or power purchase agreement, offered in response to a state renewable portfolio standard. A reduction of ten years in policy support and debt duration would increase financing costs by 11–15% of the cost of electricity.

Revenue certainty

A source of risk for renewable investors is the potential volatility in revenue streams from the sale of electricity. This may be due to variability in wind or solar resource, poor technology, or changes in the market price of electricity. Policy support mechanisms such as FiTs, which provide fixed revenue for every unit of electricity generated, mitigate this risk to some extent. Increased revenue certainty can reduce financing costs.

Variability in the market price of electricity is a greater potential risk to revenues than resource variability or technology availability. In the US, all the cases considered had long-term power purchase agreements under the renewable portfolio standard, which eliminates market price risk for the duration of the agreement. However, if power purchase agreements were replaced by long-term contracts providing a fixed premium above the market price such that expected revenues remain the same (e.g. long-term, fixed-price renewable

---

[2] A shorter term of debt than the support policy term leaves less revenue to support equity returns and hence increases financing costs, while a longer term of debt will depend on generally lower and less certain revenues after the support term has ended, also increasing financing costs.

energy certificate contracts or feed-in premium), the uncertainty in market prices would lead to debt providers provisioning less debt under such long-term contracts compared to a power purchase agreement. This would raise the cost of financing by 4–11% of the cost of electricity.

In the European cases considered, the projects rely on feed-in premiums, which expose debt investors to market risks as well as some risk related to underlying commodity price fluctuations. If these projects received fixed prices instead of a premium, the cost of finance would be lower by 1–4% of the cost of electricity[3].

Risk perception

The amount and cost of financing made available for a project depend on investors' risk perceptions. One of the factors that determine risk perception is the policy regime. For instance, a project that is not competitive without substantial policy support is likely to be perceived as more risky, and would entail a higher financing cost since investors would expect a high-risk premium.

For the investors and debt providers, risk perception would depend on multiple factors such as technology and policy regime, and would determine the investment or lending decision. Further, risk perception would also influence the cost of financing. For example, the required return on equity or the minimum debt service coverage ratio (DSCR) required by a debt provider may be higher when perceived risk is higher. Increasing the required DSCR and equity returns to the higher end of the observed ranges increase financing costs by 1–3% and 3–9% of cost of electricity, respectively.

In the US, projects depend on multiple policy supports. This exposes them to potential regulatory uncertainty (e.g. application processes and/or changing rules) and policy uncertainty (e.g. policies may be withdrawn in severely constrained fiscal environments). The extent to which the existence of multiple incentives increases risk

---

[3] The lower end of 1% is due to the impact of a price collar in the Spanish wind case, without which costs could have been 6% higher compared to a fixed-price contract.

perceptions and financing costs remains unclear, and requires further investigation.

In Europe, on the other hand, the substantial amount of revenue support required to render a solar project viable can lead to policy uncertainty and increased perceptions of regulatory or policy risks, which can increase financing costs. In response to problems in setting FiTs, governments have been forced to change policies, and in some cases changed tariffs retroactively. For many investors, this raises concerns regarding heightened risk and lack of future attractiveness of the investment, although this view is not universally shared.

Risk distribution/allocation

Different classes of investors are comfortable with different types and levels of risk. Policy can influence risk allocation among different stakeholders. For example, under public-private partnerships, the government manages risks that would deter the private sector. Appropriate risk allocation would reduce financing costs and broaden the base of interested investors.

Construction debt: Renewable energy projects have high upfront costs. Inexpensive short-term debt to cover a significant proportion of construction costs can be critical to reducing financing costs. If debt is unavailable, this cost would need to be covered by more expensive equity funding. For example, two of the cases, the US Power Tower and the Italian Utility-Scale PV both utilized construction debt as a policy, without which their financing costs would have increased by 22% and 23% of the cost of electricity, respectively. Similarly, construction debt would have lowered the financing costs of other projects by 8–15% of the cost of electricity.

Inflation risks: Policies that are linked to revenues and costs can change the allocation of a part of the project costs or revenues among stakeholders. Therefore, such policies can also affect the distribution of inflation risks among stakeholders. A number of recent studies of bond markets (for instance Hordahl and Tristani, 2010) suggest that the cost of bearing inflation risks can be measured, and has a value between 0–50 basis points in the US and Europe, increasing with the tenor of the bond.

Cost/completion certainty

Revenue generation depends on project completion and commencement of operations. Delays in project completion delay revenue generation, and may hamper the project from meeting investor return requirements. Policy can help manage or shift the burden of such risks, thereby reducing the cost of financing.

Cost and completion risks can often be managed through contractual rather than policy arrangements. However, this is often not possible for innovative, first-of-a kind projects, due to uncertainty and the possibility of catastrophic failures. This could make a project nearly impossible to finance in the private sector at any reasonable expected return. In such cases, the government may have a role in managing uncertainty. For example, in the case of US Solar Tower, a loan guarantee shifted some of the burden of a catastrophic failure of a project to the government.

Uncertainty regarding regulatory or permitting processes can lead to uncertainty in total project costs or completion schedules. The risk of project delays or additional regulatory costs can raise the financing costs. For example, a one-year delay in the project can increase financing costs by 1–5% of the cost of electricity, while a 5% cost overrun would increase financing costs by up to 3% of the cost of electricity.

Development risk

Only a fraction of the projects in the project pipeline get built. A number of barriers such as competing investments and regulatory delays hinder project development. Policies that raise the success rate and reduce development timeframes would improve investor interest as well as capital efficiency for project developers.

Increased failure rates or costs during development can result in lower competition and can drive up the returns required to attract investors. Since development only accounts for about 5% of project costs[4], policies that directly target development costs or delays do not have a significant impact on financial metrics such as equity returns.

---

[4] Based on the US Solar Tower and wind cases, where this information was available.

However, development risks can affect financing costs in other ways. Policy impacts through the development process are best understood through analysis at the portfolio rather than project level.

For example, in the case of the US Solar Tower, the development process was closely linked to regulatory processes, since the project was to be constructed on federal land and was required to meet certain conditions for availing of incentives. These incentives were essential for the project to achieve the expected rate of return. As the first at-scale facility of its kind, this process was complex. As a result, the project itself was significantly modified[5], the timeline for development and construction was extended, and the financial structure of the project was determined. The uncertainty associated with such extensive regulatory and policy interactions required for this project may have impacted the availability and cost of financing for this and future projects.

Key takeaway: *In developed economies, effective renewable energy policies would be long-term (i.e., long duration of revenue support) and take the form of FiTs (i.e., higher revenue certainty and lower risk perception).*

Similar Work in India Indicates that the Same Pathways Remain Crucial; However, All of These are Much Smaller, Given the High Cost of Capital

Figure 5.2, in addition to the cases from US/Europe, contains corresponding results for India[6].

We add two India-specific pathways: debt-cost reduction (by five percentage points) and debt-tenor increase (by six years). Two points emerge from the analysis:

First, differences between the policy impact pathways are smaller in India. This is because one important mechanism for reducing

---

[5] The original plan was to construct two 100 MW phases and one 200MW phase with several towers. It was modified to one 126 MW and two 135 MW towers.

[6] Essentially, for India, the sensitivity analysis indicated the following impact: duration of revenue support (7–11%); revenue certainty (3–8%); risk (ROE) reduction (5–8%); risk (DSCR) reduction (3%); completion certainty (4–8%); cost certainty; debt-rate reduction (12–19%); debt-tenor increase (4–6%).

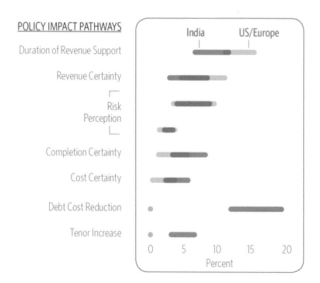

Fig. 5.2: A comparison of the range of impact of policy pathways on renewable financing cost in US/Europe and India

financing costs is reducing risks, to allow increased debt and project leverage. Given the high debt costs in India, the value of increasing leverage is lower. In addition, some of the commercial contract mechanisms to reduce construction risk may not be as reliable in India.

Second, and more significantly, all of the policy pathways discussed here are dwarfed by the potential impact of reducing debt costs. In this analysis, we have reduced the cost of debt (interest rate) by 5%, enough to cover most, but not all, of the interest rate gap with developed countries.

The higher interest rates, and shorter debt tenors, may reduce some of the effectiveness of renewable policies. Indian policymakers should therefore explore methods of reducing the cost of debt to renewable energy projects. Furthermore, they might look to countries with similar growth and interest rate environments (see Fig. 5.3), particularly Brazil and China, as inspiration for policy solutions to achieve India's ambitious renewable energy targets.

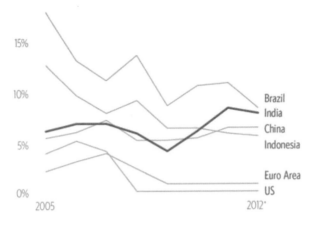

Fig 5.3:   Benchmark interest rates (%), 2005–2012

This high cost of capital is driven by the cost of debt as well as other terms of debt, such as debt tenor and the variable cost of debt

In India, the differences between debt and equity are particularly striking. Equity appears to be readily available at a reasonable cost, while renewable energy debt is both limited and expensive. Figure 5.4 highlights the differences between renewable energy debt and equity markets in India and developed markets. While equity returns in India are similar to those in the US and Europe, interest rates on debt are significantly higher.

To compound the problem, access to potentially lower-cost international debt is limited due to regulatory barriers, the high cost and risks associated with long-term currency swaps, and perceived country risks. As a result, the cost of debt to a renewable energy project in India will typically be in the 10–14% range, as compared to the 5–7% range typical in the US. In addition to the higher cost, debt in India also suffers from inferior terms, including shorter tenors (typically 10–12 years whereas project life is 20–25 years) and variable rather than fixed interest rates. This raises overall financing costs. For example, the required return on equity is much higher due to the additional risk to equity holders from variable debt rates.

* No data for solar thermal in Europe. Note: Equity is levered equity. Source: Projects in India and US CPI finance paper.

Fig. 5.4: Range of returns on equity and debt costs for renewable energy projects — India versus US and Europe

Figure 5.5 compares the financing differences of the US and Indian projects. We see that in the case of solar PV projects, higher interest rate on debt added 19% to the project cost, while it added 10% in case of the wind project.

We also see that Indian debt tenors are typically much shorter than the US or Europe. Shorter debt tenors add between 3% and 10% to the cost of the project, by forcing rapid amortization of the loan. This means that debt has to be repaid quicker, and therefore leads to lower effective leverage over the life of the project [7]. However, since the difference between the cost of debt and equity is smaller in India, debt tenor is relatively less important than it would be elsewhere. Therefore, the value of maintaining a higher level of debt throughout the life of the project decreases. If the cost of debt were lower, leading to a larger difference between debt and equity, the impact of debt tenor would increase significantly.

---

[7] The solar project used for our analysis had an uncharacteristically long tenor. Therefore, we have adjusted the debt tenor down to 13 years, which would be much more typical of Indian PV projects. The result is to increase the impact of shorter debt tenors from 3% to 6%.

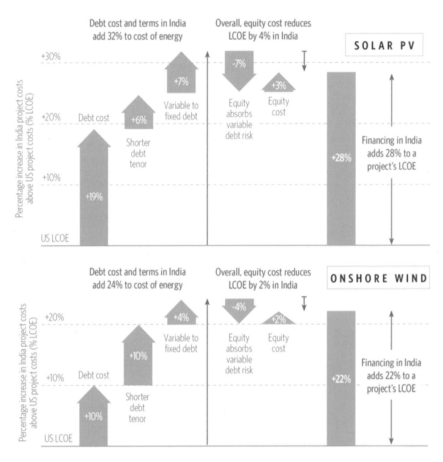

Fig. 5.5:   The impact of debt and equity costs and terms in India on overall financing costs compared to a US baseline

Since there is no liquid (variable-to-fixed) swap market in India, the rate of interest on debt is usually variable in India. In more developed markets, project developers nearly always seek fixed interest debt, and use interest rate swaps to convert variable rate debt into fixed rate debt. When combined with FiTs, or long-term power purchase agreements with a fixed price (which would provide fixed revenues per unit), a fixed interest rate leads to a high degree of certainty regarding future cash flows. An investment with well-defined cash flows is less risky, and therefore attracts lower cost finance. At the US swap rate of 2% (Federal Reserve, 2012), ten-year swap rates are currently low by historical standards. However, this cost would add approximately 7% to the finance cost of solar PV and 4% to the cost of wind on a comparable basis.

Variable rate debt means equity investors have to undertake more risk. With a fixed price power purchase agreement, an unexpected rise in interest rates could consume all of the cash flow from a project and wipe out the equity investor. While we have no accurate way of measuring the cost of the additional risk assumed by the equity investor, we can assume that the risk they take on is equal to the value of the swap used to compare India debt to US debt. The result is an exact offset between debt and equity, moving expected return from the equity column to the debt column.

As shown in Fig. 5.4, the cost of equity in India is only slightly higher than in the US or Europe, depending on the technology, in spite of the higher underlying country risks. The slightly higher return on equity adds only 3% and 2% respectively, to the total cost of financing the solar and wind project.

When all of the adjustments are made to account for the differences in terms and tenors, equity ends up being less expensive in India compared to the US or Europe, despite higher country risks. This implies that investors are buying into the market and accepting below rational returns for strategic reasons — thus suggesting that returns on equity may rise once the market matures.

Meanwhile, the total impact of debt, including terms and costs, is 24–32% of the cost of the project.

Improving cost and terms of debt can reduce the overall subsidy burden for the government, since this reduces the gap between the cost of capital for the project and the government

Renewable energy is not cost-competitive in India. This means that the direct subsidy costs, i.e. the difference between FiTs provided for renewable energy projects and the average price of electricity from other sources, are higher than they would be under favorable debt terms.

One potential policy intervention is to provide an interest rate subsidy, where the government helps provide subsidized loans. This would result in reducing (though not eliminating) the direct subsidy. However, the government would have to bear the added cost of providing low-interest loans. We next show that the benefits of providing this subsidy significantly outweigh costs.

In this sub-section, we compare the subsidy cost for the two cases: (a) direct subsidy in absence of any interest-subsidy and (b) the sum of interest-subsidy and (reduced) direct subsidy in presence of an interest-subsidy. Each of these subsidies is compared on a net present value basis by discounting at the government's cost of capital, which is assumed to be the risk-free rate — i.e., a ten-year government bond rate at 8%[8].

We find that providing an interest rate subsidy is cheaper for the government, as illustrated in Table 5.1.

Most of these gains are due to increased leverage due to the availability of cheaper debt. In other words, a reduction in the cost of debt makes it feasible for the project to employ a higher amount of debt. The project cash flows can service a larger amount of debt due to reduced per-period payments. Therefore, providing interest rate subsidies may allow more cost-effective deployment of renewable energy.

Key takeaway: *In developing economies, the most effective policies would focus on the cost and terms of debt, followed by a focus on long-term FiTs.*

There are two creative policy solutions — each of these solutions will need to be tailored to specific contexts[9].

- Reduce the cost of using debt sourced from the developed world: at present, sourcing foreign debt is expensive due to the high cost of currency swaps. If renewable energy tariffs were indexed to a foreign currency, currency hedging costs would be eliminated. This would make it possible for project developers to access low-cost, long-term debt at fixed interest rates from developed markets.

---

[8] See http://www.bloomberg.com/quote/GIND10YR:IND.
[9] See Nelson and Shrimali (2014).

Table 5.1: Impact on subsidy due to lower interest rates

	Wind				Solar			
Case	LCOE (INR)	Leverage	NPV of Total Subsidy (INR MN)	Case	LCOE (INR)	Leverage	NPV of FIT Subsidy (INR MN)
Interest rate — no subsidy	4.41	65%	2,557.4	Interest rate — no subsidy	14.24	73%	9,221.4
Interest rate — 2% subsidy	4.11	68%	2,563.7	Interest rate — 2% subsidy	13.18	76%	8,760.7
Interest rate — 5% subsidy	3.68	71%	2,143.4	Interest rate — 5% subsidy	11.39	80%	7,970.4

- Improve the cost-effectiveness of renewable energy policy supports: instead of the existing policy regime that focuses on reducing capital requirements or improving revenues, the government should focus on providing lower-cost debt. This would reduce the overall cost of financing for the developer, as well as the cost of policy support for the government.

The effectiveness of these policy solutions depends on their design and implementation in specific contexts.

Acknowledgement

The author would like to acknowledge the help of Sandhya Srinivasan, analyst, CPI-ISB Energy and Environment Program, in writing this chapter.

References

Federal Reserve (2012). '10-year Swap Rate'. Available at: http://research.stlouisfed.org/fred2/series/DSWP10 [accessed 14 August 2014].

Hordahl, P. and Tristani, O. (2010). 'Inflation Risk Premia in the US and the Euro Area', European Central Bank Working Paper.

Nelson, D. and Shrimali, G. (2014). 'Finance Mechanisms for Lowering the Cost of Renewable Energy in Developing Countries', CPI report.

Varadrajan, U., Nelson, G., Pierpont, B. and Herve-Mignucci, M. (2011). 'The Impact of Policy on the Financing of Renewable Projects', CPI report.

Chapter Six

Mobilizing Private Sector Capital in Developing Countries

Alexandre Chavarot, Managing Partner,
Clean Infra Partners
Matthew Konieczny, Vice President,
Clean Infra Partners

With over half of the estimated US$18 trillion of power and energy efficiency investment through 2035 forecast to come from outside the OECD, solutions for funding and financing emerging market infrastructure are becoming increasingly critical. It is widely acknowledged that the vast majority of such investments would need to be funded by the private sector, which should be achievable given that the annual investment requirements represent a fraction of assets under management by institutional investors[1].

Equally, it is becoming clear that public sector funding is critical to mobilizing private capital, including capital sourced from developing countries. A study by the World Economic Forum set a target of US$700 billion of incremental investment through 2020 in areas

---

[1] It is estimated that US$71 trillion of assets are being managed by institutional investors in OECD countries alone today (Nelson *et al.*, 2013).

such as clean energy infrastructure, low-carbon transport, energy efficiency and forestry, in order to transition to a low-carbon economy. Of that, US$120–$140 billion would come from public sector institutions, with the balance coming from the private sector (World Economic Forum, 2013). Interestingly, according to a Climate Policy Initiative study, the public to private sector leverage ratio was less than 1:2 globally in 2012 (Nelson *et al.*, 2013)[2].

The questions that, therefore, need to be addressed, are what additional financial mechanisms should be developed to multiply private capital deployment two- to three-fold, and what sources of private capital are most appropriate for low-carbon investments in developing countries.

This chapter starts by reviewing both generic impediments to private sector capital deployment in low-carbon investments in developing countries and the shortcomings of existing finance mechanisms targeting the sector; it then highlights the main ingredients to a new 'climate finance virtuous circle' and concludes with key implementation issues. Importantly, it stresses the need to mobilize local sources of private capital to meet the low-carbon investment challenge in developing countries.

Impediments to Private Sector Capital Deployment: A Need for Astute Policies

One can distinguish between four main generic impediments to private sector capital deployment in low-carbon investments in developing countries: inadequate risk/return propositions; a perceived lack of attractive investment opportunities; a series of market failures; and a number of policy failures.

Inadequate risk/return propositions

Many investors have flexibility choosing between investment instruments, underlying economic sectors and geographies. One of the key impediments to capital deployment in low-carbon investments is that

---

[2] US$135 billion of public versus US$224 billion of private capital.

Table 6.1: Renewable energy project return premiums (Europe vs emerging markets)

	Europe (including UK)	India	South Africa
Unlevered renewable energy project returns	6–9%	12–13%	12–13%
Ten-year government bond yield[3]	1–2.5%	8.7%	8%
Resulting premium for investors	**5–6.5%**	**3.3–4.3%**	**4–5%**

Table 6.2: OECD and non-OECD returns across asset classes

	OECD	Non-OECD
Ten-year government bond yield	1–2.5%	6–15%
Annualized return over last five years on investment in listed equities	8.30%[4]	6.18%[5]
Average returns generated by private equity (2013) (MacAurthur *et al.*, 2014)[6]	16%	13%

they often offer a poor risk-adjusted return relative to similar investments in OECD countries, and/or to other asset classes.

It is interesting to note that the premium obtained by renewable energy project investors as compared to government bonds is higher in Europe than in some key developing countries, as shown in Table 6.1. The Indian and South African projects shown correspond to the Indian National Solar Mission and the South African Renewable Energy Procurement Program.

Another way to look at the mispricing of renewable energy investments in developing countries is to look at risk-adjusted returns for different asset classes in both OECD and non-OECD countries. Table 6.2

---

[3] As of end August 2014.

[4] As of 22 August 2014; using VEA — Europe Pacific, Vanguard foreign large-cap equities in Europe, Australia and Eastern developed markets.

[5] As of 22 August 2014; using EEM iShares MSCI Emerging Markets ETF as proxy.

[6] Represents end-to-end pooled IRR for ten-year investment horizon (western European EU buy-out funds and emerging markets growth and buy-out funds).

summarizes typical returns for government bonds, listed equities, and private equity, of which infrastructure funds are a sub-set.

These numbers indicate that returns on both listed and private equity investments have historically been higher in OECD countries than in developing countries, both in absolute terms and relative to the underlying risk-free rates. This makes the case for foreign investment in developing country infrastructure and renewable energy assets difficult, unless significant risk mitigation and risk transfer can be structured through effective policy instruments and innovative financial mechanisms.

Lack of attractive investments: myths and reality

A number of policy experts and practitioners often cite the perceived lack of low-carbon investment opportunities in developing countries as a constraint. The reality is more balanced, with significant incentive programs now available in non-OECD countries to attract investments in climate mitigation and a more fragmented picture for climate adaptation.

US$429 billion has been invested in renewable energy projects in developing countries in the five-year period from 2009 to 2013. This corresponds to 38% of global investments in the sector (Aspinall *et al.*, 2014), thus demonstrating the scale of the clean energy market in these countries.

Across the developing world there are significant targets for installed low-carbon generating capacity, with an estimated US$3 trillion of investments expected through 2035 (International Energy Agency, 2014)[7]. Other climate mitigation investments in transport and energy efficiency also offer significant opportunities.

There should also be sizeable investment opportunities for private sector capital in climate adaptation areas such as water resources management, land use management, integrated coastal zone management, agriculture and forestry, and climate insurance products.

---

[7] Under the IEA's New Policy Scenario, their central scenario.

The real issue about the availability of investment opportunities is whether the projects are sufficiently de-risked to be able to attract investors and offer an adequate risk-adjusted return. The lack of proper risk-adjusted economic incentives and satisfactory regulatory frameworks is often the reason for the shortage of 'investment ready' projects. This is more to do with market and policy failures than with a lack of intrinsic investment opportunities.

Market failure: risk mispricing and macroeconomic factors

Risk mispricing

It is difficult and/or expensive for investors to price certain risks such as future regulatory changes, including changes in tax regimes or profit repatriation rules. Foreign investors can, to some extent, insure against such risks through organizations such as the Multilateral Investment Guarantee Agency (MIGA) — part of the World Bank Group — and the Overseas Private Investment Corporation (OPIC) for US investors, though the premium on political risk insurance will reduce the expected returns. There are far fewer protection mechanisms for domestic investors, apart from a limited number of guarantee schemes for local debt issuance.

There is also an asymmetry of information on risks, often leading to mispricing. Typically foreign investors will want to be compensated for what they perceive to be additional developing country risks compared to OECD investments; however this often translates into a premium that is above the spread in risk premium reflected in the difference in yield between two countries' government bonds.

Macroeconomic factors: carbon price externality and FX exposure

The fact that the cost of environmental damage created by carbon emissions is not factored into the price of fossil fuel investments, often called the carbon externality, effectively distorts the price comparison between fossil fuel and low-carbon investments. This externality keeps the cost of fossil fuels artificially low and makes it more difficult for low-carbon technologies to compete on price.

Separately, foreign exchange fluctuations and the difficulty in mitigating their impact on project returns prevent foreign direct investment in the low-carbon economy of developing countries. Most developing countries do not have a currency exchange market large enough to offer long-term cost-effective currency hedging solutions to foreign investors (unless their currency is effectively pegged to the US dollar). A few instruments have been put in place to address this issue, such as the Currency Exchange Fund (TCX), which is effectively a line of credit being made available by a number of bilateral development agencies to extend the duration of currency swaps in developing countries. It does not fully address the high cost of such swaps, which significantly affects investment returns.

Policy failures

Climate-related domestic policy failures broadly fall into five categories in developing countries:

- A lack of clarity and stability of regulatory environments.
- Long timelines for enacting and implementing policy changes.
- A lack of homogeneity of policy instruments across countries.
- Inadequacy of quantum and nature of subsidies.
- Need for one policy tool per public policy issue.

Climate mitigation and adaptation investments require a robust and stable regulatory environment, given their long-term economic cycle and associated environmental benefits. The attractiveness of such a regulatory environment is typically the single most important factor that investors look at when deciding where to deploy capital, including in relation to power purchase agreement (PPA)-based policies in developing countries.

A number of studies have been conducted to identify best regulatory practices for the renewable energy sector, with a standard form PPA having been designed to facilitate the introduction of new concepts into a contractual format that would be recognized by most international investors (Pricewaterhouse Coopers, 2012).

Governments are obviously expected to make policy changes, and many of these changes can indeed be beneficial, but we would argue that three key parameters should drive such changes: they should not adversely affect existing investments; they should be presented as part of a medium-term coherent regulatory environment, with clarity on other possible changes over a predefined timeframe; and they should be made swiftly to address particular objectives, as too often long government decision-making and implementation timelines impair their effectiveness.

Government subsidies can be useful to address market failures and to help 'kick start' a particular sector. But they can also harm the long-term stability of a market if they are not appropriately designed with a view to reducing levels over time. High level of subsidies may not be sustainable from a budgetary standpoint; or they may increase the cost of electricity to a level that is not acceptable for end-users. And, high subsidies do not help encourage innovation and cost reduction.

Finally, there are numerous situations where climate objectives are being mixed with poverty alleviation goals. While climate change mitigation and adaptation will undoubtedly help reduce poverty levels in various developing countries, or at the very least slow the increase in poverty that is directly caused by the effects of climate change, it doesn't necessarily follow that climate finance instruments should directly be tied to poverty alleviation.

This chapter doesn't include analysis of the types of policies that could be implemented to address the above failures; we acknowledge, however, that policy interventions are a necessary complement, if not a condition precedent, to the efficient deployment of climate finance.

Shortcomings of Existing Finance Mechanisms: Not Ambitious Enough, Not At Scale

The shortcomings of existing finance mechanisms mean current climate finance architecture is unlikely to adequately address the impediments to private sector capital deployment in low-carbon investments in developing countries. This applies to both traditional development finance instruments and more recent innovative climate finance mechanisms.

Traditional development finance instruments used for climate investments

Traditional public sector climate finance instruments for developing countries essentially comprise grants, concessional loans, and guarantee products. Together they amounted to US$135 billion in 2012, of which approximately US$55 billion was provided by multilateral agencies and bilateral finance institutions (including the Climate Investment Funds, but not accounting for the value of guarantees provided), while the balance was provided by national development banks, with China contributing the largest portion (Buchner *et al.*, 2013). Interestingly, 72% of climate investments in developing countries were sourced domestically according to the same study, thus putting into perspective the role of the traditional development finance instruments.

In addition, foreign governments make politically motivated infrastructure investments, though these are more common in conventional power than in low-carbon technologies. China may be the most prolific such donor, having led in the development of many of the major power infrastructure sectors throughout Africa.

Grants are provided by bilateral development institutions and by multilateral agencies, such as the World Bank Group, by some of the regional development banks and by the Global Environment Facility (GEF) to improve project economics, and/or to assist local stakeholders in funding a portion of their share of project costs.

GEF is one of the larger providers of such grants, with US$13.5 billion of cumulative grants in support of projects in areas such as biodiversity, climate change, international waters, land degradation, forest management, and waste (GEF, 2014) since its inception in 1991. It is debatable whether the provision of grants meets the grantors' policy objectives and/or whether they are an effective use of public funds. They may be more adequate for climate adaption purposes than for climate mitigation, given the higher risks and lower returns often seen in climate adaptation projects.

Concessional loans typically increase the equity return of projects, thus helping investors achieve their return target or limiting the level of revenues or subsidies required given the reduction in a project's cost of capital. Multilateral agencies have been deploying US$8 billion pledged to the CIFs, with the Clean Technology Fund attracting the bulk of this funding. The level of 'concessionality' varies greatly, with CIFs offering loans that are akin to repayable grants, with *de minimis* interest rates over very long tenors, coupled with long grace periods (e.g. 0.25%, 40-year tenor, ten-year grace period). Many bilateral agencies' concessional loans have 15–20-year tenors and an interest rate of 1–2% above their government's long-term yield.

Concessional loans can play a very useful role in a number of projects by combining improved economics with the rigorous project appraisal and de facto project de-risking that comes with development finance institution (DFI) involvement. Some loans are also linked to useful programmatic activities, as is the case with CIFs. On the other hand, concessional lenders may have other policy objectives that can occasionally be conflicting. We would suggest that one of the litmus tests of deploying concessional finance be the concurrent mobilization of private sector capital, including a clear rationale as to why concessional loans are required, and that the terms of concessional loans be defined to deliver an appropriate risk-adjusted return to investors. As an example, the Clean Technology Fund has an explicit private sector leverage objective (Climate Investment Funds, 2014).

Guarantee instruments and insurance products can be an effective way of catalyzing private sector funding and of leveraging public sector funds. Guarantees focus on non-performance by a specific party, often a state entity in the context of international finance, while insurance covers against a possible loss linked to a specific event.

Various guarantee and insurance programs exist from public sector institutions as well as from the private insurance market, including the World Bank Partial Credit and Partial Risk Guarantees, MIGA and OPIC's political risk insurance products, covers provided by Export Credit Agencies, and GuarantCo guarantees of local bank loans; but essentially the scale of these programs is not large enough or their effectiveness is severally limited by conditions that may be attached to them to adequately address the full needs of climate-related investments, as summarized in Table 6.3.

Specific climate finance mechanisms currently not attractive enough to investors

Climate finance is fast becoming a new finance activity. It has seen 'veterans' of the carbon markets (and their corresponding financing sources) turn their attention to the creation of innovative mechanisms to use public sector finance in order to de-risk projects, aggregate investments, and mobilize new sources of private capital, typically with the support of DFIs.

Many new climate finance mechanisms over the past few years relate to the creation of aggregating vehicles for climate investments, sometimes coupled with risk-absorption features whereby public sector sources of capital are exposed to more risks than private sector ones.

These aggregating vehicles are meant to facilitate the recycling of capital initially deployed to fund project construction, by pooling large and diversified project portfolios together and encouraging institutional investors and sovereign wealth funds (SWFs) to buy a portion of the equity or debt tranches they issue. This allows such investors to meet their typical minimum investment size requirements of US$50–100 million.

However, the few examples that exist of aggregating vehicles have not succeeded in mobilizing significant private capital to date. This includes the IFC Asset Management Corporation-sponsored Climate Catalyst Fund (IFC, 2014)[8]; the Asian Development Climate Public Private Partnership (CP3) fund (renamed Asia Climate Partners); and the KfW-led Global Climate Partnership Fund (GCPF). The first two aim to

---

[8] The Climate Catalyst Fund had only two private sector institutional investors as of the date of its first close.

Table 6.3: Available guarantee and insurance programs for infrastructure investment

Product	Key characteristics	Effectiveness	Main shortcomings
World Bank partial credit/ partial risk guarantees (PCGs/PRGs)	PCG: Covers private lenders against all risks during specific period of financing PRG: Cover private lenders against risks of government non-performance on contractual obligations	PCG mostly available for public sector projects PRGs typically provided for public-private partnership projects, alongside MIGA PRI and IFC loan or equity investment Close to US$5 billion of cumulative guarantees for approx. 40 transactions since inception	PCG and PRG require host government counter-guarantees, which can be time-consuming and often difficult to obtain Not more than one or two transactions in recent years
MIGA political risk insurance	Guarantee against specific and generic political risks for equity and debt instruments Typically 15-year, provided to lenders or equity investors	Helps reduce risk-capital weighting of projects, thus lowering cost of capital (e.g., guarantee premium) Infrastructure sector accounts for largest share of outstanding guarantees	Relatively high premium

(Continued)

Table 6.3: (*Continued*)

Product	Key characteristics	Effectiveness	Main shortcomings
OPIC political risk insurance	Similar to MIGA guarantees	Relatively flexible instrument	Need US investor and/or exporter/contractor Relatively high premium
Private insurer political risk cover (Lloyd's)	Insurance product (not guarantee)	Market for specific country risks can be volatile	No reduction in risk-capital weighting for lenders
ECA insurance	Political risk only or comprehensive cover provided to lenders	Can provide attractive financing terms for renewable energy projects	Tied to export of goods and services
GuarantCo (PIDG instrument)	Comprehensive guarantee of local loans	Helps extend loan tenors and reduce cost of local debt	Available to low-income country financial institutions Relatively high premium

allocate equity capital to privately managed funds in developing countries[9], while GCPF provides loans to climate-related investments in developing countries, typically alongside local financial institutions.

GCPF was a pioneer in climate-related tiered capital structure investment vehicles. Its capital base includes grants and deeply subordinated shares from the German and Danish governments, a KfW and International Finance Corporation (IFC) mezzanine loan (or B shares), and a senior tranche of capital (or A shares) provided by KfW and IFC. It is also meant to 'crowd in' international private sector lenders by issuing senior debt, though this is yet to happen.

There are a number of reasons why so few initiatives of this nature have been implemented, and why the existing ones have not managed to mobilize significant amounts of private capital:

- They are initiated by DFIs, as opposed to being 'championed' by one or several institutional investor(s) or SWFs.
- They often lack an investment focus, such as deploying capital in a limited number of sectors and/or in specific geographies.
- The risk-adjusted returns being offered to institutional investors may not be adequate.

This suggests a need for institutional investor leadership with focused climate investment strategies to help such initiatives prove effective.

Implications on cost of finance in developing countries

The shortcomings of existing finance mechanisms, together with the impediments discussed in the previous section, significantly restrict

---

[9]The European Investment Bank (EIB)-managed Global Energy Efficiency and Renewable Energy Fund (GEEREF) fund of funds is another investor in renewable energy and energy efficiency equity funds focused on developing countries, that typically requires private sector co-investors in the funds in which it invests; the IFC and the various regional and bilateral DFIs can also make direct equity investments in such funds.

the flow of capital into developing country climate investments. This in turn affects the cost of capital for such investments.

The United Nations Development Program (UNDP) estimated in a recent study that the cost of equity financing is more than 80% higher in developing countries and the cost of debt financing is a staggering ~165% higher (Waissbein *et al.*, 2013). The high cost of capital in developing countries, coupled with the capital-intensive nature of climate investments, is impeding investors from realizing appropriate risk-adjusted returns.

The aforementioned study looked at the implications of the cost of capital on the levelized cost of electricity (LCOE) for onshore wind, and found that it was 40% higher in developing countries than in developed countries; this was driven by differences in financing costs: in developed countries financing costs made up 40% of LCOE, while in developing countries it was 60%.

One obvious conclusion is that, in addition to catalyzing more capital, it is imperative to find ways of reducing the cost of capital for climate investments in developing countries. This can be achieved through the design and implementation of a 'climate finance virtuous circle', based on a targeted and judicious use of public sector funding, and assuming that investment opportunities are sufficiently de-risked.

Components of a New 'Climate Finance Virtuous Circle': Investment Aggregation, De-Risking and Capital Markets

The existing impediments to the deployment of private capital to climate mitigation and climate adaptation investments in developing countries appear daunting, given the variety of often intertwined issues, and the number and diversity of stakeholders involved. Yet there is a path towards achieving very concrete results in the next decade, based on the answers to a few simple questions:

- Where should private capital come from? Why?
- Which mechanisms can best direct capital flows accordingly? How should they vary depending on different sources of private capital?

- What should be the roles of public sector entities in developing and in funding such mechanisms? How can they work alongside international investors?

The 'climate finance virtuous circle' comprises three steps:

- Implement financial mechanisms utilizing investment aggregation vehicles to channel local sources of debt and equity in order to refinance low-carbon investments in developing countries, with appropriate uses of international and domestic public sector funding sources to de-risk such investments.
- In doing so, deliver a lower weighted average cost of capital to low-carbon investments, thus creating capital gains for project developers and their financial backers, and ensure that the capital that was used to fund project construction costs is recycled to new investments.
- Achieve scale by mobilizing international sources of private capital (including from SWFs) through the issuance by aggregation vehicles of relevant debt or equity instruments (including instruments denominated in hard currency and possibly traded on international exchanges).

Sourcing local private capital

Climate mitigation and adaptation projects require a combination of debt and equity capital in proportions that vary with, inter alia, a project risk profile and its debt capacity, the availability of debt sources and the financial objectives of the project developer.

We would argue that debt capital should primarily be sourced in the country or the region where a project takes place, with, in addition, possible funding from DFIs. The reasons for this are four-fold. First, local lenders are best able to assess the local regulatory regime; second, they should be best able to appraise the credit risk of a proposed investment, including the counterparty risks (developers, construction companies, off-takers etc); third, they are best able to allocate scarce capital according to the relative investment merits of the various sectors of a domestic economy; and fourth they often are the only counterparties capable of lending in domestic currencies.

There are a number of barriers to mobilizing local debt sources, as well as various mechanisms in place to (partly) surmount them. Table 6.4 provides a summary of these mechanisms and lists some of their shortcomings.

Equity capital typically comes from a combination of international and local developers, as well as from specialist investment platforms that together fund the development and construction phases of projects (with pure financial investors generally not involved in the development phase). These sources of equity aim to recycle their capital when the projects are operational, and realize capital gains, which means that long-term infrastructure-type investors need to be mobilized to own the bulk of these assets during their operating period.

The main barrier to the implementation of this capital recycling is the lack of long-term asset holders for climate investments in developing countries, both domestic and international. This in turn means no clear exit strategies for developers and their financiers, which leads to a shortage of equity capital during the development and construction phases, and a relatively high cost of equity during these phases.

Creating new mechanisms to adequately direct capital flows

A key measure of success for the 'climate finance virtuous circle' is to find mechanisms to mobilize significant long-term local equity and debt capital for low-carbon investments. Capital markets in the so-called 'emerging markets', and, to a lesser extent, in 'frontier markets', have reached a size relative to their GDPs that should ensure minimum levels of liquidity (Schizas, 2012)[10].

Sub-Saharan pension funds manage US$350 billion, including US$26 billion in Nigeria and US$7.8 billion in Kenya, while the mar-

---

[10] Corporate bond market capitalization stood at 18% of GDP for the median 'emerging market', compared to 26% for the median developed economy, while public or government bond markets capitalization stood at 36% of GDP, or 2% higher than for the median developed economy; and the median stock market capitalization of an 'emerging market' country was 44% of GDP.

Table 6.4: Barriers to mobilizing emerging market debt

Typical barriers	Existing mechanisms	Issues
Limited amount of capital from domestic lenders	Additional liquidity provided by DFIs to local banks through international credit lines Debt fund and guarantee facility financed by DFIs and international banks (e.g., EAIF, GCPF, GuarantCo)	Limited availability High cost unless lines of credit are in local currency Hard currency lending (debt funds) Creditworthiness of local banks (guarantee funds)
High cost of domestic bank funding, translating into high cost of project debt	Replace domestic debt with ECA and DFI project loans Concessional loans from DFIs	Borrower exposed to currency risk and/or high cost of FX swap Limited amount of concessional loans available
Limited tenors for domestic loans	World Bank and regional DFIs' partial credit guarantees (PCGs) to local banks GuarantCo guarantees to local banks	World Bank PCG typically requires host government counter-guarantee Increases cost of project debt GuarantCo focus on low-income countries
Shortage of bank expertise to appraise technical aspects of projects (new technologies)	Technical assistance grants to local banks from DFIs	Banks still at risk of technical fault during construction and operation
Lack of risk appetite for limited recourse financings	Corporate (and personal) guarantees provided by developers to domestic banks for most of project life (e.g., solar projects in India) Sector-specific partial risk guarantees (e.g., ADB Indian solar PRG)	Inefficient use of developer balance sheet No or limited risk sharing with/transfer to banks Leaves banks exposed to a portion of risks Guarantee premium translates into higher cost of project debt

ket capitalization of the Johannesburg stock exchange is approximately US$800 billion (*Financial Times*, 2014).

These new mechanisms should also serve as conduits for channeling large pools of international capital in order to provide scale.

A number of ideas for new debt and equity aggregation mechanisms are listed in Tables 6.5 and 6.6.

Table 6.5: Possible solutions to mobilizing private sector debt capital at scale

Typical barriers	Possible solutions
Limited amount of capital from domestic lenders	1. Create local/regional markets for green bond issuance by domestic banks, with DFIs/Green Climate Fund to de-risk such bonds by providing a 'first loss' guarantees 2. DFIs/Green Climate Fund to provide project subordinated debt for large-scale single infrastructure projects
High cost of domestic bank funding, translating into high cost of project debt	3. Create local/regional financing institutions to provide concessional project loans (possibly *pari passu* with domestic bank loans), with funding from local investors and DFIs/Green Climate Fund
Limited domestic loan tenors	4. Create refinancing mechanisms to transfer pools of project loans to local/regional investors post-completion (possibly via aggregation vehicles that would issue bonds): — DFIs/Green Climate Fund to de-risk aggregation vehicles through 'first loss' guarantees and/or tranches of capital 5. Aggregation vehicles to issue international climate bonds (with further FX risk mitigation as required provided by TCX and/or new FX climate mechanism), and possibly political risk guarantee from MIGA
Shortage of bank expertise to appraise technical aspects of projects (new technologies)	6. Create technology deployment mechanism to backstop use of new technologies in developing countries for initial projects, funded by DFIs/Green Climate Fund — such mechanism to wrap equipment suppliers' warranties, without creating moral hazard
Lack of risk appetite for limited recourse financings	7. Use refinancing mechanisms mentioned under 4. to transfer pools of project loans to local/regional investors post-completion

Table 6.6:   Possible solutions to mobilizing private sector equity capital at scale

Typical barriers	• Lack of long-term asset holders • No clear exit strategies for developers • Shortage of equity during development and construction phases • High cost of equity capital
Existing mechanisms	Existing mechanisms include direct equity investments in project developers by DFIs and, more recently, the creation of 'pooled' funds of funds to help mobilize international institutional investors and SWFs (e.g., IFC Climate Catalyst Fund, ADB CP3)
Issues	Limited size of direct equity investment pool by DFIs DFI-led climate equity funds of funds have so far only offered *pari passu* terms to institutional investors, thus failing to provide an attractive risk-adjusted return

Possible solutions	1. Local/regional investment funds with layered capital structure, to acquire operating assets for long-term dividend yield, funded by a combination of regional and international institutional investors and public sector institutions, possibly through regional listings
	    • DFIs/Green Climate Fund to provide contingent equity and/or a 'first loss' capital tranche
	    • Regional investors to invest in local currency stock
	    • International investors to invest in hard currency, with new FX support mechanism to be provided by DFIs/Green Climate Fund
	2. International secondary funds to acquire participation in regional funds
	    • Primarily funded by SWFs and institutional investors
	    • DFIs/Green Climate Fund to co-invest and/or provide contingent/'first loss' equity

Involving public sector entities and international investors

Our suggested solutions center on a limited number of key financial mechanisms to be funded by a combination of public and private sector grantors, investors, and lenders; none of these mechanisms have been fully tested and/or implemented at scale. These include:

- Layered capital investment vehicles: these are a creative way to use public sector funding in order to increase the risk-adjusted return of private sector investors, thus delivering expected returns. Public sector funding is subordinated to private sector funding in the investment vehicle capital structure. This layering can take the form of grant or equity, subordinated loans and senior loans, with the first two layers typically being provided by public sector institutions and the last one by commercial institutions. This can be used for both equity and debt vehicles.
- New guarantee instruments: to be provided by OECD governments, DFIs, and/or the Green Climate Fund to absorb specific risks and improve the risk-adjusted returns of private investors. They can be used for both debt and equity vehicles to mobilize local and international capital. New risk covers may include counter-guarantees of specific policies and contracts, and components of foreign exchange risks. Private insurance or reinsurance vehicles could also be set up to issue such guarantees, with financial backing from public sector institutions.
- Contingency capital instruments (including contingent convertible notes or 'Cocos'): they can be an alternative to guarantees and would typically translate into a cash injection into a company or aggregating vehicle if a predefined event occurs. Their accounting treatment should be carefully analyzed.
- Results-based instruments, including Emission Reduction Underwriting Mechanisms (ERUMs): they are typically used (though not very widely) to pay for effective reduction of CO_2 emissions achieved through the implementation of a specific project or program. ERUMs are not necessarily a mechanism to fund construction costs, but they can be effective in replacing local subsidy program and/or increasing an investment return.

Conclusion: The Effective Implementation of the 'Climate Finance Virtuous Circle' Relies on a Limited Number of Key Issues Being Addressed

The successful implementation of the 'climate finance virtuous circle' requires effective cooperation among key stakeholders, including leadership from institutional investors to develop innovative financial instruments; a transparent framework for publicizing climate finance concepts and identifying relevant investment opportunities; and an ambitious timeframe divided between short- and medium-term deliverables.

The need for effective cooperation among key stakeholders, coupled with institutional investor leadership

The climate finance world often struggles to find effective cooperation between DFIs, sources of private capital and think tanks performing climate finance analytical work. This is partly due to the diffuse nature of the stakeholder landscape with no real leadership. The risk is that government and DFI initiatives result in lengthy product development cycles mired in internal bureaucratic processes that don't ultimately deliver what investors are interested in.

The Global Innovation Lab for Climate Finance, whose secretariat is provided by the Climate Policy Initiative, is a good example of a recent cooperation mechanism among different stakeholders. The Lab, which was launched in the spring of 2014, is a public-private partnership between a few governments, DFIs, institutional investors, project developers, and climate financiers that is meant to identify, design, and help pilot a few innovative climate finance instruments.

Considering the scale of capital that is needed for low-carbon investments in a relatively short timeframe, it is critical that institutional investors take a leadership role; this includes the preparation of focused climate investment strategies and, together with public sector institutions, the development and implementation of appropriate financial mechanisms to generate adequate risk-adjusted returns for climate investments.

The Investment Leaders Group (ILG), comprising 11 investment institutions from OECD countries and hosted by the Cambridge Institute for Sustainability Leadership, recognizes the need for investors to 'scale up their allocation to green infrastructure, including the development of mechanisms for targeting opportunities in emerging markets' (Joly *et al.*, 2014). Similar calls were made on the occasion of the climate summit that was convened by the UN secretary general in September 2014. This now needs to be turned into an analytical and financial structuring phase, which should eventually see investors work with DFIs to develop the specific de-risking financial instruments they require.

Create a global database of climate finance instruments to monitor climate investments

There is a need to develop a transparent framework for publicizing existing and new climate finance instruments, including their eligibility criteria and allocation processes. We propose the creation of a global database of climate finance instruments, which would perform two roles: to inform the global financial, policy, and developer communities about the universe of climate investments available; and to monitor the 'uptake' of climate finance instruments by investors.

The database would ideally be endorsed by a combination of institutional investors, DFIs, and think tanks and/or research organizations focused on climate finance. The newly established UN Green Climate Fund may be well positioned to take the lead on this initiative. In addition to its role as a provider of innovative climate finance instruments to the developing world, the Green Climate Fund could become the gatekeeper of consolidated information on climate finance instruments.

The objective would be to avoid the duplication of efforts, to reduce donor competition, and the ensure that more 'climate finance bang can be obtained for the amount of combined public sector buck' provided by developed economies.

An ambitious timeframe

The 'climate finance virtuous circle' should show early results by the time the UN Conferences of the Parties (COP) convenes in Paris in December 2015. At a minimum, the global climate finance community needs to demonstrate proof of concepts for key innovative mechanisms, with related funding requirements in the medium-term and ways to mobilize such funding from the public and private sectors.

The annual US$100 billion of capital deployment by 2020 in developing countries that is being referred to in climate negotiations is not sufficient if the world is to close the 'climate finance gap'. The post-2015 phase therefore relates to a significant scaling-up of capital deployment for climate mitigation and adaptation in the period to 2020. This is where investor leadership is required, in close cooperation with a few public sector institutions. More climate finance instruments will need to be developed during this period, with wider sector and geographic applications.

The 2020s should see the initial fruits of the shift towards 'greener' infrastructure development. The climate finance challenge can only be met if the new mechanisms that will be developed in the next few years can be turned into recurrent capital flows at scale by the start of the next decade.

References

Aspinall, N., Mills, L., Strahan, D., Boyle, R., Cuming, V., Stopforth, K., Heckler, S. and Becker, L. (2014). 'Global Trends in Renewable Energy Investment'. Available at: http://fs-unep-centre.org/sites/default/files/attachments/14008nef_visual_14_key_findings.pdf [accessed 24 November 2014].

Buchner, B, Herve-Mignucci, M, Trabacchi, C., Wilkinson, J., Stadelmann, M., Boyd, R., Mazza, F., Falconer, A. and Micale, V. (2013). 'The Global Landscape of Climate Finance', Climate Policy Initiative'. Available at: http://cnsnews.com/sites/default/files/documents/The-Global-Landscape-of-Climate-Finance-2013.pdf [accessed 24 November 2014].

Climate Investment Funds (2014). 'Clean Technology Fund'. Available at: https://www.climateinvestmentfunds.org/cif/Clean_Technology_Fund [accessed 24 November 2014].

Financial Times (2014). 'The New Africa'. Available at: http://www.ft.com/reports/new-africa [accessed 10 March 2015].

Globel Environment Facility (2014). 'About GEF (Global Environment Facility)'. Available at: http://www.thegef.org/gef/whatisgef [accessed 24 November 2014].

International Energy Agency (2014). 'World Energy Investment Outlook', OECD/IEA, Paris. Available at: http://www.iea.org/publications/freepublications/publication/weio2014.pdf [accessed 24 November 2014].

International Finance Corporation (2014). 'IFC Catalyst Fund Completes Fundraising at $418 Million for Climate-Related Investments'. Available at: http://ifcextapps.ifc.org/ifcext/pressroom/ifcpressroom.nsf/0/0F1 6BCACFBC6D5C985257D090067EB45?OpenDocument [accessed 24 November 2014].

Joly, C., Lake, R. and Reynolds, J. (2014). 'The Value of Responsible Investment', University of Cambridge Institute for Sustainability Leadership. Available at: http://www.cisl.cam.ac.uk/~/media/Files/Business_Platforms/Investment/Investment_Leaders_Group_The_Value_of_Responsible_Investment.ashx [accessed 24 November 2014].

MacAurthur, H, Lemire, C and Rainey, B., (2014). 'Global Private Equity Report 2014', Bain and Company. Available at: http://www.bain.com/publications/business-insights/global-private-equity-report.aspx [accessed 24 November 2014].

Nelson, D. and Pierpont, B., (2013). 'The Challenge of Institutional Investment in Renewable Energy', Climate Policy Initiative. Available at: http://climatepolicyinitiative.org/wp-content/uploads/2013/03/The-Challenge-of-Institutional-Investment-in-Renewable-Energy.pdf [accessed 24 November 2014].

PricewaterhouseCoopers (2012). 'Introduction to Renewable PPAs'. Available at: http://www.pwc.com/en_US/us/technology/publications/cleantech-perspectives/pdfs/pwc-cleantech-introduction-to-renewable-ppas.pdf [accessed 24 November 2014].

Schizas, E. (2012). 'The Rise of Capital Markets in Emerging and Frontier Economies', Association of Chartered Certified Accountants. Available at: http://www.accaglobal.com/content/dam/acca/global/PDF-technical/global-economy/pol-tp-rcm.pdf [accessed 24 November 2014].

Waissbein, O., Glemarec, Y., Bayraktar, H. and Schmidt, T. (2013). 'Derisking Renewable Energy Investment', UNDP. Available at: http://www.undp.org/content/dam/undp/library/Environment%20and%20Energy/Climate%20Strategies/UNDP%20Derisking%20Renewable%20Energy%20Investment%20-%20Executive%20Summary%20%28April%202013%29.pdf [accessed 24 November 2014].

World Economic Forum (2013). 'The Green Investment Report: The ways and means to unlock private finance for green growth'. Available at: http://www3.weforum.org/docs/WEF_GreenInvestment_Report_2013.pdf [accessed 24 November 2014].

Chapter Seven

Renewable Energy Finance in China

Philip Andrews-Speed, Principal Fellow,
National University of Singapore
Sufang Zhang, Professor,
North China Electric Power University

Introduction

China has recently emerged as the largest wind power market in the world, both in terms of manufacturing and installed capacity. At the end of 2013, the cumulative installed capacity of wind power in the country reached 91.413 GW, ranking first in the world (Fig. 7.1) (China Wind Energy Association, 2014). At the end of 2011, China hosted four of the global top-ten wind turbine manufacturers (Global Wind Energy Council, 2013). Yet China's rapid growth of wind power industry has run far ahead of the power grid development scheme and the mechanism reform suitable for renewable energy deployment, which results in industrial overcapacity, immense grid connection problems and ever-growing amounts of curtailed wind generation in recent years.

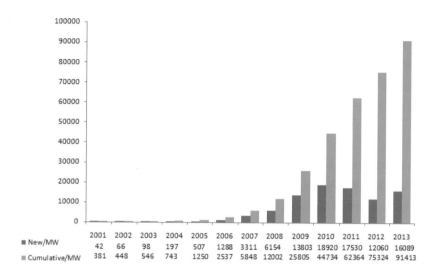

	2001	2002	2003	2004	2005	2006	2007	2008	2009	2010	2011	2012	2013
■ New/MW	42	66	98	197	507	1288	3311	6154	13803	18920	17530	12060	16089
■ Cumulative/MW	381	448	546	743	1250	2537	5848	12002	25805	44734	62364	75324	91413

Fig. 7.1: Cumulative installed capacity of wind power in China, 2001–2013 (Source: China Wind Energy Association, 2014)

At the same time, China's solar photovoltaic (PV) manufacturing industry has grown dramatically since 2004, and has taken the first position in the world in terms of production scale for many years. This success was due to incentivizing industrial policies provided by both the central and local governments of China as well as to overseas market demand simulated by governments like Germany and other European countries. By 2012, PV module manufacturing capacity and output in China had reached 37 GW and 22 GW, representing 37% and 54% of the world total respectively (Semiconductor Equipment and Materials International, 2013). China's output of solar PV cells has increased dramatically over the last decade. Since 2007, China has become the largest producer of solar PV in the world. Yet, in recent years, the industry has been facing challenges such as industrial overcapacity and financial losses resulting from shrinking overseas markets largely due to the 2008 financial crisis. It is against this context that the government started to shift its policy support focus from manufacture to deployment. Subsequently, since 2009, a series of market-incentivized policies have been put in place. The cumulative installed capacity of solar PV in the country increased

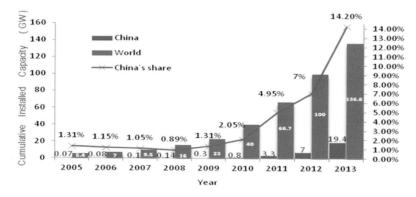

Fig. 7.2: Cumulative installed capacity of solar PV in China and the world, 2005–2013 (Source: Compiled by the authors based on the data from Semiconductor Equipment and Materials International (2013); International Energy Association, (2013); REN21, (2013); National Energy Administration, (2014))

from 0.3 GW in 2009 to 19.42 GW in 2013, taking a share in the world total from 1.31% to 14.2% (Fig. 7.2) (International Energy Association, 2013; National Energy Administration, 2014; REN21, 2013; Semiconductor Equipment and Materials International, 2013).

This rapid growth of renewable energy sector has been made possible by a range of government policies, including financial support for research and development (R&D), manufacturing, installation and deployment of wind and solar technologies. The aim of this chapter is to describe the range of different financial instruments deployed by the Chinese government and to assess the efficacy of this approach to supporting renewable energy. The account begins by reviewing the legal basis for the state funding before describing the main financial instruments. The final section provides an assessment. This account does not examine the role of international sources of funding such as bilateral or multilateral loans and the clean development mechanism (Lewis, 2010; Shen *et al.*, 2012).

Legal Basis for State-Directed Funding Since 2005

Policies to support the development of renewable energy in China date back to the 1950s, when the government promoted rural electrification through the use of small-scale hydro-electricity (Pan *et al.*, 2006). Wind and solar PV became part of rural electrification strategies from the mid-1990s, but the scale of deployment remained small (Pan *et al.*, 2006; Zhang *et al.*, 2014a).

Since 2005, the Chinese government has promulgated a series of targets and policies for renewable energies (Table 7.1). The most important of these is the Renewable Energy Law, which took effect in January 2006. It creates a framework for promoting and regulating renewable energy in China and is of great significance in that it

Table 7.1:   Selected laws and policies supporting renewable energy development in China

Year	Laws	Policy documents, plans and programs
2003		First concession bidding round for onshore wind power projects.
2005	Renewable Energy Law	
2006		Provisional Administrative Measures for the Special Fund of Renewable Energy Development China's National Mid- and Long-term Plan for Science & Technology Catalogue of High Technology Products for Export. Provisional Administrative Measures for the Pricing and Cost-Sharing of Renewable Energy Generation.
2007	Draft Energy Law	National Climate Change Program. 11th Five-Year Plan for Energy Development. Mid- and Long-Term Plan for Renewable Energy Development
2008		11th Five-Year Plan for Renewable Energy Development.
2009	Revised Renewable Energy Law	First FiT scheme for onshore wind energy. First concession bidding round for solar PV projects. Rooftop Subsidy and Golden Sun Programs (solar PV).
2011		First FiT scheme for solar PV
2012	Draft Law on Addressing Climate Change	12th Five-Year Plan for Renewable Energy Development
2013		State Council Opinion on Promoting the Healthy Development of PV Industry

provides the general direction and guidance for renewable energy development in the country, in light of which numerous regulations and policies have been issued. The law establishes three important financial arrangements for supporting renewable energy technologies:

(1) Categorized tariffs arrangement for renewable energies, under which feed-in tariffs (FiT) are set for different types of renewable energy generation. The FiT guarantees an above-market rate that the grid company will pay to the renewable generator.

(2) Cost sharing arrangements which require the cost of renewable energy generation and grid connection to be shared equitably between utilities and electricity end users. These two arrangements are illustrated in the Provisional Administrative Measures on Pricing and Cost Sharing for Renewable Energy Power Generation (Cost-Sharing Measures) issued in 2006.

(3) The Special Fund arrangement, which offers additional financial support, including subsidies and grants to renewable energy players such as manufacturers and research institutions in their production and technological innovation, among others. This arrangement is fleshed out in the Tentative Management Method for Renewable Energy Development Special Fund issued in 2006.

The Cost-Sharing Measures directs the pricing department of the National Development and Reform Commission (NDRC) to set FiTs for different types of renewable energy generation. The additional cost of the FiT over and above the cost of conventional power is paid by a national surcharge on end users of electricity. The Cost- Sharing Measures set a nationwide renewable surcharge levied on electricity users at a uniform rate, based on the users' consumption of electricity. In 2006, the surcharge was set at RMB1.00/MWh (US$0.16/MWh, but it has been raised several times, to RMB2.00/MWh (US$0.32/ MWh) in 2007, RMB4.00/MWh (US$0.64/MWh) in 2009, RMB8.00/MWh (US$1.28/MWh) in 2012, and RMB15.00/MWh (US$2.45/MWh) in 2013[1].

---

[1] Exchange rate as on 9th October 2014 US$1 = RMB 6.135.

The Special Fund provides grants and subsidies covering interest on loans, giving priority to the development and utilization of major renewable energy sources, one of which is to the diffusion of application of wind, solar and marine energy for power generation. In order to better manage the flow of funds, this Special Fund and the renewable energy surcharge were integrated into a new Renewable Energy Development Fund on 1 January 2012.

Forms of State Financial Support

The Chinese government has provided support to the wind and solar energy sectors at four points along the supply chains: R&D, manufacturing, installation and deployment. As will be discussed below, the primary emphasis has been on stimulating the manufacturing of renewable energy equipment, and even subsidies directed at installation and deployment have been introduced with the aim of supporting the manufacturers.

Government financial support for R&D

China's National Mid- and Long-term Plan for Science & Technology (2006–2020) gives top priority to developing technologies related to energy. Consistent with this plan, the 11th Five-Year Plan for Science and Technology, which provides short-term targets and goals for China's R&D and innovation activities from 2006 to 2010, lists energy technologies as a key area. Specifically, the Plan highlights three key clean technologies, one of which is the commercialization of 2–3 MW wind turbines. Among various publicly funded science and technology programs, the two most important are the National High Technology Research and Development Program (863 Program) and the National Program for Basic Research (973 Program) which were started in 1986 and 1997 respectively. These two national research projects have provided most of the direct funding sources for renewable technologies.

The 863 Program provided RMB171 million (US$28 million) of funding for research into renewable energy during the 10th

Five-Year Plan period (2001–2005), of which some 43 projects and RMB123 million (US\$20 million) were directed at wind and solar power. In contrast the 973 Program explicitly targeted only two projects at renewable energy: one focused on low-cost, long-life PV cells, and the other on hydrogen production from solar energy (Huang *et al.*, 2012). During the 11th Five-Year Plan period (2006–2010), renewable energy was one of the technology priorities for both the 863 and 973 programs. The 863 program devoted RMB29 million (US\$4.7 million) per year to renewable energy, and this included specific research into large-scale wind turbines. On average each project in the 973 program received funding of RMB22 million (US\$3.6 million) over a span of five years (Tan, 2010). One estimate places the total expenditure by the Ministry of Science and Technology on solar PV research and development between 2006 and 2010 at RMB227 million (US\$37 million) (Huo and Zhang, 2012).

In addition, the above noted Special Fund supports the R&D of domestically controlled or wholly owned enterprises manufacturing wind power machines and equipment (including spare parts such as blades, gear cases, generators, converters and bearings) within China. Wind power equipment manufacturers fulfilling the Fund's qualifications are eligible for a RMB60/kW (US\$97.80/kW) grant for the first 50 wind turbines produced (Lovells, 2008).

In recent years, the Chinese government has started to strengthen the wind power innovation system by establishing new national-level R&D centers and laboratories for all forms of new energy technologies. The central government has also funded a number of PV R&D projects (which faced many technical difficulties and uncertainties), so as to supply elemental technologies for industrial development. For example, polysilicon was in shortage in China until the state-owned Emei Semiconductor Research Institution achieved successful R&D of polysilicon technology, and transferred it to polysilicon manufacturers in China (Huo and Zhang, 2012). In 2010, a total of 38 national energy R&D centers were approved and established by the National Energy Administration (NEA) (Yang, 2010).

Government financial support for manufacturing

China's state-owned banks and local governments have provided strong financial support for the renewable manufacturing industry, ranging from loan concessions and loan guarantees, refunds of VAT and import duties, subsidies for land use rights and subsidies for electricity use.

Loan concessions and loan guarantees

In response to the central government's call for supporting strategic emerging industries, China's state-owned banks have provided a large amount of capital support to domestic PV manufacturers. For example, of the US$41.8 billion invested in the global solar industry in 2010, US$33.7 billion came from these banks (Solar Server, 2011).

The China Development Bank (CDB) has been the prime source of this capital infusion. In 2010 alone, the bank handed out US$30 billion in low-cost loans to the top-five PV manufacturers in the country. The Chinese government also supports its PV industry as one of a number of key industries identified in the Catalogue of Chinese High-Technology Products for Export, updated in 2006. As a result, solar PV manufacturers are eligible for additional financial support for R&D and provision of export credits at preferential rates from the Import–Export Bank of China, as well as export guarantees and insurance through the China Export and Credit Insurance Corporation (Solar Server, 2011).

Refunding of VAT and import duties

For the purpose of promoting self-sufficiency in renewable energy equipment, since 1 January 2008 the government has begun refunding value-added tax (VAT) and import duties on core parts, components and materials that are imported for the development and manufacturing of domestically made large-scale wind turbines (Ministry of Finance, 2008).

Subsidies for land use rights

In China, the government has the ownership of the land and is entitled to sell the right to use the land for tens of years. Local governments have granted subsidies to solar PV companies in their purchase of the land. For example, when a particular company, 'Company A', was established, the local government approved 1,000 hectares of land at a very favorable price. The annual report of the company shows that during the period 2006–2012, the company spent a total of US$302.5 million on purchasing land in various provinces and obtained US$90.6 million in subsidy from its local government, accounting for 30% of the total purchase price (Qi, 2014).

Subsidies for electricity use

Local electricity distribution companies have strong ties to local governments. This allows local governments to provide favored companies with electricity tariffs below the prevailing levels. For example, the above-mentioned Company A enjoyed such subsidies in its production of silicon chips. In August 2006, the local government agreed to grant it an electricity tariff of RMB0.40/kWh (US$0.065/kWh) for its production of silicon chips, RMB0.15 /kWh (US$0.024/kWh) lower than the normal industrial electricity tariff. The agreement was extended for three years when it expired in March 2009. In March 2013, the government agreed to continue to provide subsidies (Qi, 2014).

In addition, in September 2009, the local government agreed to grant Company A an electricity tariff of RMB0.25/kWh (US$0.04/kWh) for its production of silicon feedstock. This price was half of the normal industrial electricity tariff in that area. According to the calculation, during the years from 2006 to 2012, this electricity subsidy accounted for 1.3%, 0.9%, 0.3%, 1.8%, 3.0% and 1.6% of the selling cost of Company A's product respectively (Qi, 2014).

Schemes to support the installation of renewable energy

The national wind power generation market is mainly shared among the 'Big Five' power producers[2] and a few other major state-owned enterprises. These firms account for more than 80% of the total wind power market. Most of the foreign-owned and private enterprises have only a limited presence in the market (IREA and GWEC, 2012).

The Chinese government has been dedicated to the construction of large-scale wind farms. The total subsidies provided for such wind farms in China increased dramatically from RMB138 million (US$22.5 million) in 2002 to RMB2.377 billion (US$387 million) in 2008 (Sino-Danish Wind Energy Development Program Office and Chinese Renewable Energy Industry Association, 2009). According to the China National Renewable Energy Center (CNREC), in 2012 the installed capacity of the state-owned enterprises reached 50.77 GW, accounting for 80% of the state total (Fig. 7.3) (China National Renewable Energy Center, 2014).

Historically, the high cost of solar PV has restricted China's PV market growth. As a consequence, China's PV power market developed very slowly for many years, and China's solar PV manufacturing industry has been heavily dependent on imported components and materials. The global financial crisis of 2008 hit China's solar PV manufacturing industry severely. In response, between 2009 and 2011 the government launched two national solar subsidy programs, the Rooftop Subsidy Program and the Golden Sun Program, both of which were supported by the Special Fund.

The first solar subsidy program, the Rooftop Subsidy Program was announced jointly by the Ministry of Finance and the Ministry of Housing and Urban-Rural Development of China (MOHURD) in March 2009. The program provided a subsidy of 50% of the bid price for the supply of critical components and required that the scale of the solar PV project be no less than 50 kW.

In July 2009, the second subsidy program, the Golden Sun Demonstration Program, was jointly initiated by the Ministry of

[2] China Hueneng Power Group, China Datang Power Group, China Huadian Power Group, China Guodian Power Group, and China Power Investment Corporation.

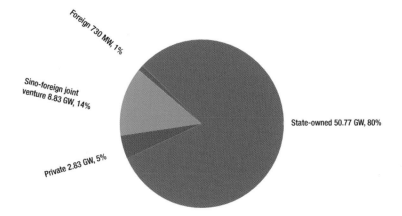

Fig. 7.3: Installed capacity of wind power enterprises in 2012 (Source: China National Renewable Energy Centre, 2014)

Finance, the Ministry of Science and Technology (MOST) and the NEA. The Program provided a 50% upfront subsidy on the investment cost for grid-connected systems and a 70% upfront subsidy for off-grid PV systems over the period of 2009–2011. It also set a cap of 20 MW for each province, including installations under the Building Integrated Photovoltaics (BIPV) subsidy scheme. The program emphasized the on-site consumption of PV electricity. Excess electricity could be sold to the utility at the local benchmark coal-fired grid tariff. As of 2012, both programs have gone through four phases (Table 7.2).

Despite its achievements, the Golden Sun Program came under heavy criticism from China's PV industry for its flaws. This includes the lack of criterion for project approval; the failure of the one-off upfront payment of the subsidies to provide incentives for the companies to build high-performance systems; severe fraud and abuse of subsidy funds arising from the lack of oversight of project implementation; and delays in the payment of subsidies (Yu, 2013). A report released by China's National Audit Office in June 2013 showed that seven solar PV projects received a total of RMB207 million (US$33.7 million) of the Golden Sun subsidy (Yu, 2013). To win more subsidies, companies used tactics such as exaggerating the capacity of the projects proposed in order to generate more subsidy than was actually needed, winning subsidies for non-existent projects conjured up on false contracts and

Table 7.2: Rooftop Subsidy Program and Golden Sun Demonstration Program

Solar PV integrated building demonstration program (BAPV* & BIPV**)		
Project phase	Scale	Upfront subsidy (RMB/W)
Phase I 2009	111 projects, 91 MW	BIPV: 20 BAPV:15
Phase II 2010	99 projects, 90.2 MW	BIPV: 17 BAPV: 13
Phase III 2011	106 projects, 120 MW	BIPV: 12
Phase IV 2012	250 MW	BIPV: 9 BAPV: 7.5
Total	Approx. 550 MW	
Golden Sun Demonstration Program		
Project phase	Scale	Upfront subsidy (RMB/W)
Phase I 2009	98 projects, 201 MW	Solar PV building :14.5 off-grid: 20
Phase II 2010	99 projects, 90.2 MW	Solar PV building: 17 off-grid: 16
Phase III 2011	106 projects, 120 MW	C-Si 9.0, a-Si 8.5
Phase IV 2012	220 MW	Solar PV building: 5.5 off-grid>7.0
Total	2,870 MW	
Integration period of the two programs		
Project phase	Scale	Upfront subsidy (RMB/W)
Phase V	2,830 MW	BIPV: 7 BAPV: 5.5
Total	6,250 MW	

* BIPV: Building integrated PV.
** BAPV: Building applied PV.
Data source: Li *et al.* (2013).

documents. On account of these deficiencies, the government sought to replace the one-time capacity-based subsidies with generation-based subsidies. This change of strategy was combined with an increased emphasis on promoting distributed solar PV[3].

---

[3]The major installations of solar PV are ground-mounted (utility scale) and distributed solar PV which comprises mainly rooftop and small, local plants that are either not attached to a grid or may be dispatched to a local distribution network rather than to a high-voltage grid. The advantage of distributed solar PV is that the total energy and economic efficiency of the energy system is enhanced by reducing or eliminating line losses and the investment costs in the transmission infrastructure.

Subsidies for the deployment of renewable energy

Feed-in-tariff (FiT)

The FiT guarantees an above-market rate that the grid company will pay to the renewable energy generator. In the wind sector, a comprehensive nationwide program providing FiT for wind projects was launched in July 2009 after several rounds of concession bidding. In the concession programs, developers bid on the right to construct wind farms by putting forward a proposal that included a proposed sale price for the electricity generated. The comprehensive FiT schedule for wind released by the NDRC in July 2009 has eliminated the need to bid on the sale price for wind projects on a project-by-project basis. The tariff schedule contains four different tiers, with the highest tariffs available for projects in regions with the least abundant wind resources. The four different tiers are RMB0.51/kWh (US$0.083/kWh), RMB0.54/kWh (US$0.088/kWh), RMB0.58/kWh (US$0.095/kWh) and RMB0.61/kWh (US$0.099/kWh) (National Development and Reform Commission, 2009).

Two years later, in July 2011, the NDRC announced its first nationwide FiT scheme for solar PV power which was warmly received by project developers and project lenders. According to the FiT scheme:

(1) Projects approved prior to 1 July 2011, which have completed construction and have achieved commercial operation prior to 31 December 2011, were entitled to a tariff of RMB1.15/kWh (US$0.187/kWh).

(2) Projects approved after 1 July 2011 or approved prior to that date but not completed before the end of 2011 were entitled to a tariff of RMB1/kWh (US$0.163/kWh). Exceptions were granted to projects located in Tibet which, under certain circumstances, could still receive a FiT of RMB 1.15/kWh (US$ 0.187/kWh).

(3) Bid tariffs would continue to apply to grid-connected solar PV projects through the concession bidding procedure. Bid tariffs should not exceed national solar PV benchmark on-grid tariff.

(4) Local desulfurized coal-fired benchmark on-grid tariffs would continue to be on-grid tariff of solar PV projects under the two subsidy programs (National Development and Reform Commission, 2011). However, this FiT scheme failed to take into account the variability of solar resources.

As such, in August 2013, the government adjusted the FiT scheme to support ground-based PV power stations. The ground-based PV power stations will receive a FiT of RMB0.90/kWh (US$0.147/kWh), RMB0.95/kWh (US$0.155/kWh) or RMB1.00/kWh (US$0.163/kWh), depending on the local solar resources. The standards, scheduled to last 20 years, apply to all PV power stations registered after 1 September 2013. Power stations that were registered before the date, but that will only start power generation after 1 January 2014, are also eligible for the subsidies.

Excluded from the new subsidies are distributed PV projects that directly receive an investment allowance from the government budget. Distributed solar PV projects will receive a subsidy of RMB0.42/kWh (US$0.068/kWh) for all generation which is supported by the Renewable Energy Development Fund. For surplus generation connected to the grid, the purchase price paid by the grid enterprises is the same as local benchmark on-grid price of coal powered units, which is on average less than RMB0.40/kWh (US$0.065/kWh) (National Development and Reform Commission, 2013). The renewable energy electricity surcharge and subsidy payments in China during 2006–2013 are shown in Table 7.3.

Subsidy for electricity integration

As laid down in the Interim Measures for Allocation of Income from Surcharges on Renewable Energy Power Prices (National Development and Reform Commission, 2007), appropriate subsidy will be granted for the investment, operation and maintenance costs of construction projects specifically built for the integration of renewable energy to the grid as follows:

Table 7.3: Renewable energy electricity surcharge and subsidy payments in China

	2006	2007 (Jan–Sept)	Oct 2007– June 2008	2008 (July–Dec)	2009 (Jan–June)	2009 (July–Dec)	2010**	2011**	2012	2013
RE subsidy payments from the electricity surcharge fund (RMB million)										
Wind	227	489	1382	1468	299	3026	N/A	N/A	5,85	9,315
Biomass	24.7	237	569	379	N/A	769	N/A	N/A	723	2,438
Solar	0.1	N/A	3	2.3	3,35	7.8	N/A	N/A	2,02	3,055
Total*	260.3	741	2,078	2,047	3,35	4,105	N/A	N/A	8,69	14,811
Electricity surcharge (RMB/kWh)										
	0.001	0.002	0.002	0.002	0.004	0.004	0.00	0.00	0.00	0.008***
Estimated funding deficit (RMB million)										
	N/A	N/A	N/A	N/A	1,30	N/A	2,000	10,00	N/A	N/A

Source: Fischer (2014).

* Total includes subsidies for biomass, grid integration costs and independent public power systems.

** Data on subsidy payments were not available at the time of writing.

*** This was raised to 0.015 RMB/kWh on 25 September 2013.

- RMB10.00/MWh (US$1.60/MWh) of electricity integration for distances of less than 50 km.
- RMB20.00/MWh (US$3.20/MWh) for distances of 50–100 km.
- RMB30.00/MWh (US$ 4.80/kWh) for distances greater than 100 km.

As of 2010, the integration subsidies were granted to projects spanning five phases, including five projects, 32 projects, 82 projects, 134 projects and 190 projects in each phase, involving RMB1.16 million, 15.08 million, 48.50 million, 57.55 million and 115.63 million respectively (US$0.19 million, 2.46 million, 7.91 million, 9.38 million and 18.9 million). The share of integration subsidy in the total surcharge of renewable energy electricity price was relatively low. For instance, the subsidy for the projects in the last phase only took a share of 3.46% of the total surcharges. In addition, compared with the total revenue of the power grid enterprises, this income is minimal and not sufficient to encourage grid enterprises to actively accommodate wind power (Energy Research Institute, 2010).

Assessment

This comprehensive range of government financial support has brought substantial and direct benefits to the country and, in some respects, to the rest of the world. These policies played a vital role in accelerating the installation and deployment of wind and solar energy within China after 2005 following a rather slow build up over the previous decade. The massive and continuing expansion of wind and solar power adds to the domestic supply of energy, increases the diversity of sources of energy supply, and provides clean energy. In these ways, the growing production of renewable and solar energy enhances national energy security and helps to constrain the rising level of greenhouse gases and of local air pollution.

The emphasis placed by the government on supporting technological innovation and manufacturing has led directly to the creation of the world's largest manufacturing industry for wind and solar PV equipment. This   boosted   the   innovative   capacity   of the sector, provided employment and supplied tax revenues to local governments. More importantly, the rapid expansion of manufacturing capacity, combined with the subsidies for manufacturers, drove down the cost of wind and solar PV materials and equipment. This in turn assisted the installation and deployment of wind and solar energy across the country. The benefits of lower-cost equipment are now being spread across the world, as Chinese companies increase their global sales and investments.

China's ability to successfully undertake such a bold strategy has its roots in a number of factors. These include the plentiful availability of state and corporate funds, and the willingness of the government to provide financial support along the full length of the supply chain from scientific research to electricity dispatch. This reflects the equivalent importance to China's leaders of policies for industry, technology and energy supply. A strong pre-existing technological base and R&D capacity resulted in effective absorption and diffusion of new technologies (Lewis, 2013; Watson *et al.*, 2011). In addition, the government was able to react to policy weaknesses and external events through the incremental adaptation of policy priorities and instruments (Zhang *et al.*, 2014a).

However, these successes have been achieved at considerable cost. The most obvious of these is the sheer scale of the funds that have been deployed by the government, which must amount to tens of billions of US$. For example, government expenditure on solar PV research and development between 2006 and 2010 amounted to RMB227 million (US$37 million). Between 2006 and 2013, the subsidies related to the installation and generation of wind and solar PV energy between 2006 and 2011 probably amounted to at least RMB30 billion (US$4.9 billion) (see Table 7.3; also Zhao *et al.*, 2014). As described above, equipment manufacturers have received so many different types of financial support that making an estimate of the total is impossible, but two statistics give an indication of the scale: the CDB made US$30 billion in low-cost loans to the top-five PV manufacturers in the country in 2010; and at the end of 2012 the central government pledged RMB30 billion (US$4.9 billion) in subsidies to keep the large, loss-making solar PV manufacturers afloat (Goossens, 2012).

The significance of the scale of this financial support lies in the opportunity cost of this investment; in other words, could these funds have been directed to other causes? This question might have been moot had it not been for the massive overcapacity that emerged in the country's wind and solar PV manufacturing industry, which has led to financial losses, bad debts and bankruptcy. Excessive levels of state investment and subsidy have indeed resulted in the inefficient allocation of resources. The subsidies and overcapacity have been key contributors to the low cost of China's renewable energy equipment and resulted in the trade disputes over the price of solar PV equipment brought by the US and the EU in 2012.

Whilst the manufacturing sector drew great benefits from government support, the deployment of wind and solar PV energy faced more challenges. Targets for wind energy were set in terms of installed capacity, and local governments were keen to encourage the installation of wind farms. But this approach took no account of the need to coordinate effectively with the grid companies. In addition, the siting of wind farms has not always been optimal and technical failures have been common (Zhang *et al.*, 2013a). In the case of solar PV, installation of new capacity was slow to pick up, on account of the relatively high cost of the equipment and the initial lack of a FiT. This was compounded by the government's initial preference for relatively large-scale installations (Zhang *et al.*, 2014a).

These costs can be traced to the nature of government policy and of policy implementation. The top priority for the government has long been economic growth and industrial development with a strong scientific component. As a consequence, the greatest effort and investment was directed at the manufacturing industry rather than on renewable energy generation. This strategic approach in combination with the Renewable Energy Law led to investment and subsidy programs which were excessive in scale and in speed of deployment. Implementation was eased by lack of powerful actors that stood to lose in the short term (Andrews-Speed, 2012) and by additional support and protectionism provided by local governments (Zhang *et al.*,

2014b). State ownership, soft budgetary constraints and a low cost of capital further stimulated manufacturers to over-expand their capacity.

This enthusiastic support for the manufacturers was not matched by equivalent measures further down the supply chain for wind and solar PV project developers, nor by effective policy coordination between project developers, the grid companies and local governments. In general terms, the government managed the interaction between industrial and energy policies rather poorly and have struggled to improve this coordination (Zhang *et al.*, 2013b).

References

Andrews-Speed, P. (2012). *The Governance of Energy in China, Transition to a Low-Carbon Economy*, Palgrave Macmillan, Basingstoke.

China National Renewable Energy Center (2014). 'China Renewable Energy Outline 2012' (in Chinese). Available at: http://www.cnrec.org.cn/english/publication/2014-01-20-408.html [accessed 15 October 2014].

China Wind Energy Association (2014). 'Statistics of Wind Power Installed Capacity 2013' (in Chinese). Available at: http://www.cwea.org.cn/download/display_info.asp?id=55 [accessed 15 October 2014].

Energy Research Institute of the National Development and Reform Commission (2010). 'Research on the Guarantee Policy for China's Large Scale Integration of Renewable Energy'. Available at: http://www.efchina.org/csepupfiles/report/201012222651665.8754952527133.pdf/ [accessed 15 October 2014].

Fischer, D. (2014). 'Green industrial policies in China — the example of solar energy', in Pegels, A. (ed.), *Green Industry Policy in Emerging Countries*, Routledge, Abingdon, pp. 69–103.

Global Wind Energy Council (2013). 'Global Wind Report: Annual Market Update 2012'. Available at: http://www.gwec.net/wp-content/uploads/2012/06/Annual_report_2012_LowRes.pdf [accessed 15 October 2014].

Goosens, E. (2012). 'The Downside of China's Clean Energy Push. Business Week, Focus on Energy'. Available at: http://www.businessweek.com/articles/2012-11-21/the-downside-of-chinas-clean-energy-push [accessed 23 October 2014].

Huang, C., Su. J., Zhao, X., Sui, J., Ru, P., Zhang, H. and Wang, X. (2012). 'Government Funded Renewable Energy Innovation in China', *Energy Policy*, **51**, 121–127.

Huo, M. L. and Zhang, D. W. (2012). 'Lessons from Photovoltaic Policies in China for Future Development', *Energy Policy*, **51**, 38–45.

International Renewable Energy Agency and Global Wind Energy Council (IREA and GWEC) (2012). '30 Years of Policies for Wind Energy'. Available at: http://www.irena.org/DocumentDownloads/Publications/IRENA_GWEC_WindReport_Full.pdf [accessed 15 October 2014].

International Energy Agency (2013). 'National Survey Report of PV Power Applications in China 2012'. Available at: http://www.iea-pvps.org/index.php?id=3&no_cache=1&tx_damfrontend_pi1%5BshowUid%5D=1534&tx_damfrontend_pi1%5BbackPid%5D=3 [accessed 15 October 2014].

Lewis, J. I. (2010). 'The Evolving Role of Carbon Finance in Promoting Renewable Energy Development in China', *Energy Policy*, **38**, 2875–2886.

Lewis, J. I. (2013). *Green Innovation in China: China's Wind Power Industry and the Global Transition to a Low-Carbon Economy*, Columbia University Press, New York,

Li, J., Wang, S., Wang, B. and Ma, L. (2013). 'China Solar PV Development Report' (in Chinese). Available at: http://www.creia.net/publish/report/161.html [accessed 15 October 2014].

Lovells, H., Robinson, S. and Sun, J. (2008). 'China's Central Government Sets Up Special Fund to Support Development of the Wind Power Industry'. Available at: http://www.lexology.com/library/detail.aspx?g=0f16ad7f-0446-4d7a-a566-2671efba6084 [accessed 15 October 2014].

Ministry of Finance (2008). 'Notice on Adjusting the Import Tariffs on Large Size Wind Turbines and Core Parts, Components and Raw Materials for Producing These Wind Turbines' (in Chinese). Available at: http://jx.mof.gov.cn/lanmudaohang/zhengcefagui/200807/t20080728_59029.html [accessed 15 October 2014].

Ministry of Finance (2012). 'Notice of Printing and Distributing the Interim Measures for Administrating the Subsidy Fund from Renewable Energy Surcharges'. Available at: http://jjs.mof.gov.cn/zhengwuxinxi/zhengcefagui/201203/t20120329_638930.html [accessed 15 October 2014].

National Development and Reform Commission (2009). 'Notice on Improving On-grid Wind Power Pricing Mechanism' (in Chinese).

Available at: http://www.gov.cn/gzdt/2009-07/24/content_1373827. htm [accessed 15 October 2014].

National Development and Reform Commission (2011). 'Notice on Improving the Policy Regarding Feed-in Tariff for Solar PV Generation' (in Chinese). Available at: http://www.ndrc.gov.cn/zcfb/zcfbtz/ 2011tz/t20110801_426501.htm [accessed 15 October 2014].

National Development and Reform Commission (2013). 'Notice on Promoting the Healthy Development of Solar PV Industry through Price Leverage' (in Chinese). Available at: http://www.sdpc.gov.cn/zfdj/ jggg/dian/t20130830_56127.htm [accessed 15 October 2014].

National Energy Administration (2014). 'Statistics of Solar PV Installed Capacity in 2013' (in Chinese). Available at: http://www.nea.gov. cn/2014-04/28/c_133296165.htm [accessed 15 October 2014].

Pan J., Peng W., Li M., Xianyang, W. and Lishuang, W. (2006). 'Rural Electrification in China: 1950–2004, Program on Energy and Sustainable Development', Working Paper No. 60, Stanford University. Available at: http://iis-db.stanford.edu/pubs/21292/WP_60,Rural_Elec_China.pdf [accessed 15 October 2014].

Qi, Y. (2014). *Annual Review of Low-Carbon Development in China*, Social Sciences Academic Press, China.

REN21 (2013). 'Renewables 2013: Global Status Report'. Available at: http://www.ren21.net/Portals/0/documents/Resources/GSR/2013/ GSR2013_lowres.pdf [accessed 15 October 2014].

Semiconductor Equipment and Materials International (2013). 'Solar PV Industry Development in China in 2013'. Available at: http://www. semi.org.cn/admin/img/news/file/pv_white_book_2013.pdf [accessed 15 October 2014].

Shen, B., Price, L., Wang, J., Li, M. and Zeng, L. (2012). 'China's Approaches to Financing Sustainable Development: Policies, Practices and Issues', Ernesto Orlando Lawrence Berkeley National Laboratory, Report LBNL-5579E.

Sino-Danish Wind Energy Development Program Office and Chinese Renewable Energy Industry Association (2009). 'Study Report on Development of Policy of Chinese Wind Power Tariff' (in Chinese). Available at: http://.www.cdm.ccchina.gov.cn/WebSite/CDM/UpFile/ File2364.doc [accessed 15 October 2014].

Solar Server (2011). 'Chinese government to change solar industry support, encourage restructuring to eliminate outdated PV production'. Available at: http://www.solarserver.com/solar-magazine/solar-news/current/

2012/kw51/chinese-government-to-change-solar-industry-support-encourage-restructuring-to-eliminate-outdated-pv-production-capacity. html [accessed 15 October 2014].

Tan, X. M. (2010). 'Clean Technology R&D and Innovation in Emerging Countries — Experience from China', *Energy Policy*, **38**, 2916–2926.

Watson, J., Bryne, R., Stua, M. and Ockwell, D. (2011). *UK–China Collaborative Study on Low-Carbon Technology Transfer, Sussex Energy Group*, University of Sussex, Brighton.

Yang, H. X. (2010). 'Build a National Team of Energy Research: An exclusive interview with Li Ye, Director of the Bureau of Energy Conservation and Technology Equipment of the National Energy Bureau' (in Chinese), *Journal of China Investment*, **8**, 42–47.

Yu, R. (2013). 'Vast Subsidy Fraud Revealed in Chinese PV Industry'. Available at: http://solarpvinvestor.com/spvi-news/503-vast-subsidy-fraud-revealed-in-chinese-pv-industry [accessed 15 October 2014].

Zhang, S., Zhao, X., Andrews-Speed, P. and He, Y. (2013a). 'The Development Trajectories of Wind Power and Solar PV Power in China: A Comparison and Policy Recommendations', *Renewable and Sustainable Energy Reviews*, **26**, 322–331.

Zhang, S., Andrews-Speed, P., Zhao, X. and He, Y. (2013b). 'Interactions between Renewable Energy Policy and Renewable Energy Industrial Policy: A Critical Analysis of China's Policy Approach to Renewable Energies', *Energy Policy*, **62**, 342–353.

Zhang, S., Andrews-Speed, P. and Ji, M. (2014a). 'The Erratic Path of the Low-Carbon Transition in China: Evolution of Solar PV Policy', *Energy Policy*, **67**, 903–912.

Zhang, H., Li, L., Zhou, D. and Zhou, P. (2014b). 'Political Connections, Government Subsidies and Firm Financial Performance: Evidence from Renewable Energy Manufacturing in China', *Renewable Energy*, **63**, 330–336.

Zhao, H. R., Guo, S. and Fu, L. W. (2014). 'Review on the Costs and benefits of Renewable Energy Power Subsidy in China', *Renewable and Sustainable Energy Reviews*, **37**, 538–549.

Chapter Eight

Measuring the Carbon Delta of Investment Performance

Celine McInerney, Lecturer, University College Cork
Derek Bunn, Professor of Decision Sciences,
London Business School

Incorporating carbon price risk in valuation and investment decisions poses significant challenges for power sector investors. To the extent that carbon emissions are a cost of production for fossil fuel generators, capital markets theory would suggest that a rising price for any factor of production would lead investors to revise their expectations of future profits, leading to lower company valuations (Veith, 2009). Thus, in principle, carbon emissions create a contingent liability for carbon-intense generators and the valuation implication of this depends upon the extent to which these liabilities can be passed on to consumers. This chapter explores how carbon pricing changes the competitive dynamics of fossil fuel and renewable energy technologies in European power markets.

Background

Regarding the long-term liability of the so-called 'unburnable carbon', the Carbon Tracker Initiative (2013) suggests that either investors do not understand carbon valuation implications or that they not do not believe policymakers will follow through on carbon targets. This is because the prospect of burning the known fossil fuel reserves of the world's leading oil and gas companies is incompatible with meeting international climate change targets. If burnt, there will be increases in world temperatures which would be catastrophic in some regions. As a consequence of this analysis, should policy interventions prove successful and prevent the burning of these reserves, there would be significant reductions in valuation of some of the world's largest companies leading to stranded assets.

The lack of accounting standards has made it difficult for investors to estimate both short-term and long-term carbon liabilities. An attempt by the International Accounting Standards Board (IASB) to introduce guidance on accounting for carbon emissions was withdrawn in 2005 six months after its introduction, following lobbying by major EU Emissions Trading System (ETS) participants, Lovell and MacKenzie (2011). This has made it difficult for investors to assess carbon liabilities, and indeed there is substantial research which suggests that carbon liabilities are not fully evaluated (ACCA 2010; FTSE4Good, 2012; Goldman Sachs, 2009; Lovell and Mackenzie, 2011; Stern, 2011). Cook (2009) highlights the various ways existing accounting standards can be interpreted, and these have resulted in significant variations in how individual companies account for carbon liabilities. Kolk *et al.* (2008, p3) suggest that 'carbon accounting is not very useful in understanding the market and technological risks and opportunities ... it is still hard to examine the linkages between corporate climate change strategies, financial performance, and greenhouse gas (GHG) emissions'. Further, estimation of company-specific carbon liabilities is hindered by the fact that the European Commission's Community Independent Transactions Log (CITL) reports allowances and emissions produced by each of 12,000 installations and not by company.

Research suggests that while unaccrued liabilities may be disclosed in notes to the accounts, the effect of these will only be fully incorporated in share prices once the liabilities impact on earnings (Picconi, 2006; Schneider *et al.*, 2011). Furthermore, regarding debt, it is not clear if the traditional methodologies employed by ratings agencies can capture the inherent risk associated with carbon-intense generation. Moody's (2010a, p. 1) highlights that 'the disclosures provided rarely allow us to make quantitative adjustments'. Standard and Poor's (2010) looks specifically at how climate policy impacts on credit quality and suggests that companies that can pass emissions costs onto customers will be least affected by the regulations. Standard and Poor's (2012) examined the impact of carbon liabilities on utility company cash flows and found that with carbon prices of €14/tonne, even if 80% of costs were passed on to consumers, carbon payments could have been as high as 20% of 'earnings before interest, taxes, depreciation, and amortisation' (EBITDA) for some companies, but concluded that the ability to pass on emission costs to customers and the low European Union Allowance (EUA) prices at the time would delay the effect on credit quality.

Overall, the rating agencies, since 2012 have been less concerned with the specific effects of carbon liabilities on cash flows and more with the general outlook for the sector, as weak demand, lower power prices, narrow clean spark spreads and growing output from renewables reduced thermal generation load factors, as well as the regulatory risk hanging over the sector (Moody's, 2010b, 2012a, 2012b, 2013). Figure 8.1 shows 87 European corporates rated by Moody's in the electric and gas utilities, and highlights how over the six years to 2013, the largest European utilities have seen deteriorations in credit ratings of three to four notches from the Aa/high single A rating level. This rapid deterioration in credit quality and access to capital of the utility sector is of particular concern given the scale of investment required to maintain generation adequacy, to 'keep the lights on', and to meet European renewable energy targets. The International Energy Agency (IEA) estimates the European energy sector will need €1 trillion of investment by 2020 and €3 trillion up to 2030 (IEA, 2012). A report by the House of Lords subcommittee on climate change (2013) expressed concern that the balance sheets of utilities had slumped and that the 'crisis of investment' needed to be overcome if the estimated €1 trillion of investment required in the EU's energy system to 2020 is to be achieved.

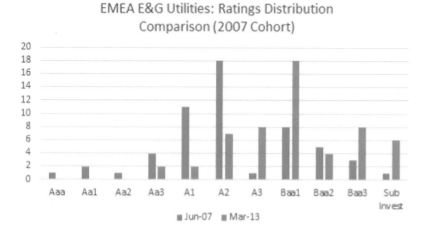

EMEA E&G Utilities: Ratings Distribution Comparison (2007 Cohort)

■ Jun-07 ■ Mar-13

Fig. 8.1:   European Utilities: Ratings in Decline, Moody's (2013)

These financial challenges for the power utilities are exacerbated in the third phase of the EU ETS, with the fundamental change in power companies' cost exposure to carbon emissions. From 2013, European power companies no longer received free EUAs as they did in Phases I and II, but have to purchase them. This creates a contingent liability for carbon-intense generators and the valuation implication of this depends upon the extent to which these liabilities can be passed on to consumers.

A number of prior studies have examined the impact of carbon pricing on power prices, and in particular the impact of carbon cost pass-through to electricity prices. Representative studies include (Fabra and Reguant, 2013; Fezzi and Bunn, 2009; Jouvet and Solier, 2013; Keppler and Mansanet-Bataller, 2010; Sijm *et al.*, 2008, Zachmann and von Hirschhausen, 2008). As power producers are profit maximisers, regardless of whether they purchase allowances or receive them free, they should factor these carbon costs into electricity prices. Furthermore, there are regulatory precedents which allow for full carbon cost pass-through, for example Australia (Frontier Economics, 2012) and Ireland (SEM, 2008). Therefore there is a general assumption that depending on market conditions, 100% of carbon costs are passed through to wholesale electricity prices

(Lise *et al.*, 2010; Zachmann and von Hirschhausen, 2008). Veith *et al.* (2009) showed that for Phase I of the EU ETS, the returns on common stock for the power generation sector were positively correlated with rising EUA prices. This work builds on earlier work by Koch and Bassen (2013) who examined the impact of carbon prices for firm-specific costs of capital for 20 European utilities between 2005 and 2010. They found that whilst the majority of power producers displayed no carbon price risk, the extremely high-emitting utilities did have significant risk premia, resulting in higher costs of capital. Research on the free allocation of EUAs in the first two phases of the EU ETS reports significant profit windfalls and increases in equity valuations of European power companies (Keppler and Cruciani, 2010; Lise *et al.*, 2010; Oberndorfer, 2009; Sijm *et al.*, 2006). Thus, a reasonable expectation is that subsequent payments for carbon emissions in Phase III would create contingent liabilities for these firms. While the impact of EUA prices on cost of equity for Phases I and II of the EU ETS has been extensively researched, the Phase III analysis remains open. Also open is the question of how relevant EUAs are for debt investors. While the academic literature has not addressed the issue of carbon pass-through impact on company cost of debt and credit quality, there are practitioner studies. However these make arbitrary assumptions about the percentage of carbon cost increases that can be passed on to consumers. For example, Standard and Poor's (2012) assume 80%, Carbon Trust (2006) assumes 50% whilst Harris (2006) assumes 100%. From an investor's perspective, the simple measure of evaluating carbon exposure based on tonnes of carbon emitted is therefore a rather crude way to estimate company-specific carbon risk. For example, a company could be very carbon intense but have a low carbon delta (i.e. carbon price impact on cash flows) if it also has some low carbon generation which provides compensating benefits from the full carbon cost pass-through by the marginal price-setting generators.

Because of these challenges in identifying EUA liabilities, and because carbon intensity of generation may provide a poor and inconsistent empirical measure of carbon exposure, a bottom–up rating agency cash flow model is therefore developed in our research to analyse whether EUAs are price relevant for debt investors. Using a range of future carbon price scenarios, a cash flow model may provide a more reliable estimate of carbon exposure. This is the first research outside of the rating agencies' own analysis to assess the extent to which carbon liabilities will impact on company cash flows and hence cost of capital and credit quality. The potential impact of EUA costs is examined using two different approaches, the first based on actual emissions in 2011 and the second based on the carbon intensity of the individual company's generation portfolio. The latter analysis assumes that carbon costs are passed through based on a portfolio-weighted carbon intensity for each generator relative to the marginal. The approach of this analysis is therefore more conservative than prior studies, which assumed all costs were passed on and hence had no cash flow effect. Full carbon cost pass-through is assumed for marginal generators which are understood to be gas, consistent with previous analyses by Sijm *et al.* (2008) and Jouvet and Solier (2013). Electricity generation that is more carbon intense than marginal generation (i.e. coal) is likely to be cash flow negative, and any generator with carbon intensity less than marginal generation (i.e. renewables) will benefit from infra-marginal rent and so will be cash flow positive. These two are netted off (based on the carbon intensity of generation) to estimate the 'net' carbon impact on company cash flows (in tonnes of carbon). It is anticipated that EUA liabilities will have the least impact on companies with a balanced portfolio including low carbon generation assets.

To complement this fundamental analysis, two separate econometric analyses are conducted to examine capital markets' value assessment of carbon liabilities. In the first, equity markets' assessment of carbon impairment are examined with regressions of company share price returns as the dependent variable and EUA price returns, country-specific electricity price returns and returns on a broad-based equity market index as the independent variables. In the second analysis, debt markets' assessment of carbon impairment is examined. Credit default swap (CDS) data is available for 11 of the 20 companies in the sample. Regressions of the CDS as the dependent variable and EUA prices, a proxy for default risk (discussed below) and country-specific electricity prices as the independent variables are conducted.

The Company Analysis

Total carbon emissions in the EU-27 in 2011 were 4,550 Tg (million tonnes). A sample of the largest emitters in the power sector was identified using DataStream country codes for publicly traded power generating firms incorporated in the EU-27 which earn over 50% of their revenues from electricity generation, and then cross-referencing this list with a previous study by Veith *et al.* (2009). From this list, 20 companies for whom emissions data was available were identified. The 20 companies included in this analysis represent €243 billion in market capitalisation (based on market value at 24 October 2013) and €294 billion in debt at the balance sheet date (31 December 2012) for all companies except SSE, which has a balance sheet date of 3 March 2013. The sample firms represent 78% of total power sector emissions in 2011.

The proposition of price relevance of EUAs for debt and equity investors relies on efficient markets: if markets are 'weak form' efficient (Fama,1970), then investors may use a simplistic analysis such as looking at the carbon intensity of generation. In reality the situation is more complex than that, as many generators with carbon-intense generation also have low carbon generation, such as nuclear and renewables. If markets are 'strong form' efficient, we might expect that a portfolio-based approach to estimating carbon exposure might be a more precise way to understanding carbon exposure and the effect of EUA prices for share prices and cost of debt. Portfolio theory has been in employed previously in the power sector to determine the optimum generation mix (see, for example, Awerbuch and Berger, 2003; Bar-Lev and Katz, 1976; Bazilian and Roques, 2008; Roques *et al.*, 2008). The net impact on cash flows depends to what extent high carbon generation is balanced by low carbon generation in the company's overall generation portfolio.

In order to determine the likely impact of carbon liabilities on company cash flows and cost of debt, the company's net exposure to

Table 8.1:   Characteristics of the sample firms

Company	Market	Tonnes of Emissions	Share of Total Emissions	MV Equity € m	Book Value of Debt € m
A2A	Italy	5,416,423	0.4%	1,959,630	5,024,000
BKW	Switzerland	267,291	0.0%	1,333,996	1,106,693
Centrica	United Kingdom	8,361,421	0.7%	23,488,579	6,299,362
CEZ	Czech Republic	38,906,000	3.2%	10,007,113	7,686,438
Drax	United Kingdom	21,465,607	1.8%	3,098,037	107,236
EON	Germany	146,200,000	12.1%	25,534,770	25,944,000
EDF	France	71,016,962	5.9%	37,888,370	58,592,000
Edison	Italy	18,852,847	1.6%	94,900	3,506,000
ENBW	Germany	45,500,000	3.8%	7,545,770	20,211,725
EDP	Portugal	18,237,580	1.5%	7,781,100	6,761,200
Endesa	Spain	51,046,755	4.2%	17,839,980	10,425,000
ENEL	Germany	123,871,330	10.2%	23,470,770	63,295,000
Fortum	Finland	23,900,000	2.0%	13,147,830	8,777,000
Jberdrola	Spain	41,382,000	3.4%	24,922,440	32,499,306
PKA	Poland	59,793,129	4.9%	6,965,262	464,841
Public Power	Greece	46,880,821	3.9%	1,547,440	5,104,980
RWE	Germany	166,200,000	13.7%	13,533,460	22,648,000
SSE	United Kingdom	26,119,153	2.2%	18,527,619	9,779,853
Tauron	Poland	24,669,241	2.0%	1,846,913	1,364,152
	Austria	4,503,481	0.4%	2,596,060	4,321,100
Verbund		942,590,541	78.0%	243,130,039	293,917,886

Total EU-27 Power Sector Emissions 2011					1,209,000,000

Source: Company data various, total emissions from EU Emissions European Commission (2012 and 2013).

EUAs which it cannot pass on to customers is evaluated. This is done by compiling the generation mix for each company in terms of MWh generated from each technology. This information is identified for individual companies from several sources including annual reports, company websites, company presentations to equity research analysts and company sustainability reports. The carbon intensity of each MWh of generation is estimated by technology type using standard conversion factors for German power plants from CDC Climate Research (2013). Each MWh of gas generation is assumed to be cash flow neutral on the basis that the marginal generation unit is assumed to be gas and the full cost of carbon for the marginal unit is passed on to the electricity consumer. For coal, each MWh of generation results in 0.96 tonnes of CO_2 being emitted. However because gas at the margin results in 0.37 tonnes of CO_2 costs being passed on to electricity consumers, the incremental carbon liability as (0.96–0.37) x the MWh of coal generation is assessed. This is then netted off against MWh of low carbon generation, multiplied by 0.37 which is the pass-through of carbon price for gas which all low carbon generators benefit from.

Table 8.2 shows the carbon intensity of generation based on tonnes of CO_2/MWh produced. It also shows the carbon intensity of generation on a portfolio-weighted basis.

Ratings Model

Having established the net carbon exposure in tonnes of carbon for each company, a credit rating model is used to measure the credit quality impact of these carbon liabilities. Moody's (2009) 'Rating Methodology — Unregulated Utilities and Power Companies' provides the ratings framework in which the impact of carbon liabilities on power companies' ability to service debt and on credit quality and cost of debt is evaluated. When analysing credit risk in the power sector, Moody's focuses on the key rating factors shown in Tables 8.3 and 8.4 (Moody's, 2009, p. 7).

The first three sub-factors in the rating model are market assessment, cash flow predictability and financial policy all of which are subjective; we focus on the financial strengths metrics which are based on actual ratios calculated using historic financial data. Using the ratings methodology outlined above, the 'base case' credit rating (based on financial strengths metrics) is calculated for each of the 20

Table 8.2: Carbon intensity of generation

	Based on 2011 Actual Emissions				Based on Generation Mix (Negative indicates buying EUAs — positive means net low carbon generation)	
	2011 CO_2 Emissions/Tons	2011 Total MWh Generated	Tonnes of Emissions/MWh	Ranking	2011 Ranking	2012 Ranking
A2A	5,416,423	10,137,000	0.534	13	663,264 10	41,955 8
BKW	268,291	9,865,000	0.027	20	3,389,940 6	3,824,320 6
Centrica	8,361,421	26,726,000	0.313	17	4,348,610 5	4,638,690 5
CEZ	38,906,000	69,200,000	0.562	12	-10,396,000 16	-6,176,000 13
Drax	21,465,607	26,400,000	0.813	5	-12,281,280 17	-13,387,400 17
EON	146,200,000	628,200,000	0.233	18	171,835,000 1	167,403,726 1
EDF	71,016,962	208,700,000	0.340	16	-7,399,000 15	-11,796,000 16
Edison	18,852,847	22,462,000	0.839	4	1,256,969 8	1,153,509 7
ENBW	45,500,000	59,029,000	0.771	7	1,353,190 7	-755,509 9
EDP	18,237,580	41,424,000	0.440	14	1,059,800 9	-3,211,810 10
Endesa	51,046,755	72,679,000	0.702	8	-2,015,480 11	-3,420,470 11
ENEL	123,871,830	182,477,000	0.679	9	-7,330,540 14	-9,693,120 15
Fortum	23,900,000	55,300,000	0.432	15	14,321,900 2	16,235,510 2
Iberdrola	41,382,000	65,485,000	0.632	10	9,778,450 4	10,385,300 4
PKA	59,793,129	56,520,000	1.058	3	13,774,820 3	15,869,360 3
Public Power	46,880,821	41,500,000	1.130	2	-3,996,370 12	-5,484,060 12
RWE	166,200,000	205,700,000	0.808	6	-31,169,300 19	-30,915,700 19
SSE	26,119,153	46,373,000	0.563	11	-14,799,315 18	-14,727,635 18
Tauron	24,669,241	21,380,000	1.154	1	-55,160,000 20	-66,561,000 20
Verbund	4,503,481	29,754,000	0.151	19	-6,948,400 13	-9,363,480 14

Table 8.3:   Rating factor/sub-factor weighting — power companies

Broad rating factors	Broad rating factor weighting	Rating sub-factor	Sub-factor weighting
Market assessment, scale and competitive position	20%	Market and competitive position	15.0%
		Competitive position and market structure	5.0%
Cash flow predictability of business model	20%	Hedging strategy	10.0%
		Fuel strategy and mix	5.0%
		Capital requirements and operational performance	5.0%
		Contribution from low-risk/high-risk businesses	10.0%
Financial policy	10%	Financial policy	10.0%
Financial strengths Metrics	50%	Cash flow interest coverage	15.0%
		Cash flow/debt	20.0%
		Retained cash flow/ debt	7.5%
		Free cash flow/debt	7.5%
Total	100%		100.0%

companies (assuming carbon prices are zero). Normally Moody's uses three-year averages of financial statement information with the latest period on a trailing 12-month basis to capture improving or deteriorating trends (Moody's, 2009, p. 8). In this analysis, just one year of data is used on the basis that decarbonisation of the European power market has made historic data redundant. The rating methodology is applied to calculate the 'base case' rating. After mapping the letter ratings to a numeric scale (with higher ratings corresponding to lower ratings as described in Moody's (2009, p. 9), the average credit rating is calculated as a simple average of the corresponding numerical

Table 8.4: Moody's power company ratings criteria

Rating category	Aaa	Aa	A	Baa	Ba	B	Caa	Sub-factor weighting
Cash flow interest coverage (10%) CFO pre-WC + interest / interest	≥ 18.0x	12.0–18.0x	7.0–11.9x	3.6–6.9x	2.0–3.5x	1.0–1.9x	<1.0x	15.0%
Cash flow / debt (10%) CFO pre-WC / debt	>90%	61–90%	36–60%	21–35%	13–20%	5–12%	<5%	20.0%
Retained cash flow / debt (10%)	≥ 60%	45–60%	25–44%	15–24%	8–14%	3–7%	<3%	7.5%
Free cash flow / debt	≥ 50%	35–50%	22–34%	12–21%	0–11%	(30%)–0%	< (30%)	7.5%

rating. This is not the actual current company rating, but the rating implied by putting each company's cash flow and debt metrics through the financial metrics model. Carbon prices are then adjusted for by holding 50% of the base case rating constant, as factors such as competitive market position, size and scale, financial policy, etc. are unchanged by the price of carbon. This allows the impact of changing carbon prices on the overall company credit rating and not just on the financial metrics to be assessed. Based on the debt profile of the firms in the sample, the cost of debt for maturities between five and seven years is used. Cost of debt is deduced for the credit ratings between the bands shown in Table 8.5 through interpolation.

Using data for actual emissions in 2011, company accounts data for 2012 and the IEA EU 450 Scenario for 2014 with carbon prices of €20.6/ tonne, results suggest that the cost of debt increases for 15 of the 20 companies as a result of having to pay for carbon emissions. On a debt-weighted basis (based on the book value of debt outstanding at 31 December 2012), an increase in cost of debt for those companies whose debt cost increases of 39.4 basis points is found. However based on the portfolio of generation, where high and low carbon generation is netted off at their respective carbon intensities, only two of the 20 companies have a net cash flow exposure from carbon. This is because most companies have a balanced portfolio of both high carbon and low-generation assets, so they effectively self-hedge their carbon risk, and the average weighted increase in cost of debt is just 20 basis points.

Table 8.5:   Historic credit spreads by rating — spreads over the London Interbank Offered Rate (LIBOR) (Source: Moody's, 2015)

Duration	Aaa	Aa	A	Baa	Ba	B	Caa
>=1 and < 3	25	37	59	109	353	534	695
>=3 and < 5	49	66	94	175	398	599	802
>=5 and < 7	90	94	119	216	386	477	675
>=7	148	146	179	251	372	437	805

To put these in context, Table 8.5 shows the historic spreads over LIBOR for each credit rating. In reality, while rating drives the spread, the cash flow model provides relevance to the increase in cost of debt arising from power companies having to pay for carbon emissions. In the context of the average credit rating for the European utility sector being Baa1 (from Table 8.5), an increase in cost of debt of 20–40 basis points is unlikely to change the overall credit rating for a company comfortably in the middle of a rating band, particularly for maturities between five and seven years. However if a company is more highly rated, its sensitivity to cash flows is greater as the spread over LIBOR is much tighter for shorter dated securities. For example for credits rated Aaa, the spread over LIBOR is just 25 basis points for issuances with maturities between one and three years. Also, if a company's rating has a negative credit outlook; it may also be more sensitive to changing cash flows. Findings indicate that increasing cost of carbon has some implications for debt holders but perhaps not to the extent anticipated. Also, given the gap between forecast and actual EUAs in 2014, the cash flow impact is likely to have been much lower than estimated in this analysis.

Market Assessment of Carbon Impairment

To further explore the hypothesis that a balanced generation portfolio reduces financial risk for utility investors, we use a secondary econometric analysis to examine if carbon liabilities are value relevant for equity prices and cost of debt. The two analyses are not contemporaneous: one looks at the cash flow impact of net carbon exposure based on generation mix over a two-year period 2011 and 2012, the second examines how capital markets assess the impact of carbon liabilities on share valuation and cost of debt in Phases II and III of the EU ETS.

The intuition in the analysis is that in efficient capital markets, all value relevant information will be reflected in share prices (Fama, 1991) and that stock prices represent the discounted value of future cash flows (Fama, 1970). Against the background of liabilities for carbon emissions reducing cash flows to the company, the price of EUAs affects the value of power companies where EUAs could be interpreted as an indicator of stringency of regulation shrinking future cash flows (Orbendorfer, 2009). The theoretical framework used by Veith *et al.* (2009) based on an arbitrage pricing theory-style model (Ross 1976) and used extensively in prior literature cited in Veith *et al.* (2009) is followed. For the equities analysis, the value relevance for power company share price returns of EUA liabilities is estimated for each company using ordinary least squares (OLS) (with robust standard errors) based on daily prices with returns on the market portfolio, country-specific electricity prices and the price of EUAs as explanatory variables for company share prices. All series were rendered stationary by using returns and the augmented Dickey–Fuller confirmed this.

The second part of the analysis looks at EUA prices as explanatory variables for company cost of debt as measured by credit default swaps. A similar regression is run using credit default swaps as the dependent variable and EUA prices, a proxy for default risk (outlined below) and country-specific base-load daily electricity spot prices as the independent variables for 11 of the 20 companies that have traded CDS on their debt. First differences for all variables are used in the debt analysis. The results of the econometric analysis are presented in Table 8.6. Empty cells indicate that EUA prices were not significant explanatory variables for share prices and cost of debt. CDS are used as it is difficult to compare cost of debt (in terms of yield to maturity) on corporate bonds in a meaningful way due to different terms to maturity and coupon rates for different issuers. A CDS is the most common type of credit derivative and the price represents the effective cost of insuring against default for debt holders (Wallison, 2009). Longstaff *et al.* (2005) show that the majority of the corporate spread in a credit default swaps is due to default risk. Following Duffie (1999) and Duffie and Liu (2001) who show that the credit default premium (or 'spread' between riskless German government debt and risky corporate debt) should equal the spread between corporate and riskless floating rate notes, a proxy for default risk is estimated by deducting the yield to maturity on a notionally riskless Germany government bond (with a constant yield to maturity) (GVBD03(CM10)) from the yield to maturity on the Barclays Euro Aggregate German Corporate bond index (LHADCIE(RY)).

Table 8.6:   EUA prices as explanatory variable for share prices and CDS

Dependent variable	Share prices				CDS			
Explanatory variable	EUA spot prices		EUA future prices		EUA spot prices		EUA future prices	
Period	Phase II	Phase III	Phase II	Phase III	Phase II	Phase III	Phase II	Phase III
A2A								
BKW								
Centrica		0.031*	0.037*		−0.424*		−0.451***	
Cez			−0.053*	0.031*				
Drax	0.011**							
EDF								
E.ON		0.041**		0.034**	−0.677***			
Edison								
EDP								
ENBW						0.815***		
Endesa					−1.077***		−0.627**	
ENEL								
Fortum	0.018***	0.069***		0.067***				

Iberdrola			1.277***		-5.134***
PKA					
Public Power					
RWE				0.767***	0.374***
SSE	0.031*				-.0849***
Tauron		-0.034*			
Verbund	0.014**	0.056***	0.054***		

This table reports coefficients and p-values for a two-tailed t-test for EUA spot and futures prices estimated as a linear regression with robust standard errors. For share prices the regression equation is: $R_{it} = a + \beta_1 R_{market\ t} + \beta_2 R_{electricity} + \beta_3 R_{carbon\ t} + e$ where a = the intercept, R_{it} = daily return on the common stock for firm at the end of period t (i.e., between t and t-1), $R_{market\ t}$ = daily return on the market portfolio at the end of period t. R^2 is the adjusted coefficient of determination. $R_{electricity\ t}$ = daily return on country-specific base-load spot electricity prices at the end of period t, $R_{carbon\ t}$ = daily return on emissions allowance at the end of period, e = the error term. For CDS the regression equation is: (d) CDS_i = a + (d) β_1 Spread + (d) β_2 carbon + (d) β_3 electricity + e where a = the intercept, (d) CDS_i = first difference between daily prices for CDS, (d) β_1 Gov t = first difference on the spread between risk corporate and risk free German government debt, (d) β_2 carbon = first difference of daily EUA prices and e = the error term. Observations are daily. Significance at 1% indicated by ***, at 5% indicated by ** and at 10% indicated by *.

Overall, one might expect for generators who are net low carbon generation that if the coefficient is significant it should be positive (this would indicate that rising EUA prices would have a positive impact on share prices) and vice versa. We would also anticipate a change in the sign of the coefficient between Phases II and III for companies who are net short of allowances as these will represent a drain on cash flow in Phase III when companies have to pay for allowances. However there was no consistency in either the type of generator (net long or short EUAs based on a hedged portfolio of generation assets) for whom the EUA price was value relevant for share prices or the sign of the coefficient for either spot or future EUA prices. For some companies, the results of the equities analysis are internally consistent. For example for Centrica, EUA futures prices are significant explanatory variables for share prices in Phase II and also significant explanatory variables for CDS in Phase II. The positive sign of the coefficient for equities indicates that rising EUA prices should result in increasing share prices. The negative sign on EUAs as explanatory variables for CDS is consistent with the positive sign on EUAs as explanatory variables for equities: as CDS effectively represent the cost of insuring corporate debt, a negative sign on the coefficient suggests that increasing EUA prices reduces cost of debt.

The results for other companies are less consistent. For example, Drax is predominately a coal generator (with a certain amount of biomass) but is very carbon intensive and does not have any low carbon or carbon-free generation to reduce the carbon delta to cash flows. On this basis, one might expect for there to be a negative coefficient for EUAs as explanatory variable for share prices, however this is not the case. Also, the analysis suggests that EUAs are not significant variables for cost of debt which is not what one would anticipate for a carbon intense generator.

The results differ from those of Orbendorfer (2009) and Veith (2009). These studies identify a positive relationship between carbon prices movements and stock market returns on utilities in the EU ETS trading period 2005–2007 (Phase I). However, they do so using an equal-weighted portfolio and a pooled panel data framework. Koch and Bassen (2013) note that while these studies suggest that EUA price developments matter for the stock performance of utility port-folios, they do not look at the economic effects for individual firms within the European utility industry. This analysis uses company-specific data and while the Koch and Bassen (2013) study covers Phase I and part of Phase II and so is not contemporaneous with this one (also the frequency of data differs), the results for relevance of carbon for share prices show some consistency. Had an industry index or portfolio approach been used some of the company-specific noise might be eliminated. Also, a number of variables have been omitted in the analysis; for example the growing role of renewables and decar-bonisation in the sector; reduced demand due to the recession; regu-latory interventions; general outlook for the sector; reducing power prices; the reserve margin and capacity 'tightness', narrow clean spark spreads; downgrading of credit quality by rating agencies; asymmetric pass-through. Further (Boyer and Filion, 2007; Orbendorfer, 2009; Sardorsky, 2001) show that crude oil and gas prices constitute signifi-cant sources of risk for energy stocks. These variables have not been included in this analysis. Further modelling work might account for these variables to control for their effects and facilitate parameter identification and estimation.

The results of the CDS analysis show that EUAs are significant explanatory variables for some companies. It is noteworthy that the coefficients of EUAs are negative in most instances and the coefficients are much larger than for the share prices. Both the market coefficient and the overall coefficient of determination are low. However previous studies including Veith *et al.* (2009), point to the fact that this is con-sistent with prior research in the electricity sector using similar models. Also, for reasons specific to the electricity industry, the risk of this industry is lower than overall market risk (and power companies typi-cally have betas less than one) and profits depend less on economic cycles (Competition Commission, 2006). In the CDS analyses, the results must be caveated as the R^2 are low in general, indicating that the model may be poorly specified and that neither the spread between riskless government and risky corporate bond yields nor EUA prices are good explanatory variables for the CDS. Recent research from Coro *et al.* (2013) shows that the role of liquidity risk has become more important than credit risk in explaining CDS price changes during recent crisis periods. So pricing of CDS may be less driven by fundamentals such as the impact of carbon on company cash flows and credit quality, than it is by the liquidity of the CDS market for particular maturities. On the basis that there may be a time lag before capital markets process information on EUA prices, following earlier work by Keppler and Mansanet-Bataller (2010) and Fezzi and Bunn (2009), further analysis is conducted using lagged EUA price data. However, no consistent pattern emerged using lagged variables.

The most notable finding of the econometric analysis is that coefficients on CDS are higher than on equities. One possible explanation is that debt market investors may be more attuned to default risk based on reduced cash flows from rising EUA prices, and so EUA prices are more value relevant for debt market investors. Also, debt investors may have a more short-term focus and may be more sensitive to changes in cash flows, because rating actions are infrequent meaning that ratings are sticky as it is a slow and challenging process for a company to have its rating revised upward. Nonetheless the results from the debt analysis are broadly consistent with the findings in the equity analysis; for Centrica, E.ON and Endesa, positive coefficients on EUAs as explanatory variables for share prices are associated with negative coefficients for CDS (indicating that rising EUA prices are associated with a reduction in the cost of debt) where the CDS as a measure of the cost of insuring corporate debt is taken as a proxy for the cost of debt. However, we do not see consistent evidence of a change in the sign in coefficient of EUAs as explanatory variables for either share prices or cost of debt between Phases II and III. However, based on the portfolio-weighted carbon exposure of the utility companies and the subtle nature of the carbon delta we would not really have expected to see significant results in the econometric analyses.

Conclusion

Lack of accounting standards resulting in inconsistent reporting has made assessing carbon liabilities rather elusive. Yet in Phase III of the

EU ETS, these liabilities may be significant from a cash flow perspective for a number of European utilities. Notwithstanding variable carbon prices, even if investors can estimate actual carbon emissions, we propose that a more coherent way to consider carbon liabilities is to estimate the portfolio-weighted carbon delta, i.e. the impact on cash flow from net carbon exposure (where high and low carbon are netted off at their respective carbon intensities) rather than on the carbon intensity of each MWh of power produced. A bottom–up rating agency cash flow model is used as a theoretical framework to test this empirically. If the cash flow impact of carbon liabilities is relevant for debt investors, this should be demonstrated in an increase in cost of debt if companies have to pay for carbon emissions. Using IEA central carbon prices and actual emissions in 2011, results indicate that for 15 of the 20 leading European power utilities, there is deterioration in credit quality and a debt-weighted increase in cost of debt of 39.4 basis points as result of increasing carbon prices. This is based on attributing just 50% of overall credit ratings to financial metrics. However analysing companies' carbon exposure based on their generation mix, the impact of carbon costs is only relevant for two of the 20 companies with an average increase in cost of debt of just 20 basis points. These increases in cost of debt are not very significant in the context of spreads for different rating bands yet demonstrate the cost of debt benefit of having a diversified generation portfolio. This fundamental analysis is supplemented by empirical analysis aimed at exploring how sensitive debt and equity investors are to changing EUA prices. The econometric analyses indicate comparatively little and rather inconsistent effects, but given the portfolio effect of balanced high and low carbon generation mixes and the rather subtle and elusive nature of carbon accounting these results are not surprising. While the cash flow model underestimates the apparent demise of the power companies, it may be a more valid approach to estimating carbon exposure than the empirical analysis. The regression results indicate that carbon prices are only value relevant for a handful of company share prices and the coefficients are not always in the direction anticipated. Perhaps the topic is not well understood or has not received adequate coverage by the equity research community. It may be that the price of EUA allowances is considered too low generally to be of significance, which is the view of the ratings agencies. Or, on the contrary, it may be that equity investors and research analysts understand the portfolio nature of companies quite well, and, in the short term, for a diversified portfolio, rising prices may have a positive impact on share prices.

Notwithstanding the mixed results from the regression analysis, regulatory risk associated with carbon emissions is value relevant for power company share prices. For example, the share prices of E.ON and RWE dropped by 5% and 2% respectively on 16 April 2013, following the EU Parliament rejection of a CO_2 'back loading' plan (*Financial Times*, 2013). Perhaps equity investors assess carbon price risk less as fuel price risk and more as a regulatory, carbon sentiment or implicit risk.

From a policy perspective, the approach to date of attempting to reduce carbon emissions via the EU ETS has failed due to over generous allocation of allowances and falling electricity demand because of the recession. The increased penetration of wind in most European power systems has also exacerbated the oversupply of EUAs. Ironically, of the two major policy initiatives introduced to incentivise a structural shift in the asset base from high to low carbon generation, it may be that renewable energy finance (in the form of subsidies for low carbon investments) has succeeded where the EU ETS has failed. The merit-order effect of 'must run' renewable generation displacing mid-merit and peak plant resulting in reduced load factors and profitability for thermal generation may prove a much greater incentive to decarbonise generation than EUA liabilities.

References

ACCA (2010). 'Accounting for Carbon, Research: Report 122', ACCA working in partnership with the International Emissions Trading Association.

Awerbuch, S. and Berger, M. (2003). 'Applying portfolio theory to EU electricity planning and policy-making', IEA Research Paper, Paris, February 2003. Available at: www. iea.org/techno/renew/port.pdf [accessed 9 March 2015].

Bar-Lev, D. and Katz, S. (1976). 'A Portfolio Approach to Fossil Fuel Procurement in the Electric Utility Industry', *Journal of Finance*, **31(3)**, 933–947.

Bazilian, M. and Roques, F. (2008). *Analytical Methods for Energy Diversity and Security: Portfolio Optimization in the Energy Sector: A Tribute to the work of Dr.Shimon Awerbuch*, Elsevier, Oxford.

Boyer, M. and Filion, D. (2007). 'Common and Fundamental Factors in Stock Returns of Canadian Oil and Gas Companies', *Energy Economics*, **29**, 428–453.

Carbon Tracker Initiative (2013). 'Unburnable carbon 2013: Wasted capital and stranded assets', Carbon Tracker Initiative in collaboration with the Grantham Research Institute on Climate Change and the Environment, London School of Economics. Available at: http://carbontracker.live. kiln.it/Unburnable-Carbon-2-Web-Version.pdf [accessed 9 March 2015].

Carbon Trust (2006). 'Climate Change and Shareholder Value'. Available at: http://www.carbontrust.com/media/84952/ctc602-climate-change-and-shareholder-value.pdf [accessed 9 March 2015].

CDC Climate Research (2013). 'Tendances Carbone — Methodology'. Available at: http://www.cdcclimat.com/IMG//pdf/methodologie_tendances_carbone_en_v8.pdf [accessed 9 March 2015].

Competition Commission (2006). 'Domestic bulk liquefied petroleum gas'. Available at: http://www.competition-commission.org.uk/rep_pub/reports/2006/514lpg.htm [accessed 9 March 2011].

Cook, A. (2009). 'Emission Right: From Costless Activity to Market Operations', *Accounting, Organizations and Society*, **34(3–4)**, 456–468.

Coro, F., Dufour, A. and Varotto, S. (2013). 'Credit and Liquidity Components of Corporate CDS Spreads', *Journal of Banking and Finance*, **37**, 5511–5525.

Duffie, D. (1999). 'Credit Swap Valuation', *Financial Analysts Journal*, **51**, 493–526.

Duffie, D. and Liu, J. (2001). 'Floating-Fixed Rate Credit Spreads', *Financial Analysts Journal*, **57**, 76–87.

European Commission (2012). 'Emissions trading: annual compliance round-up shows declining emissions in 2011', European Commissions press release, IP/12/477. Available at: http://europa.eu/rapid/press-release_IP-12-477_en.htm [accessed 9 March 2015].

European Environmental Agency (2013). 'Annual European Union green-house gas inventory 1990-2011 and inventory report 2013', Submissions to the UNFCC Secretariat. Available at: http://www.eea.europa.eu/publications/european-union-greenhouse-gas-inventory-2013 [accessed 9 March 2015].

Fabra, N. and Reguant, M. (2013). 'Pass-Through of Emissions Costs in Electricity Markets'. Available at: http://idei.fr/doc/conf/eem/papers_2013/fabra.pdf [accessed 9 March 2015].

Fama, E. (1970). 'Efficient Capital Markets: A Review of Theory and Empirical Work', *Journal of Finance*, **25(2)**, 383–417.

Fama, E. (1991). 'Efficient capital markets: II', *Journal of Finance*, **46**, 1575–1617.

Fezzi, C. and Bunn, D.W. (2009). 'Structural Interactions of European Carbon Trading and Energy Prices', *The Journal of Energy Markets*, **2(4)**, 53–69.

Financial Times (2013). 'Europe's carbon market left in disarray'.

Frontier Economics (2012). 'Carbon Pricing in the NEWM: Day One, Energy and Climate Change Client Briefing'. Available at: http://www.frontier-economics.com/australia/au/publications/396/ [accessed 21 March 2012].

FTSE4good (2012). 'FTSE4good Climate Change Criteria'. Available at: http://www.ftse.com/Indices/FTSE4Good_Index_Series/Downloads/FTSE4Good_Climate_Change_Criteria.pdf [accessed 21 March 2012].

Goldman Sachs Sustain (2009). 'Change Is Coming: A Framework for Climate Change — A Defining Issue Of The Twenty First Century', Goldman Sachs Equity Research.

Harris, C. (2006). *Electricity Markets — Pricing Structures and Economics*, Wiley and Sons, Chichester.

House of Lords (2013). 'No Country is an Energy Island: Securing Investment for the EU's Future', 14th Report of Session 2012–13, HL Paper 161, published by the Authority of the House of Lords. Available at: http://www.publications.parliament.uk/pa/ld201213/ldselect/ldeucom/161/161/161.pdf [accessed 9 March 2015].

International Energy Agency (2012). 'World Energy Outlook 2012', IEA, Paris. Available at: http://www.worldenergyoutlook.org/media/weowebsite/2012/WEO2012_Renewables.pdf [accessed 9 March 2015].

Jouvet, P. A. and Solier, B. (2013). 'An overview of CO2 cost pass-through to electricity prices in Europe', *Energy Policy*, **61**, 1370–1376.

Keppler, J. H. and Cruciani, M. (2010). 'Rents in the European Power Sector Due to Carbon Trading', *Energy Policy*, **38(8)**, 4280–4290.

Keppler, J. H. and Mansanet-Bataller, M. (2010). 'Causalities between CO_2, Electricity, and Other Energy Variables during Phase I and Phase II of the EU ETS', *Energy Policy*, **38(7)**, 3329–3341.

Koch, N. and Bassen, A. (2013). 'Valuing the Carbon Exposure of European Utilities: The Role of Fuel Mix, Permit Allocation and Replacement Investments', *Energy Journal* **36**, 431–443.

Kolk, A., Levy, D. L. and Pinkse, J. (2008). 'Corporate Responses in an Emerging Climate Regime: The Institutionalization and Commensuration of Carbon Disclosure', *European Accounting Review*, **17(4)**, 719–745.

Lise, W., Sijm, J. and Hobbs, B. F. (2010). 'The Impact of the EU ETS on Prices, Profits and Emissions in the Power Sector: Simulation Results with the COMPETES EU20 Model', *Environmental and Resource Economics*, **47(1)**, 23–44.

Longstaff, F., Mithal, S. and Neis, S. (2005). 'Corporate Yield Spreads: Default Risk or Liquidity? New Evidence from the Credit Default Swap Market', *The Journal of Finance*, **60**, 2213–2253.

Lovell, H. and MacKenzie, D. (2011). 'Accounting for Carbon: The Role Of Accounting Professional Organisations in Governing Climate Change', *Antipode* **43(3)**, 704–730.

Moody's (2009). 'Rating Methodology — Unregulated Utilities and Power Companies', Moody's Global Infrastructure Finance. Available at: http://www.moodys.com/research.

Moody's (2010a). 'Accounting for Emissions Allowances: Up in Smoke', Moody's Investor Service. Available at: http://www.moodys.com/research/global corporate finance.

Moody's (2010b). 'Unregulated European Utilities: Investment & Political Risk Add to Mood of Caution', Moody's Global Investor Service. Available at: http://www.moodys.com/research.

Moody's (2012a). 'Wind and solar power will continue to erode thermal generator's credit quality', Global Credit Research. Available at: http://www.moodys.com/research/European-Utilities-Wind-and-Solar-Power-Will-Continue-to-Erode--PBC_146913.

Moody's (2012b). 'EMEA Electric and Gas Utilities: Negative outlook for unregulated utilities on weak market conditions and rising euro area risks'. Available at: https://www.moodys.com/research/Moodys-Negative-outlook-for-unregulated-EMEA-utilities-on-weak-market--PR_259134.

Moody's (2013). 'European Utilities: Ratings under Pressure', Presentation by Helen Frances, VP Senior Credit Officer to MBA Class, London Business School, 17 April 2013.

Moody's (2015). 'Research and Ratings'. Available at: http://www.moodys. com/researchandratings/viewall/statistical-data/marketdata/003 00A004/4294963670/4294966848/0/0/-/0/-/-/-/-/-/-/-/-/en/ usa/pdf/-/rra [accessed 9 March 2015].

Orbendorfer, U. (2009). 'EU Emission Allowances and the Stock Market: Evidence from the Electricity Industry', *Ecological Economics,* **68(4)**, 1116–1126.

Picconi, M. (2006), 'The Perils of Pensions: Does Pension Accounting Lead Investors Astray?', *The Accounting Review*, **88(4)**, 925–955.

Roques, F. D., Newbery, D. M. and Nuttall, W. (2008). 'Fuel Mix Diversification Incentives In Liberalised Electricity Markets: A Mean-Variance Portfolio Theory Approach', *Energy Economics,* **30(4)**, 1831–1849.

Ross, S. A. (1976). 'The Arbitrage Theory of Capital Asset Pricing', *Journal of Economic Theory*, **13**, 341–360.

Sardorsky, P. (2001). 'Risk Factors in Stock Returns of Canadian Oil and Gas Companies', *Energy Economics*, **21**, 17–28.

Schneider, D., McCarthy, M. and Austen-Jaggard, L. (2011). 'Change in Reporting the Funded Status of Pensions? Impact of Debt: Asset and Debt: Equity Ratios', *The Coastal Business Journal*, **10**, 31–40.

Sijm, J. P. M., Hers, S. J., Lise, W. and Wetzelaer, B. (2008). 'The impact of the EU ETS on electricity price', Final report to DG Environment of the European Commission, Energy Research Centre of the Netherlands (ECN). Report ECN-E--08-007, December 2008.

Sijm, J. P. M., Neuhoff, K. and Chen, Y. (2006). 'CO$_2$ Cost Pass Through and Windfall Profits In the Power Sector', *Climate Policy* 6, 49–72.

Single Electricity Market Committee (2008). 'Bidding the Opportunity Cost of Carbon Allowances A Decision Paper'. Available at: http://www. allislandproject.org/en/market-power-consultation.aspx?article= dea8125b-8b4e-4b27-bc1f-554c1e33a4a0 [accessed 9 March 2015].

Standard and Poor's (2010). 'Does Climate Policy Matter to Credit Quality?', Presentation by Michael Wilkins, Managing Director, Global Carbon Markets to London Energy Forum, Royal Society London, 22 November 2010.

Standard and Poor's (2012). 'Europe's Tightening CO2 Emission Rules Add Costs and Uncertainties for Utilities'. Available at: www.standardandpoors.com [accessed 9 March 2015].

Stern, N. (2011). 'A profound contradiction at the heard of climate change policy', *Financial Times*, 8 December 2011.

Veith, S. and Werner, J. R., (2009). 'Capital Market Response to Emission Rights Returns: Evidence from the European Power Sector', *Energy Economics*, **31**, 605–613.

Wallinson, P. (2010). 'Everything You Wanted to Know About Credit Default Swaps: But Were Never Told', CFA Digest. Available at: http://www.cfainstitute.org/learning/products/publications/dig/Pages/dig.v40.n1.28.aspx [accessed 9 March 2015].

Zachmann, G. and von Hirschhausen, C. (2008). 'First Evidence of Asymmetric Cost Pass-Through of EU Emissions Allowances: Examining Wholesale Electricity Prices In Germany', *Economics Letters*, **99(3)**, 465–469.

Section III

Chapter Nine

The Growing Role for Private Equity

Brian Potskowski, Policy & Strategy Advisor, Riverstone LLC
Chris Hunt, Managing Director, Riverstone LLC

An Introduction to Private Equity

Although it may not be apparent at first glance, private equity is an integral component of the energy sector. The role of private equity could include investing in an onshore wind farm from which your local utility purchases power, funding a solar photovoltaic (PV) manufacturer whose panels sit atop your workplace, or perhaps even backing a technology developer which allows you to manage your home's energy settings from the touch of a mobile phone. The diversity of private equity involvement in the clean energy sector reflects both the wide opportunity set of this burgeoning space, and the varying risk and return profiles within this asset class.

The term 'private equity' typically refers to an investment approach whereby an investor takes ownership in a non-public company. Unlike the public equity markets which are accessible to anyone with a brokerage account, private equity firms generally draw their funds from institutional investors such as pension funds and high net worth individuals. They then invest these funds, often with the use of debt, in exchange for ownership (equity) in non-listed companies. While there is no all-encompassing investment style among private equity firms, they often seek to grow or restructure businesses, in order to better position them for their eventual exit, whether that is to a strategic buyer (such as a utility), a listing on a stock exchange through an initial public offering (IPO) or a sale to another private investment fund.

Private equity has existed in various forms since the beginning of the financial markets. However, the modern form of private equity came to prominence in the 1960s with the creation of limited partnerships whereby a group of limited partners (LPs) provide capital to a general partner (GP) made up of investment professionals. As the investor and asset manager, the GP typically charges an annual management fee to its LPs of 1–2% of committed capital and then receives a performance fee of up to 20% of returns.

The private equity industry as a whole has grown rapidly and there are now over 5,000 funds globally with $3.5 trillion of assets under management (see Fig. 9.1).

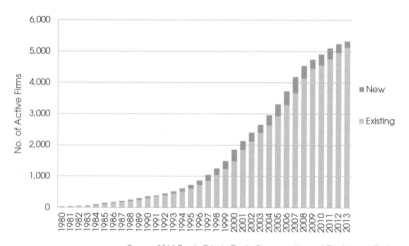

Source: 2014 Preqin Private Equity Compensation and Employment Review

Fig. 9.1: Number of active PE firms globally (by vintage of first fund raised) (Source: Prequin)

Some might ask, why is there so much demand by investors for this asset class, and why are they willing to pay significant fees to a private equity firm when they can invest in public companies or mutual funds with much lower fees?

Private equity is a unique asset class — fund managers actively manage and grow companies, exerting greater control over strategic decisions such as management teams and capital structure than is possible by passive investors. Moreover, specialist funds are likely to have access to proprietary deal flow, which can allow them to source investments opportunistically, being able to deliver value where other companies cannot. Because the companies they invest in are private and not subject to the whims of the equity market on a daily basis, managers can sometimes sit-out challenging public markets and exit when valuations become more attractive. On the other hand, funds can capitalize on market corrections by providing capital when public markets are unable to do so. All of these factors can contribute to higher returns for investors willing to sacrifice liquidity for a longer investment horizon (see Fig. 9.2).

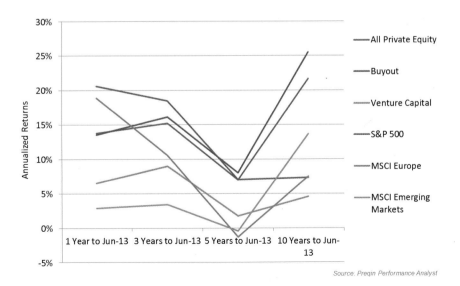

Source: Preqin Performance Analyst

Fig. 9.2: PE performance vs benchmarks (Source: Prequin)

Investing in private equity

Private equity funds are not for the impatient. The process of sourcing investments, committing capital, actively managing companies and their ultimate exit can take ten years, or even longer. Typically, limited partners agree to commit a certain amount of capital, say US$50 million, to a fund for a minimum duration of around ten years. And because they have little control over when investments are exited, they must also be willing to face unpredictable distributions.

Once the fund is established and begins identifying investment opportunities, it will begin 'capital calls', in which the investor transfers funds to the GP for investment. There is generally a set period when the company can invest in new companies. Often, the investor will not receive any distributions during this period while companies are being acquired and funded. However, once investments reach maturity, the GP will begin returning cash to investors. These cash flows continue until the last investment has been completed. The resulting shape of an investor's cash flows is called the 'J-curve' as shown in Fig. 9.3.

Limited partners shoulder a number of risks often not present in other investments. As mentioned above, this can include less flexibility

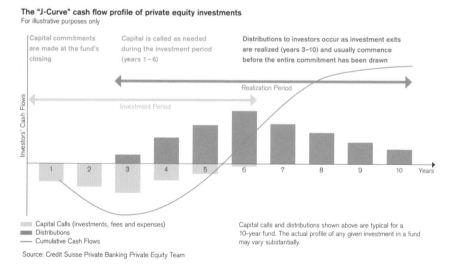

Fig. 9.3: J-curve for private equity (Source: Credit Suisse Private Banking)

due to a long lock-up period and uncertainty of cash distributions. Many investors have limited control over investment decisions and, unlike buying and selling shares through a stock exchange, there is low liquidity for limited partners to sell their investment in a fund. Companies in a private equity portfolio are also often subject to less scrutiny than public companies as they have fewer reporting requirements, offering investors less transparency. All of these factors limit the suitability of private equity to only certain investors — however, with these risks comes the potential for more attractive returns than alternatives.

Private equity in clean energy

Private equity involvement in clean energy has evolved along with the wider renewables sector. Before the early 2000s, clean energy investment was largely considered risky and exotic, as renewable deployment remained limited and poorly understood by investors and banks. This confined private investment in clean energy to funds with the highest appetite for risk. However, as favorable policy mechanisms encouraged attractive returns and the rapid deployment of renewable capacity, interest by limited partners increased, as did the willingness of funds to enter this rapidly changing sector (see Fig. 9.4).

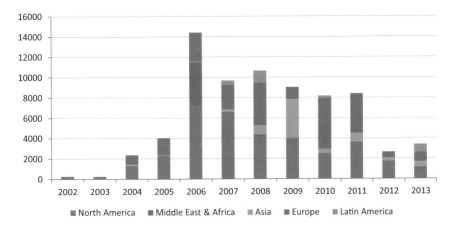

Fig. 9.4: Private equity transactions in clean energy (US$m) (Source: Bloomberg)

As renewables have become more mainstream, so has interest among investors. There are several fund managers with specialist funds focusing solely on renewables and clean energy, but larger generalist funds investing across multiple sectors also now consider renewables alongside more traditional investments such as hotels or retailers. This reflects a number of drivers including a better understanding of clean energy by investors, growing capital for deployment by generalist funds, and attractive valuations following the 2009 credit crisis.

Varying approaches by private equity in clean energy

With both specialist and generalist funds investing in clean energy, the private equity fund space offers a diversity of strategies and return profiles to investors. However, we can assign funds to three broad categories based on their focus along the risk-reward. At one end are yield-seeking *infrastructure funds*, which aim to offer investors stable, low-risk returns by investing in assets with predictable cash flows. This asset class is especially attractive to pension investors who have long-term inflation-linked liabilities. In order to deliver these returns, infrastructure funds typically invest in only the most mature, low-risk assets and then hold them for a long period — up to 20 years in the case of a wind farm, for example. In clean energy space, these funds focus on operational renewable energy projects (where there is little development or construction risk) which are fully hedged through a high-creditworthy offtaker, guaranteeing it will purchase the power generated from the project. The project will often be structured through multiple contractual agreements such as operations and maintenance (O&M) agreements and power purchase agreements (PPAs) which leave investors with high visibility of cash flows. In the end, this makes the asset very similar to other typical infrastructure investments such as toll roads and airports.

For investors seeking higher returns, *growth capital funds* invest in projects and companies at an earlier stage and therefore target a higher rate of return to compensate for the additional risk associated with less mature investments. This type of investing is most commonly associated with the term 'private equity' and can involve investments in both assets and companies, which will typically be held for between three and seven years. As the name suggests, this style of investing involves funding a strategy to allow a company to grow to a stage suitable for exit. One example of this approach is investing in an onshore wind developer, whereby a portfolio company takes a development project through construction by overseeing a number of key milestones such as obtaining land options for a suitable location, obtaining planning consent and grid connection, agreeing contracts with landowners and turbine suppliers, providing equity funding and agreeing debt for construction, overseeing construction and then selling an operational wind farm which has largely been de-risked to a utility or another investor (such as an infrastructure fund). Developing a large-scale portfolio of wind farms would take several years and require hundreds of millions of dollars of investment — however, this will typically offer investors higher returns to compensate for the numerous risks inherent in taking a renewable project through construction and an operational phase (see more below).

Finally, *venture capital* funding seeks out early stage investments with high potential for growth and disrupting the status quo. Often these funds will commit small amounts of capital (below US$25m) in several stages to start-ups targeting prototype technology or new markets. The investment horizon is likely to be slightly longer than growth capital funds (5–7 years) due to the nature of growing nascent businesses to wider adoption. These will often be binary bets: investments often flop as they fail to achieve scale and become profitable. However, some investments can be wildly successful and deliver double-digit returns of invested capital, as was the case of the investment in Nest by Kleiner Perkins Caufield Byers and Shasta Ventures.

Figure 9.5 shows the types of private equity funds on the risk and reward spectrum, though there are no hard-fast rules for where a fund will fit onto this spectrum.

The Private Equity Approach to Investing in Clean Energy

There is no one-size-fits-all approach to investing — and the same holds true for the private equity industry. Nevertheless, there is a broad process whereby firms invest in companies and position them

Fig. 9.5: Risk-return spectrum of investors (Note: Data based as of December 2014)

for exit. The section below sets out the life-cycle of a private equity investment.

Investment process

Every investment begins with an idea. This could originate with a strategic decision to enter a specific market or an approach by a management team with an investment idea. Alternatively, there could be a sales process as an owner looks to divest part of a business. Regardless of how the opportunity is generated, investors will ask a number of questions to better understand the company's prospects, such as:

- Market: What are the growth prospects for the industry? Who are the main competitors and what are the barriers to entry? What are the main risks to the industry?
- Fit: How well does the opportunity fit within the fund's stated strategy? Do the potential returns coincide with the fund's target returns? Will limited partners have appetite for this type of transaction? Are there sufficient funds available?
- Company: How suitable is the management team for growing the business? If not, are their suitable alternatives? How stable are the finances? Will the company require large funding requirements?
- Support: What is the policy support and how likely is this to endure?

In a world of imperfect information, it is impossible to arrive at a full understanding of a business from the outside looking in. However, through a combination of research, meetings with management and industry contacts, investors will be looking to identify the major risks and ensure the opportunity is an attractive fit with the fund before proceeding. Indeed, few opportunities which end up on an investor's desk pass the initial screening stage.

Valuation and due diligence

The next stage is highly time intensive, as the deal team spends days and nights seeking to understand the nuts and bolts of the business and evaluate potential returns to the fund. Depending on the type of investment, investors will use a range of valuation methodologies including discounted cash flow analysis, comparable companies and transactions, and leveraged buy-out analysis to value the company. Here the investor will be looking at how robust projected returns appear under various scenarios by flexing growth and cost profiles, business strategies and capital structures.

In parallel with developing a financial snapshot of the company and its potential evolution, investors will conduct due diligence on the opportunity, involving a comprehensive evaluation of the business from a legal, technical, commercial and financial standpoint. Oftentimes, they will engage outside lawyers and consultants to perform independent studies. This is a crucial step in order for a potential buyer to confirm the information the seller is presenting about the business and to uncover any material items which could lower the valuation or impede the purchase. For example, a buyer of a solar plant would want to know about a pending lawsuit by a landowner, as the business could face a large payment once it is owned. The risk profile for an opportunity increases significantly in markets where there are fewer precedents and less information available, resigning the opportunity to investors with higher risk appetites.

The results of the due diligence will help better inform the assumptions underpinning the investor's 'base case' outlook for the business. Over the course of this process, which can take several months, the investor will also be evaluating the optimal capital structure for the business. This involves deciding the mixture of equity and debt for purchasing the business. In general, the use of debt increases returns to private equity investors because it is a cheaper form of financing (equity is subordinated to debt when a company is liquidated). The availability of cheap and plentiful debt drove many private equity funds to embark on large leveraged buy-outs (LBOs) in the years running up to the credit crisis. However, the resulting withdrawal of cheap debt, increased capital requirements at banks and a number of high-profile bankruptcies of LBOs (one of the most notable being the US$45 bn bankruptcy of TXU Energy Holdings) has led to more modest leverage among private equity firms for the time being.

Negotiation and purchase

At this point, the investor will have a thorough understanding of the company and the market in which it operates. The financial modeling will support returns which exceed the fund's so-called 'hurdle rate' or minimum return to investors before collecting fees. At this stage, the buyer will also be well known to the seller, having participated in due diligence. Negotiations may have already begun with an indicative offer for the business, but the push for reaching a binding agreement will now be more pressing.

No two transactions are alike. An investment bank managing a sales process will try to encourage competition among bidders for highest offers. On the other hand, negotiations over funding a new business through a known management team will take on a different nature. Regardless of the process, the various parties will be looking to agree a *term sheet*, outlining the key terms of a transaction such as the purchase price or funding amount, management and their equity share; exclusivity, voting rights and dividends associated with shares; board membership and IPO/exit agreements, among others. Many of these points are likely to be contentious and can derail an investment despite months of countless hours spent by all parties. However, once the headline terms are agreed, lawyers can begin drafting a detailed share purchase agreement that, once signed, will provide the legal basis for the purchase.

Funding growth and delivering value for shareholders

Private equity firms are often characterized in the media as vultures, slashing jobs and stripping assets after purchasing a company. While there are certainly examples to support this, the majority of private equity firms deploy their operational and financial expertise to grow businesses in ways which increase the value of the business and consequently for their investors. There are a number of methods in which they might do this, such as:

- Providing equity to fund the development of a wind or solar PV portfolio.
- Refinancing the business to achieve a more optimal capital structure.
- Funding the acquisition of a competitor and merging it with a portfolio company.
- Combining multiple companies within a private equity fund to take advantage of strong management teams and synergies among similar businesses.

   Private equity firms are in a unique position to enhance value due to their extensive network that offers them access to industry best practices, proprietary deal flow and access to capital which might not be available to traditional corporates constrained by balance sheets and the pressures of public shareholders. Furthermore, the very nature of private equity ownership allows funds to be opportunistic about exiting their investment in order to maximize value.

Exit

Although 'exit' is listed here almost last, it is pervasive throughout the life of an investment. Even before choosing to invest, a fund will need to consider how it will ultimately deliver value to its own investors. This could take a number of options: a 'trade-sale' to an industrial company, a sale to another financial investor, an IPO, or other routes such as selling specific assets or a merger with another company and retaining a stake in the new entity. The actual exit is often different from the one imagined while investing as market conditions shift over the life of the investment. However, a benefit of private equity ownership is the flexibility investors have to choose the exit option that maximizes value based on market conditions. For example, many investors in renewable companies throughout around 2010 would not have foreseen the rapid growth of the 'yieldco' model which is one of the leading exit strategies for investors in renewables as of 2015.

Mitigating Risk

By their very nature, private equity investments face numerous risks — without risk, these investments would not offer the returns which make them attractive. As one might expect, many risks are inherent in *any* investment, such as the possibility that a counter-party does not honor their obligation, or the danger of cost and time overruns for a project. However, in addition to these general risks, clean energy investments face specific risks relating to policy support, technology and in some case, commodities. A key element private equity firms create value is by mitigating risk, thereby opening an investment to a wider range of lower cost of capital buyers.

An overview of these risks and how private equity investors might address them is outlined in Fig. 9.6.

Policy risk

As of 2015, the majority of clean energy projects are inextricably linked to policy as they require some incentive beyond the wholesale market in order to drive investment. While technology costs continue to decline and approach 'grid parity' in select locations, many forms of renewables are likely to continue requiring policy support for the near future. There are multiple ways in which policymakers

	Planning	Construction	Operations
General Project Risks	• Will there be strong public opposition? • Can developers secure land options? • Will the authorities grant planning consent?	• Is debt finance available? • Will the project experience delays? • Will the costs of building the project be higher than expected?	• Will counterparties honor contracts? • Will changes in interest rates or currency adversely impact cashflows?
Clean Energy Risks	• Will the wind study prove feasible? • Will policy support remain stable?	• Will grid connection be available on time? • Availability of a power offtakeron attractive terms? • Will policy support remain stable?	• Will turbines perform as expected? • Will market conditions for power offtake change? • Will policy support remain stable?

Fig. 9.6: Risk considerations for investors

incentivize clean energy projects, whether through feed-in tariffs (FiTs) and green certificates, auctions, tax measures or carbon pricing.

The risk that policies supporting clean energy are subject to change — for both new assets and existing ones — is the greatest risk to investors in clean energy. This is particularly the case for private equity investors who might hold an investment under successive governments. The potential for policy changes creates uncertainty as investors create business plans and look to allocate capital. Will a project developer still earn sufficient returns under a new offshore wind tariff? What will happen to order books for solar panels in a country changing its solar policy? Abrupt policy shifts make it challenging for businesses to make decisions about staffing, equipment orders and investment.

While it is a given that policies will evolve as technology costs and governments shift, retroactive changes to existing tariffs are the most damaging to investment. Investors will have purchased or developed assets with a view to making a certain return on the basis of a government contract for a specific tariff level or incentive. When the government defaults on its promise, there can be catastrophic consequences for businesses. This is especially the case with investors that have used leverage, thereby making equity project returns highly sensitive to even small changes in tariff levels. Despite the consequences to existing investors and a country's reputation for future investment, a handful of governments have implemented retroactive changes to clean energy laws in recent years with severe consequences for clean energy investors (see Case Study: Private Equity Distress in Spain).

Case Study: Private Equity in Distress in Spain

Anyone who has visited Spain will quickly realize it benefits from an abundance of sunshine. In the mid-2000s, politicians looking for ways to meet their renewable energy targets devised a plan which they hoped would lead to the installation of 400 MW of solar PV. Because of the large upfront costs for solar projects during this period, the wholesale price of around US$50/MWh was insufficient to provide project developers with the certainty that they would be able to earn a sufficient return on their investment. Policymakers therefore established a system of FiTs, offering a fixed-price to renewable generators for up to 25 years. In 2007, for example, Spain offered around US$550 per MWh to those generating power from rooftops.

Spain's FiT worked spectacularly. Between 2000 and 2010, Spain installed 23 GW of wind and solar capacity — the rapid growth of solar PV can be seen in Fig. 9.7. This placed Spain third globally in clean energy investment at US$75 bn, behind only the energy behemoths of the US and China. However, there were two key faults with the system as designed by Spain. First, the costs of solar PV experienced rapid declines in the late 2000s driven by technological advances and increased supply globally. The FiTs offered by the government did not adjust at the same pace — this led to a boom whereby developers locked in favorable tariffs while their costs had declined significantly. Second, the Spanish government in an attempt to keep prices for consumers low, did not allow utilities to pass on the full cost of renewable subsidies onto their customers. These costs accumulated and resulted in a tariff deficit that reached €26bn by 2012 (Figs. 9.8 and 9.9).

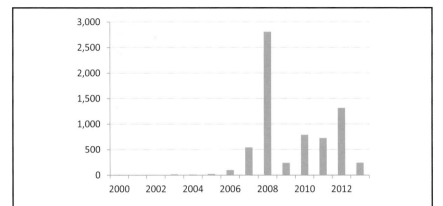

Fig. 9.7: Spanish solar PV new build (MW), 2000–2013 (Source: Bloomberg New Energy Finance)

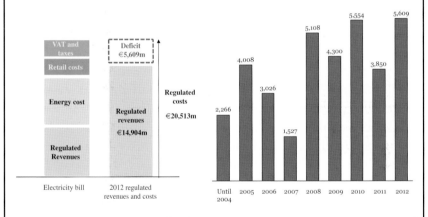

Figs. 9.8 & 9.9: Spanish tariff deficit and evolution (Source: Comisión Nacional De Los Mercados (CNMC); PricewaterhouseCoopers (PWC))

While the utilities initially shouldered the burden of the tariff deficit, it was clear this was not sustainable as these companies already faced strained balance sheets as Spain dipped into recession. At the same time, several years of economic malaise meant that consumers were less able to stomach price increases on their utility bills. Another effect of the recession, falling power demand, meant that the high fixed costs were spread over fewer kilowatt hours.

The government securitized the deficit with state guarantees, however, this placed the Spanish government in a precarious position with investors viewing it as sovereign debt, and pushing up Spain's borrowing costs.

This confluence of events led the Spanish government to seek ways to tackle its deficit and the high costs it had locked into its power system. What ensued from 2010 through 2014 were a series of emergency measures targeting existing renewable operators through production caps, generation taxes and ultimately retroactive cuts in tariff levels. In 2014, the government passed measures imposing a 'reasonable return' of 7.4% on projects. Those which it deemed to have already met this return would cease to receive support — impacting over 35% of existing wind projects.

The measures in Spain have been devastating to the renewable sector. Both foreign and domestic investors funded projects with leverage on the basis of predictable, long-term cash flows. However, due to the sharp reduction in revenues, many of these projects were threatened with default on their debt payments. Meanwhile, investors hoping to recover some of their investment initiated lawsuits against the Kingdom of Spain over its broken contracts. As the saga looks to drag on for several years, the damage of the Spanish government's policy is set to be long lasting with investor trust unlikely to be rebuilt anytime soon.

However, there are some ways to mitigate policy risk. An investor in the supply chain, in wood pellets for example, might have long-term supply contracts with purchasers who remain obligated to offtake cargoes even in the case of a policy change. The availability of insurance, government guarantees and support from international institutions can also mitigate policy risk. However, private equity investors in clean energy will be unlikely to be able to insulate their investments completely from policy instability. In such cases, portfolio managers will have to continue monitoring the political situation to anticipate changes in policy that could adversely impact investments.

At a wider level, portfolio diversification among technologies and geographies, offers the best remedy for policy risk.

Technology risk

Investors in renewable projects will want to insulate their investment from technology failure, which can reduce cash flows and consequently valuations. Clean energy investments are particularly exposed to technology risk, though the extent of this varies considerably within the industry. Companies backed by venture capital firms, for example, are often at an early stage and will be developing a concept or technology that is not yet widely established. The failure rate for these types of businesses is high and the best way for investors to mitigate this risk is to have a thorough understanding of the technology and the marketplace in which it operates and limit their concentration to any given technology within their fund. However, at the end of the day, there is no way to ensure that the technology is widely adopted and there is little one can do to mitigate against a competing technology securing a leading market share.

Within renewable energy projects, there is also a spectrum of technological risk, from well-established onshore wind and solar PV projects to less-establish marine technologies. All investors in these projects will need to consider the following:

- Is the equipment supplier able to deliver its product on-time and as expected?
- What is the credit rating of the supplier? Is the chance of them going bankrupt and replacement parts being hard to source?
- How reliable is the technology? Can the supplier guarantee a baseline level of performance?

When investing in technology, investors will seek to mitigate the risks of technology underperformance through contracts offering certain guarantees around operations and maintenance. This will improve visibility of project returns and make the project more attractive to a wider universe of investors. Long-term O&M contracts are now standard practice for energy projects though bespoke insurance products can also be arranged.

Commodity risk

Renewable generation projects, with the exception of biomass, are different from fossil fuel generation in that they do not need to pay for their fuel. However, they can bear commodity risk through exposure to power prices. Renewable assets that are on FiTs fixing the power price will generally not have commodity risk. However, many projects will have some exposure to the wholesale market if they are incentivized using green certificates or a feed-in premium. At least in Europe, policymakers are generally moving in this direction as they look to minimize wholesale market distortions.

For investors, a predictable revenue stream which underpins project cash flows is crucial to increasing value. Typically an investor in a project will agree PPA with an offtaker who purchases power generated by the asset for a set duration of time (often between ten and 20 years). A range of parties enter into PPAs including utilities, commodity trading houses and investment banks which might purchase power at a fixed price or a discount to the wholesale price to compensate the offtaker for the risk of the long-term obligation. For the project owner, this offers some certainty about the revenue stream for the project which can allow it to take on additional debt. However, a significant barrier to investing in these projects can be a lack of liquidity in the market for PPAs, which will mean that investors either agree prices on unfavorable terms or have to shoulder the volatility of wholesale power pricing.

The Future of the Industry

Perception of PE renewables investments as an asset class

In the run-up to the global recession of 2009, clean energy funds were considered a 'hot' asset class, easily able to attract investment based on the vision of high returns backed by generous government support and a rapidly transforming energy sector. Unfortunately for many investors, abrupt shifts in policy and technology meant that the reality did not live up to the promise. With the credit crisis and ensuing recession, many governments which offered generous support found renewables to be a luxury good, no longer a priority for an age of austerity. Even worse, a handful of governments reneged on their promises and implemented retroactive changes to the tariffs they had promised investors (see the case study above). These investors were severely impacted by these changes and forced to make significant write-downs to asset valuations. Funds holding a large concentration of assets in these markets were especially damaged, unable to return shareholders their initial capital.

In addition to policy shocks, rapid changes to the structure of the clean energy industry disrupted the business models of many portfolio companies. This was particularly acute among technology manufacturers where rapid growth of suppliers, some subsidized by governments, rapidly drove down module prices. In Germany, for

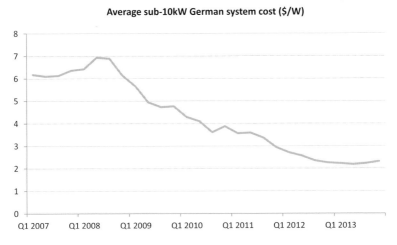

Fig. 9.10: System cost for solar PV (US$/W) (Source: Bloomberg New Energy Finance)

example, consumers benefitted from a 65% decline in system costs between 2007 and 2013 (see Fig. 9.10). However, companies which faced a higher cost base — whether due to their location or choice of technology — were unable to compete against lower priced solar PV modules. This led to, by some counts, over 75 private equity and venture capital backed solar companies facing bankruptcy or restructuring between 2009 and the end of 2013[1]. Perhaps the most high profile of VC-backed bankruptcies was Solyndra, which had received US$536m in loan guarantees from the US Energy Department, resulting in losses to US taxpayers.

The future is bright for private equity funds in clean energy

Despite the challenges faced by many funds investing in clean energy throughout the cycle, the future is bright for the industry. Clean energy has undoubtedly become mainstream and one can now find private equity fund portfolios investing in renewables alongside restaurants, toll roads and technology businesses. Moreover, the need is ever greater for private investors to fund the growing demand for low-carbon and reliable energy across the world by 2030. This is especially true as many utilities, long considered the traditional investors in the space, have retrenched, as their balance sheets have become strained by rapid changes in the industry. By providing capital to grow companies investing and innovating in clean energy across multiple business cycles, private equity investors will continue to play a major role in transforming the world's energy mix.

---

[1] For more information, see http://www.greentechmedia.com/articles/read/ Rest-in-Peace-The-List-of-Deceased-Solar-Companies.

Chapter Ten

Project Finance and the Supply of Credit from Commercial Banks

Alejandro Ciruelos Alonso, Executive Director, Santander
Global Banking and Markets

Introduction

This chapter examines the role of the commercial banking sector in the debt financing of renewable energy projects. Firstly, we analyze the role that commercial banks have played to date in the development of the renewable energy finance industry. Secondly, we identify the reasons behind the rapid uptake of non-recourse project finance debt by renewable energy borrowers. Thirdly, we discuss the specific characteristics that have made renewable energy project — as opposed to corporate — debt financing an attractive investment instrument for commercial banks. Finally, we outline the consequences of the long-term nature of renewable project financing and recent regulatory changes introduced by Basel III to the future contribution role of the commercial banking industry to this sector.

Project Finance and the Role of Commercial Banks in the Renewable Energy Industry

Private equity firms and venture capitalists devote their resources to new investments with high return prospects, undertaking a significant amount of risk of failure which they seek to diversify through a portfolio approach. As one successful project may compensate for the loss caused by others, the risk appetite of this type of investor has allowed capital to be displayed into commercially unproven technologies and more difficult ventures, which otherwise would not have made progress.

Despite their lower risk tolerance, commercial banks have also played a pivotal, and perhaps even more important, role in the development of the renewable energy sector. While the flaws of commercial banking lending practices could be part of a completely different book, and bank capital does not always flows where it is most needed, by focusing on low-risk fixed-income instruments such as commercial loans, banks have made possible the access of this industry to large amounts of inexpensive capital and contributed to its rapid expansion over the last decade.

As the safe-keepers of the deposits made by small savers, commercial banks have traditionally focused in the lower end of the risk spectrum lending only to established technologies with a minimum level of operational track record. This investment approach allows for the creation a virtuous cycle of innovation where, as less mature projects and technologies become commercially sound, they gain access to lower-return funding paving the way for mass scale roll-out. In fact, having access to bank financing, beyond the unintended consequences of intense lending competition, represents in many occasions the ultimate proof of solid business fundamentals.

The financial conduit of choice used by commercial banks to deploy their balance sheet directly into the renewable energy industry has historically been non-recourse project finance debt and, most notably, project finance loans. Project debt financing is a fixed-income instrument which relies solely on the ability of the project cash flows to repay the amounts borrowed. It has limited or no recourse to its shareholders and is secured only against the assets and the revenues that underpin the relevant project.

This form of financing matches the tangible, immovable and capital-intensive nature of renewable energy projects, which demand significant levels of investment that need to be committed upfront with the expectation of achieving pay back over a long-term horizon. Given the lower cost of debt against equity, project debt tends to represent the bulk of the capital deployed in renewable energy financing.

While the risk of insolvency remains a limiting factor in determining the adequate levels of debt when financing a new project on a non-recourse basis, gearing ratios in project finance typically average 7.5:1 (expressed as the ratio of debt to equity) but they can reach up to 9:1 (Blanc-Brude and Ismail, 2013). These multiples are substantially higher to those observed in corporate finance. Under normal circumstances this would result in lower credit quality, making debt investment in this asset class more expensive and, ultimately, constraining the overall availability of debt financing to this sector.

However, historical data shows that the opposite picture is true. Volumes of project finance debt have increased materially over the past ten years even at the worst of the global economic downturn, suggesting a low risk and attractive investment profile. Using data from Projectware-Dealogic, including a sample of 2,216 renewable energy projects which achieved financial close from 2003 to 2013, we estimate that US$385 billion of new investment was financed (both debt and equity) on a non-recourse basis with circa 75% or US$292 being project finance debt. This represents roughly 26% of the total US$1.45 trillion of new investment deployed into large scale renewable energy projects estimated by Bloomberg New Energy Finance to have occurred over that same period.

Literature on this topic (Esty, 2002; Moody's, 2012) outlines that while in traditional corporate financing debt is used to increase equity returns (and risk) to shareholders, in project financing, debt is used to minimize the cost of capital to make a project feasible. The thesis made by financiers is that in project financing higher leverage does not necessarily entail higher risk and in certain cases, actually the opposite. This counterintuitive notion can be mainly explained due to the endogenous nature of project debt financing which we describe in detail in the second section of this chapter.

Although literature in the field of project finance is scarce, amongst the most cited reasons used to explain the uptake of non-recourse debt financing is the desire of project sponsors to insulate their existing operations from the uncertainties related to investing in a specific project such as political or certain commercial risks. In a research paper published in 2006, Heinz and Kleimeier (2006) find that the share of project financing as a proportion of total syndicated lending provided by commercial and development banks increases in more political unstable geographies, because project financing usually creates a legally binding network of contractual relationships that substitutes weak national institutions. In other cases, it is the sheer size of the capital commitments that need to be made in a single project what has favored the use of project finance debt instead of corporate financing. As Esty (2003) points out, 'in contrast to corporate-financed investment, which exposes a sponsoring firm to losses up to the project's total cost, project-financed investment exposes the firm to losses only as large as its equity commitment'.

However, when we examine the use of project finance debt in renewable energy projects it is hard to present either the overall size of the capital commitments to be made or political risk as the key drivers for its increased relevance. In fact, in comparison with large infrastructure or oil and gas projects, renewable energy transactions are of a limited scale. In addition to this, a large portion of the overall volumes of renewable energy project finance have been deployed in developed economies with relatively lower levels of embedded political risk.

It is the nature of the sponsors typically involved in renewable energy projects that explains the high use of project rather than corporate financing. As a nascent industry, renewable energy is widely viewed as a cross-over sector between infrastructure and independent power generation, attracting sponsors of different nature and with different return objectives. On the one hand, the fact that government intervention in renewables is limited to creating incentive structures that accommodate a certain rate of deployment supposedly aligned with nationwide or international objectives, has attracted entrepreneurs and small firms into the sector. This is different to large infrastructure projects, where governments allow a nationally or regionally significant project to be financed by the private sector and are, therefore, more concerned by the identity of its future owner.

Given the limited amount of capital that a small- or medium-sized development firm has access to, project finance is the least expensive and, perhaps, the only form of debt financing available to them. This type of investor is usually interested in exiting its investment at an early stage when it can maximize its return and recycle capital which can ultimately be reinvested into new assets. It is at this stage where the institutional equity market comes into play.

Over the past decades, numerous investment (listed and private) vehicles, ultimately funded by institutional investors such as pension funds and insurance companies, have been raised to channel investment into infrastructure-like assets, of which renewable energy is part. This second investor profile is looking for long-term, cash-yielding, low-risk assets which it can hold to maturity to mirror the liabilities of their ultimate shareholders. Many of these vehicles have been set up under a fund structure which usually has a limited life and no other unencumbered assets to use as collateral to raise additional debt. In addition to this, non-recourse project financing also allows for this second kind of investor to deploy the equity they have raised across a larger number of investments.

In both cases, the limited size of the balance sheet of small developers and equity investment vehicles explains the use of project rather than corporate financing. In other words, when the credit quality of the project owner on a standalone basis is worse than that of the project itself, project debt financing becomes the most economically efficient and accessible source of financing. This not only applies to funds or development firms but also to large corporations.

For example, Abengoa S.A. a B/Ba3 rated (Standard and Poor's (S&P)/Moody's) renewable technology and development firm operating across Latin America, Europe and the US tends to rely on project debt rather than corporate financing to fund new projects, whereas Iberdrola S.A. (BBB/Baa1) a vertically integrated utility who owns one of the largest renewable energy generation portfolios, tends to finance projects on balance sheet. As we will see over the following sections of this chapter, behavioral analysis of project finance loans undertaken by Moody's and S&P tends to place this type of lending product in the low BBB or high BB arena, corroborating the rationale behind the funding strategy of these two companies.

The involvement of the commercial lending sector from the advent of the renewable energy industry can be characterized as the effort made by the banking industry to follow the needs of credit-constrained clients into a new asset class that is extremely capital intensive. Non-recourse project debt financing is a bespoke financial product that has achieved a high level of penetration predominantly amongst project developers, sub-investment grade corporates and institutional equity investors, given their lack of access to traditional corporate debt financing at competitive levels.

The Supply of Credit in the Form of Non-Recourse Project Financing

In the previous section we outlined the factors that have led to an increase in the demand for project debt financing by different type of renewable energy equity investors. This was a borrower rather than a creditor perspective. In this second section, we look at the reasons behind the matching increase supply of credit in the form of non-recourse lending provided by commercial banks into the renewable energy sector.

Commercial banks usually have somewhat similar asset investment strategies to each other, with their balance sheets being allocated to different mixes of loans made available to individuals (personal lending, consumer financing and mortgages) or corporations (corporate lending). As the borrower in a non-recourse project financing is a firm rather than an individual, project financing could be viewed as a sub-category of corporate financing. However, when we look into the main attributes of project finance debt and compare it to that of traditional corporate finance debt, we find that there are certain differentiating characteristics between both forms of debt investment that can help us to understand why non-recourse lending has become an attractive debt instrument to large financial institutions:

1) Projects tend to have limited life either due to technological, regulatory or contractual restrictions and, therefore, negligible terminal or residual value. In the specific case of renewable energy project financing, the operational life of the assets (which tends to not exceed 20 or 25 years, depending on the technology), combined with the time-limited access to underlying support schemes, constrains the maximum horizon in which an investment can attain its targeted return or, in the case of debt financing, be repaid.

2) As projects are time-bound, lenders play an active role in the design of an efficient risk allocation framework across all stakeholders before (*ex-ante*) any investment decision is made, resulting in lower levels of adverse selection. This opposes the traditional approach in corporate debt financing, where all decisions are delegated to the management of the company and creditors usually only tend to get involved in how cash flow is allocated between shareholders, management and debt providers only when the borrower is already underperforming (*ex-post*). This is usually referred to as endogenous credit risk given that creditors in project financing determine at the outset what their maximum level of acceptance to risk is, not only on day one but over the entire life of the financing.

3) The active involvement of lenders in project financing also helps to reduce one of the key issues in corporate financing, the asymmetry of information existing between the management of a company and its creditors. In project finance, during the due diligence phase banks have complete access to all the aspects of commercial sensitive information around the commercial strategy of the borrower and can make their own independent assessment of the risks connected to it.

4) The higher leverage associated with project financing typically means that more of the cash is used to debt service than to return capital to shareholders and management. This translates into

tighter controls on dividend policy and incurrence of additional debt.

5) The firm is insulated from other risks unrelated to the nature of its business. This entails that the company that raises the debt will be a newly constituted firm, usually a special purpose vehicle (SPV), with no pre-existing operations and whose sole purpose will be limited to constructing, owning, operating and financing the relevant renewable energy project.

6) The single purpose, time-constrained activity of the SPV results in a contractual structure that provides an efficient risk allocation amongst all project participants including contractors, offtakers and technology suppliers allowing cash flow visibility over the long term with a high level of predictability limiting being the downside, but also the upside in terms of return. In the context of renewable energy generation projects this is usually best demonstrated by long-term offtake agreements, in the form of power purchase agreements (PPAs) or government-sponsored frameworks such as feed-in tariffs (FiTs) or market plus premium schemes, where a substantial or all of the output of produced by the asset is sold at a fixed price or a minimum guaranteed level.

A study by S&P (2014) using a sample of 573 projects across a diverse range of sectors shows about two thirds were originally investment grade rated (BBB or higher) with an additional c. 20% in the BB area despite the high leverage multiples observed. Similarly, Moody's (2014), using data from a pool of 4,425 projects representing 54.2% of all project finance transactions originated globally during a 30-year period from 1 January 1983 to 31 December 2012, reveals that the ten-year cumulative default rate for project finance bank loans is consistent with ten-year cumulative default rates for corporate issuers of low investment grade/high speculative grade credit quality (Baa/Ba), which is in line with S&P's findings.

Most importantly, over 30 years of observational experience Moody's found that while — during an initial three-year period post-financial close, associated with the construction phase of projects — marginal annual default rates for project finance bank loans perform in line with a high grade speculative corporate ratings (Ba), towards year ten from financial close they fall significantly achieving marginal default rates associated with a single-A category rating (high investment grade). This characteristic of project finance bank loans is significantly different from that of corporate loans where the marginal rate of default remains stable over time. As argued by Blanc-Brude and Ismail (2013), the risk profile of project finance debt is dynamic because of the continuous improvement of its credit profile over time.

In addition to this, ultimate recovery (the amount of capital that is recovered after a loan has defaulted) of project finance loans is in average c. 80% and broadly similar to ultimate recovery rates for senior secured corporate bank loans. However, project finance loan default rates when compared to those of corporate loans are largely uncorrelated to the jurisdiction where the borrower is incorporated, the level of capitalization (debt cushion) existing in the capital structure and the economic cycle. Although, the Moody's study is not sector specific, the largest contributing industry to the data sample is power, of which renewable energy project finance loans represent a significant portion and therefore, its conclusions can be extrapolated to the industry subject of this book.

These two pieces of research provide a very relevant insight as to why commercial banks have been able to deploy substantial volumes of new lending into this sector. The credit quality of project finance debt improves over time and results in high recovery rates that are uncorrelated to the level of debt that is initially injected into the SPV or the economic cycle. It is the direct involvement of financiers at the inception of the project, when choices are made about the optimal risk allocation across all stakeholders and the project structure is defined, that allows this asset class to be resilient to the changes that each of variables that impact project performance over time.

The Sources of Credit Risk in Renewable Energy Financing

While in the previous section we argue that non-recourse debt financing of renewable energy projects has certain characteristics that have allowed it to be perceived as a resilient investment for commercial banks, this does not mean that it is exempt from credit risk. As a matter of fact, in its brief history, this industry has already experienced a number of renowned defaults which in turn have helped to shape the face of commercial banking's lending appetite.

According to S&P (2014) there are six broad categories that outline the main causes of project finance defaults:

1) Technology or design problems during the construction and ramp up phase.
2) Ongoing operational underperformance.
3) Exposure to market prices or lack of raw materials or project output (price or volume).
4) Failure of a parent company.
5) Counterparty issues.
6) Changes to existing regulation or new regulations.

The one category that explains the largest number of defaults analyzed by S&P over the past 20 years is market exposure (26.5% of the total) whereas, surprisingly enough, changes to regulation is the least representative one with c. 3% (one default out of 34). While this data sample is probably too small to draw very relevant conclusions, it can help us to classify the key issues that commercial banks have encountered when financing renewable energy projects.

At the inception of the industry, technology and operational risk together with the uncertainty related to the availability of renewable energy fuel (volume risk) were the three key credit considerations that commercial banks devoted their attention to when analyzing their participation in renewable energy transactions. During these initial years, very little attention was placed on counter-party, price and regulatory issues, given that most countries came up with government-guaranteed FiT regimes that provided long-term price stability. Decarbonization, security of supply and employment were at the top of the political agenda and governments felt that by promoting the creation of a new national industry they would reap the benefits of the green revolution.

However, even when at the core of the analysis, the financing industry struggled to get some of these issues adequately addressed. A good example was the €371 million bond issued by Breeze Finance S.A. to fund the financing of a portfolio of mostly operational wind farms located across Germany and France. While a significant portion of the securities issued were guaranteed by a monoliner (MBIA), the non-guaranteed subordinated notes managed to attain a Ba1 (high speculative grade) rating on the back of the supportive regulatory framework in these two countries, the diversification of risk across a portfolio of assets, and the resilience of the structure to downside wind resource and operational scenarios. After a few years, extremely poor conditions, which meant the project was never able to get close to the overly optimistic output estimates initially made, together with lower than expected turbine availability levels, resulted in a series of rating downgrades tainting the reputation of renewable power generation and closing its access to the capital markets for a number of years. In more recent times, Continental Wind LLC successful issue of US$635 million of senior secured notes (Baa3) and the US$850 million Topaz Solar Farms LLC's (Baa2) senior secured bond issue, mark the ability of this industry to learn from its past mistakes.

While the more established technologies (solar and wind) have encountered teething issues, in other circumstances, investors and project finance debt providers have suffered important losses after committing funding to incipient technologies. In one case, EnerTech Environmental, a plant located at a landfill site in California designed to convert biosolids into a coal substitute, suffered technical problems causing the plant to produce only one third of its contractual commitments, and eventually shutting it down completely. Another example is Northeast Biofuels, an ethanol production facility that did not achieve completion and filed for bankruptcy under Chapter 11 (of the US Bankruptcy Code) in 2008 after design issues impacted the construction schedule.

As commercial banks learned through experience about technology, volume and operational risk, their attention turned into those areas that were deemed to be less exposed to these issues. In effect, capital quickly moved into what were perceived to be safer investments more in line with the infrastructure-type of returns that debt and equity providers required. This allowed for the large-scale development of solar PV, concentrated solar power, onshore wind and, eventually, offshore wind projects. It is, at this point in time, triggered by the squeeze that consumers and taxpayers were withstanding as the result of the global economic crisis that the question of affordability became the epicenter of the political debate. The international finance community had, once again, overlooked a major credit issue.

In certain jurisdictions like the UK, Sweden, Germany or Finland, infrastructure regulated assets, such as electricity, water and gas distribution, receive a regulated return that is reviewed cyclically by an independent regulator and is usually protected from certain risks inherent to renewable energy power generation, such as volume risk. Although at the time of the crisis some experienced investors believed that the ultimate goal of regulation was to provide stable returns to the private sector, as a matter of fact regulation is in many occasions aimed to protect consumers against the monopolistic position of asset owners. If not controlled, unreasonable price increases in access tariffs to the transportation of gas, water and electricity, could make essential utility services unaffordable or simply curb competition by treating different utility service providers unequally. Those are the reasons behind the unbundling regulations set out by the European Commission which prevent vertically integrated utilities from ownership of generation and transmission or distribution networks under the same legal entity.

Against this, the objective of regulation in renewables, at least in those geographies where grid parity has not been achieved yet, is to attract private capital into the sector, but not necessarily to ensure customer protection. From the perspective of the regulator, viewing renewable energy as another type of regulated investment is, therefore, conceptually incorrect. In fact, power generation, has for quite some time been a liberalized market activity in many Western economies and, therefore, exposed to the fluctuations of supply and demand of electricity.

However, when commercial banks and equity investors started to finance renewables, they drew a parallel between the regulated tariffs set out for renewable energy power projects and those already in place for regulated utilities, with the added positive that the former was not exposed to periodic regulatory reviews while the latter was. Very few players focused on the fact that renewable power generation, being a non-monopolistic, liberalized activity that requires additional consumer support above the market clearing price, had a different type of inherent credit risk to that of a monopolistic asset where the system needs to ensure customer access to essential services. This is not to blame the private sector for the retroactive changes to the renewable support schemes that unfortunately have been implemented in countries like Italy or Spain, but just pointing out the fact that at the time there was a broad misconception as to what exactly regulatory risk was.

As Blanc-Brude (2013) points out, given the long-term horizon required by infrastructure investments to achieve an acceptable rate of return, one of the key problems that renewable energy investors (equity and debt) encounter when committing capital upfront is that of time inconsistency, where the preferences of each of the multiple stakeholders involved (regulators, operator, etc) may change over time, potentially affecting the risk-reward dynamics that the investor used when making its investment decision. This problem can only be mitigated through the creation of a legally binding contractual structure that re-establishes time consistency across all project participants.

In the case of renewable energy financing, the risk of time inconsistency has materialized as regulators changed their preferences by favoring short-term consumer needs (i.e. avoiding increases in electricity bills) to the detriment of long-term choices about the future impact of growing CO_2 emissions in the welfare of their citizens. While commercial banks believed that the legal framework for renewable energy power would remain inalterable, they took this view at a time when the global state of the economy supported the long-term objective of decarbonization, ignoring the fact that if the economy started to underperform and unemployment increased, the short-term objective of affordability would dominate the decisions to be made by the regulator.

The future ability of governments to attract private capital into their renewable energy markets will depend upon the perceived risk of time inconsistency occurring. In order to assess such risk, the private sector is already focusing on countries whose legal systems protect the principle of grandfathering, and those technologies and countries where the short- and long-term objectives are not mutually exclusive. As a consequence, certain emerging economies highly dependent on expensive coal and diesel power generation where renewable energy sources are more abundant are increasingly attracting more capital.

Renewable Energy Project Financing: Duration, Pricing and the Impact of the Credit Cycle

While credit risk in renewable energy debt financing has been at times misunderstood by commercial banks and other financial institutions, the intrinsic characteristics of project finance debt as a proxy for overall renewable energy financing have allowed an unparalleled growth in the availability of debt for this sector.

However, credit risk is only one part of the equation. As banks have a finite amount of capital to be deployed, the attractiveness of the returns related to renewable energy project finance lending need to be considered in the context of a multi-asset allocation strategy, and benchmarked against that of other alternative investment instruments both in terms of price, herein referred as credit spreads or margin, and duration.

When we compared the key differences between project debt financing and corporate debt financing we outlined that empirical evidence has demonstrated that credit risk in project debt financing is dynamic, and tends to improve over time through deleveraging and as some of the initial uncertainties (i.e. construction risk) dissipate. Secondly, we have pointed out that renewable energy projects require a large amount of capital to be deployed upfront, and this is only recovered in the long term. Finally, we have also mentioned that projects have a limited life and negligible or zero residual value, which results in contractual structures that are designed to afford a high level of predictability about the ability of the project generate stable cash flows over a long-term horizon. These three features combined lead to longer average maturities in project finance loans than in corporate debt financing. Using data extracted from Projectware-Dealogic we estimate that the average loan maturity for renewable energy non-recourse loans is close to 12 years for the period 2003–2014.

Several authors have analyzed the relationship between credit spreads and long-term maturities in project finance loans, following the model developed by Merton (1974) which outlines that the price of a certain debt security depends upon its underlying characteristics, such as maturity or seniority and its probability of default, which is connected to the degree of indebtedness of the borrower and the uncertainty of the value of the assets of the firm at maturity. The dynamic credit profile of non-recourse project debt should lead to lower spreads as maturity increases, given that assets de-lever over time, resulting in a diminishing value of debt relative to the total value of the firm. In typical project financing structures, the repayment profile of the debt is not fully stretched through the total operational life of the asset, leaving a substantial element of residual cash flow after debt is fully repaid — commonly known as a 'tail'. As debt is repaid, the value of the tail increases, reducing leverage. In addition to this, in assets that bear construction risk, the value of the firm increases as the project advances through construction until it becomes fully operational. However, longer maturities also increase the level of uncertainty about the future value of the firm, acting as a counterbalancing effect to the firm's deleveraging profile.

For a borrower with low levels of gearing, the effect of the reduced value of debt over the total value of the firm will be limited and therefore as maturity increases the yield curve should be upward sloping. However, for a highly levered borrower, like an SPV that enters into long-term debt financing arrangements to finance a renewable energy project, the reduction in gearing and the improvement in its credit profile as it becomes operational should dominate over the increase in maturities, resulting in a hump-shaped credit spread curve. Sorge and Gadanecz's (2004) findings are in line with the predictions made by the Merton model for a sample of project finance borrowers in industrialized and developing economies, establishing that there is no linear statistically significant relationship between credit spreads and maturities in non-recourse project debt financing.

A study conducted by Blanc-Brude (2013), using granular data about different type of project finance loans, concludes that average credit spreads within loans vary as a function of the specific risks related to each project. This author classifies systematic credit risk in project finance within three different categories:

1. Availability-based payment schemes, where the public sector promises to make a fixed payment over a certain period in exchange for the construction and operation of the asset. Public-private partnerships (PPPs) would comprise the bulk of this category.
2. Commercial schemes which allow the project finance SPV to enter into a long-term contract in exchange for variable amount of income that varies with volume and/or price. This would be the case of tolled transportation assets where the owner full discretion to change tariffs but takes complete volume risk.
3. Capped commercial schemes: which are effectively the same as commercial schemes but which include some form of sharing mechanism with the public administration (capped and floored revenues). This is the case for shadow toll roads where effectively the borrower takes an element of volume risk in exchange for a fixed payment per user.

Revenue risk drivers are found to be statistically significant for the sample of data used, which is skewed towards transportation and PPP/PFI assets. For example a real toll road (full price and volume risk) is expected to increase the cost of debt by 41.2 basis points in average when compared to that of an availability-based revenue scheme with limited or no price or volume risk.

Using this framework, renewable power generation assets would typically fall into the third category, as the renewable energy support mechanisms afforded by governments, together with the common practice of renewable energy power projects to enter into long-term

PPAs to sell the electricity produced at a minimum or fixed price, reduce the potential revenue downside. Full merchant power plants, however would fall into the second category. If a similar analysis was conducted amongst different type of renewable energy projects, its findings would most likely result in similar findings to the ones observed by Blanc-Brude, establishing a clear differentiation between those projects that bear both volume and price risk and those which only withstand volume risk.

This provides an important insight about the determinants of the price of project finance debt; uncontrollable credit risk related to inner nature of each different project drives pricing, rather than maturity itself. Following Merton's insight, the revenue risk profile of each specific asset is what drives the uncertainty about the potential value of the claim to be made by project creditors over the total value of the firm at any point in time in the future, and that effect is greater than the uncertainty created by longer maturities, given that project finance borrowers have limited scope for re-leveraging, and as debt amortizes their credit profile improves.

This could help to explain the results obtained by Kleimeier and Megginson (2005) who find that there is a statistically significant and inverse relationship between credit spreads and maturities for project finance loans (i.e. as maturities increase while credit spreads decrease). In fact, in project finance loans with lower credit risk profiles (for example in availability-based revenue schemes), maturities tend to be longer, as the level of uncertainty about the future value of the assets is reduced, driving credit spreads down. If the analysis corrected for an accurate proxy of credit risk for each specific project the results would probably be consistent with those of Blanc-Brude. While most of the research available focuses on the relationship between credit risk and pricing, very little research has looked at the relationship between loan maturity and credit risk in project financing.

Beyond differences in credit quality (probability of default and recovery rates) across different type of renewable energy projects, the other significant variable that many authors point out as one of the influencing factors in determining credit spreads is the impact of changes in the macroeconomic environment and particularly, in the credit cycle. Using two different data sets which cover the pre- and post-crisis period, Blanc-Brude (2013) shows that both 2008 (Lehman collapse) and 2012 (European debt sovereign crisis) had a positive statistical impact in the evolution of credit spreads.

Moody's (2014) comprehensive study on historical performance of project finance loans states that recovery rates tend to be substantially independent of both the economic cycle at default and the economic cycle at emergence from default. If this holds true, that means that the credit quality of project finance borrowers should be relatively insulated from the fluctuations in the business cycle. This outcome is supported by the contractual attributes of project finance structures, which afford stability to the value of the borrower's assets and its ability to generate predictable cash flows almost independently from what happens to the economy as a whole, as long as time consistency is maintained. However, it is worth noting that projects with full revenue exposure to price and volume risk may be more exposed to the fluctuations in the economic cycle, whereas the results of Moody's analysis should hold, *ceteris paribus*, relatively accurate to most renewable energy financings, where prices are supported by long-term fixed prices, especially in those geographies where regulatory risk is deemed to be low or the support schemes prove to be sustainable in terms of consumer affordability.

Merton (1974) also points to the risk-free rate as the third variable necessary to determine price of a security (i.e. as the risk-free rate or interest rate increase, the value of debt decreases). However, the overall pricing of most project finance loans is calculated adding a fixed credit spread to a market reference rate such as the London Interbank Offered Rate (LIBOR) or the fed funds rate. This provides a natural protection against movements in interest rates and therefore, should not impact the credit spread element of project finance loans.

This leaves us with a puzzling question. If the credit quality of renewable energy projects is preserved from fluctuations in the credit cycle through the contractual structures put in place, why would be loan spreads be positively correlated with the credit cycle? One straightforward answer is that more empirical analysis is required, as research in this topic is evidently anecdotal. The other rational explanation is the interdependency of renewable energy project financing and the supply of credit by commercial banks.

As previously discussed, while the credit quality of renewable energy project finance loans should prove to be acyclical, the health of commercial banks' balance sheets is not. During downturns, the net worth and collateral of most other commercial banks' clients (individuals and firms) deteriorates with the change in macroeconomic conditions. This leads to the tightening of credit terms, with the supply of credit becoming more restrictive and expensive, which in turn exacerbates the consequences of the recession. This is commonly known as the 'financial accelerator' hypothesis. The increasing levels of non-performing loans sitting in the balance sheet of commercial banks' during sustained recessionary periods eventually results in a negative spiral, affecting the confidence of savers in the financial system, leading to a reduction in deposits and forcing banks to either raise additional equity or sell off assets to de-lever.

A banking crisis like the one that still resonates in our heads, has a greater impact in those sectors that are more reliant in access to the credit supplied by commercial banks. While most sizeable low investment grade or high speculative grade corporate borrowers have recurrent access to the capital markets allowing them to circumvent the struggles of the banking sector, in the case of renewable project financing the almost exclusive relationship held with the banking sector leaves the availability of debt for new financings completely exposed to the evolution of the banking market. This certainly seems like a plausible explanation to the increase in spreads observed in project finance loans during the crisis.

Although the link between lending pricing conditions for renewable energy projects and the swings in the credit cycle is evident, the reality is that the implications should not be as severe as one could initially think. In fact, the tightening of credit terms will primarily affect the marginal borrower but not all borrowers. Most renewable energy projects have historically been successful in securing long-term lending facilities from commercial banks. This effectively affords them complete protection to changes in the availability of credit as once a 15- or 20-year loan is signed — as long as it is performing — it can only be refinanced at the borrower's option. This reduces the need for refinancing and therefore, the exposure of the sector to the changes in the macroeconomic environment. While this is a powerful counterbalancing argument, the reality still remains that the marginal borrower, the one that is seeking new financing or needs to be refinanced, will be affected.

One obvious conclusion about all of this is that as the renewable energy industry matures and the creditworthiness of project financed assets becomes more widely understood, the migration of a portion of the existing banks' renewable energy lending business to the institutional capital and loan markets would be both a natural and necessary step. While this is the subject of other chapters in this book, the intrinsic characteristic of project finance debt both in terms of maturity and credit quality should make it an attractive asset class for pension funds and insurance companies.

Despite the fact that the overall size of the renewable energy debt market is three times larger than the equity raised, until very recently the focus of institutional investors has been the latter rather than the former. Using the dataset from Dealogic, we estimate that out of the US$292 billion of non-recourse debt raised during the period 2003–2013, roughly 90% was provided in the form of commercial bank loans. The remaining amount was supplied by the institutional debt capital markets in a project bond format.

We would expect this picture to change gradually over time for the reasons outlined in this section. The increase in credit spreads during the credit crunch sparked the interest of a large number of institutional investors, including amongst others Aviva, Allianz, Blackrock, Legal & General and Prudential, have now publicly announced their intention to increase their participation in the infrastructure and energy project debt market.

The Impact of the Long-Term Nature of Project Finance in Commercial Banks

In the previous section we briefly discussed the implications of the long-term maturities available in project financing for renewable energy projects and borrowers. While this industry has probably been overly reliant on the ability of commercial banks to supply credit, the fact that banks have been able to offer long-dated financing in the form of non-recourse project finance loans provides a certain degree of protection to renewable energy borrowers against the swings in the credit cycle. In this section, we will examine the implications of this lending practice from a commercial bank perspective and how this could shape the future financing landscape for the renewable energy industry as a whole.

As we discussed earlier, commercial bank loans and, more particularly, project finance loans afford the borrower the option to refinance early, incurring in no additional cost. According to Mian and Santos (2012), who analyze the behavior of borrowers in the wider corporate loan market in the US, there is a strong correlation between the credit cycle and the propensity to refinance early. When credit markets are most fluid, creditworthy borrowers tend to refinance more frequently in order to extend maturities and benefit from lower spreads. However, when times are tougher, the propensity to refinance reduces drastically. This signals an active management of financing costs and maturities by borrowers that have good access to capital supplied by banks.

Although, no similar analysis has been conducted for the project finance loan market to date, the long-term maturities of this type of lending instrument should make this effect even more acute. As renewable energy project finance borrowers tend to lock tenors that in average exceed those of a complete business cycle, this effectively allows them to avoid refinancing when credit market conditions are more restrictive. On the other hand, when the market recovers renewable energy projects and borrowers can realize the benefits of improved market conditions as there limited cost involved in refinancing.

The consequence of all of this is that commercial banks tend to fund projects at spreads that in average should converge with those available at the low end of the credit cycle when their funding costs are lower but, in exchange, there is no reciprocal price increase when their funding costs peak. This is very different to what issuers and borrowers encounter in the public and private capital markets. Typically bond investors require prepayment protection through the introduction of what is commonly known as a *spens* clause. Under this formulation, if refinanced ahead of maturity, bond investors are entitled to receive a cash payment equivalent to the principal outstanding in the bond plus an amount equivalent to the foregone coupon, discounted at a yield commensurate with that of risk-free asset of a similar maturity. In the corporate finance debt market, maturities tend to be shorter due to the uncertainty over the future value of the assets of the borrower. This implies that the lack of prepayment protection is less relevant for this type of lending product, given that borrowers still need to manage their relatively shorter maturities allowing banks to re-price loans according to their effective cost of capital in the not too distant future.

The long-term maturity of project finance loans prevents banks from re-pricing in the near term, which in turn leaves them sitting on a portfolio of assets yielding low spreads for a long period of time. This should have led banks to include prepayment protections in line with those of the international capital markets when deploying funding for long tenors, but competitive market dynamics have not allowed for the inclusion of this mechanism in project finance lending. Banks however, have been keen to introduce pricing step-ups to incentivize early refinancing. While this has proved to be an effective way to make sure that most loans do not reach their ultimate maturity and are repaid ahead of time, the reality is that unless those step-ups are sufficiently significant their only consequence is an increase the pro-cyclicality of borrower behavior to refinance.

The renewable energy equity investor reader of this chapter could think that this is a positive feature of the bank financing and it definitely is. However, the repercussions for commercial banks involved in project financing are exactly the opposite. When the cycle bottoms down, project finance becomes one of the most questioned lending practices, triggering a complete retreat of certain market participants and making the availability of long-term financing even scarcer for those projects that are ready to be built and are seeking new financing. As argued previously, the marginal renewable energy project is the one who bears the pain.

In the recent times, changes to bank regulation and in particular those introduced by Basel III, have exacerbated the consequences of long-term lending in project finance. The new framework established by Basel III aims to improve the resilience of banks against downturns in the credit cycle by: (1) enhancing the levels of liquid assets they hold in their balance and (2) reducing their leverage ratios to ensure that banks can remain solvent even when they have to absorb large levels of impairments.

This has translated into the introduction of the liquidity coverage ratio (LCR), whose goal is to ensure that banks hold an adequate level of unencumbered high credit quality assets that they can easily convert into cash under a 30-day stress scenario. This ratio which will be introduced as of 1 January 2015 (BCIS, 2013) will be initially set at 60% and gradually increase by 10% until 1 January 2019 when it reaches 100%. The implications for project finance lending provided by commercial banks are two-fold — firstly project finance loans as illiquid unrated instruments do not get any type of beneficial treatment for the calculation of this ratio (including any undrawn commitments which need to be considered as if they were drawn), and secondly, as banks will need to hold a higher proportion of liquid assets in their books, it is likely that less capital will be available for illiquid products such as project finance assets.

The second measure to be adopted and which could affect the ability of banks to provide project finance loans is the net stable funding ratio (NSFR), which is directed to reduce the reliance of banks in short-term funding and will implemented as of 1 January 2018. This new requirement will force banks to ensure that they are able to fund 100% of their stable funding requirements with a sufficient amount of stable available funding sources, such as capital, preferred stock and liabilities with a maturity of greater than one year, and selected deposits and wholesale funding with shorter maturities. As project finance loans to renewable energy assets are long-term and illiquid in nature they require an equivalent amount of stable funding forcing banks to hold larger amounts of more long-term stable liabilities.

Taking a step back we can see that the argument is simple. Commercial banks tend to obtain the bulk of their funding through relatively short-dated deposits made by savers. The short-term nature of those deposits means that the cost of financing for banks can adjust quickly to changes in macroeconomic conditions while their long-term assets cannot. In addition to this, deposits can quickly evaporate if the lack of confidence in the financial system increases. On the other hand, if the majority of the assets held by a bank are long-term and illiquid in nature the ability of banks to re-price or sell those assets to meet the short-term demands of savers becomes limited, making commercial banks vulnerable to the business cycle. The new regulation is aimed to address these issues in an effective manner.

The consequences of the new regulation, combined with obsolete lending practices such as the lack of prepayment protection when providing long-term financing cannot be overlooked. Banks, whose project finance books, together with other illiquid, unrated and long-term assets, represent a sizeable proportion of their overall portfolios, will gradually need to shift their holdings towards more short-term liquid assets. In addition to this, banks should try to adjust their maturity profile by increasing the amount of long-term funding that matches the amount of long-term assets that they hold in their balance sheet. This could ultimately result in higher costs of financing or the introduction of shorter maturities in renewable energy financing. Both of these are undesirable outcomes that need to be resolved to ensure the ongoing access of this industry to long-term and economically efficient capital levels.

The Future Role of Commercial Banks in Renewable Energy Financing

In this chapter we have argued that the intimate relationship between the commercial banking sector and the renewable energy industry has proved to date to be extremely successful in achieving a high rate of development. Despite having experienced major issues such as technological or political risk, the certainty provided by project finance structures over the long-term value of the future cash flows of renewable energy assets have allowed the access of this industry to considerable volumes of long-term debt at a reasonable cost. However, banks' regulation and capital structures could lead to severe changes in the availability of long-term funding for new renewable energy capacity, affecting its bright outlook. At the light of these issues, in this final section, we describe what the role of commercial banks could be in a more balanced future.

Over the past 20 years project finance banks have accumulated a vast amount of knowledge about the lights and shadows of renewable energy financing. The experience of renewable energy project finance practitioners in scrutinizing and understanding the risks inherent to each different project is, and will remain a critical success factor in determining what should be an acceptable risk-adjusted return for any given investment.

However, the intrinsic characteristics of renewable energy project finance debt makes this fixed-income instrument less suitable for commercial banks as long as maturities remain in line with those historically observed and no prepayment protection is afforded to project finance creditors. Eventually, this may play out in endless phases of boom and bust where commercial banks expand and contract the availability of credit depending on what end of the cycle we sit at.

A more reasonable alternative to historical bank behavior would be commercial banks allowing new entrants in what has been to date both their backyard and a stable source of revenues. The advent of long-term institutional debt investors capable of deploying long-term capital has multiple benefits, but its implementation is not particularly straightforward. In a similar analysis to the one presented in these pages, Narbel (2013) suggests that banks should 'provide loans to capital-intensive renewable energy projects, pool these loans, tranche them and sell them down to various groups of investors', in what would be a typical collateralized loan obligations (CLO) structure. While there is merit in this approach, the outcome of this type of model could result in asset bubbles like the one created by the subprime mortgage asset backed securities in the US real estate market. The lack of knowledge of the ultimate risk taker can lead the originator into a moral dilemma, as it will continue to underwrite new business as long as the market can take it, rather than to what an acceptable level should be. This could of course, be addressed by macro-prudential regulation that sets the parameters under which new business is originated. However, this always takes time, and can result in market inefficient limits that are not necessarily sensible, given the tendency of regulators to overreact to new developments.

A more sensible approach would involve institutional debt investors committing capital directly into new projects, rather than indirectly through securitization vehicles. This would lead to an increased level of understanding of the asset class by this type of funder, which could ultimately help the renewable industry to reduce its dependency on the commercial banking market. This could clearly damage the ability of commercial banks to continue generating positive net interest margins from their renewable energy project finance activity, and perhaps it is the reason why most literature remains silent on this topic. However, the relationship between both types of financing institutions does not necessarily mean a worse outcome for the commercial banking sector on a risk-adjusted basis. While the knowledge around risk allocation and structuring remains in the commercial banking sector, that function should stay with the banks. What is more difficult to argue is why long-term maturities typical of renewable energy project finance loans should be left with commercial banks.

If banks are to remain the primary holders of the relationships with renewable energy borrowers, not only because of their understanding of the industry but also due to their ability to provide essential ancillary services such as cash and account management, agency roles, risk management (hedging products) or undrawn committed facilities, it is also essential that they retain a portion of the risk that they underwrite, to avoid the unintended consequences of a completely disintermediated risk transfer model. Retaining a junior or equity slice in a CLO model like the one proposed by Narbel could be an option.

Another alternative, that I personally find very compelling, would involve a hybrid bank and institutional structure. Under this type of financing arrangement, banks provide a short-term amortizing tranche, allowing the borrower to benefit from the ability of commercial banks to provide funding at competitive levels in the shorter end of the yield curve while not eroding their long-term profitability. An institutional term loan tranche with a longer maturity is then provided alongside. The institutional lender benefits from a higher credit spread, in compensation for the longer duration of this tranche. This symbiotic solution is not a new invention, but a concept brought from the traditional corporate finance debt market where the near end of the maturity spectrum has traditionally been funded by banks and the long term by the institutional capital markets. As opposed to scaling back maturities all together, this model means that there is no refinancing risk for the borrower as both tranches are fully amortizing. The bank retains a significant slice of the risk and returns derived from lending which also prevents morally hazardous behavior.

The risk of increased penetration by the institutional market to new renewable energy financing remains that rather than having a collaborative relationship with banks, their arrival to the market results in increased competition which, while beneficial to borrowers in the near term, in the long term results in excess credit supply and indulgence in credit terms.

Following the most essential principle of project finance, in a more sustainable future for the financing of the renewable energy industry, risk should be allocated to the party that is most capable of understanding it and absorbing it. On that basis, commercial banks should be able to remain an important source of funding for this sector without compromising their future by adjusting their role and term of funding where it is more economically efficient for them to undertake it.

References

BCBS (2012). 'Basel III: A global regulatory framework for more resilient banks and banking systems', Basel Committee on Banking Supervision.

BCBS (2013). 'Basel III: the LCR and liquidity risk monitoring tools', Basel Committee on Banking Supervision.

Blanc-Brude, F. (2013). 'Towards efficient benchmarks for infrastructure equity investments', EDHEC-Risk Institute.

Blanc-Brude, F. (2014). 'Unlisted Infrastructure Debt Valuation & Performance Measurement. EDHEC-Risk Institute'.

Blanc-Brude, F. and O. R. H. Ismail (2013). 'Who is afraid of Construction Risk? Portfolio Construction with Infrastructure Debt. EDHEC and NATIXIS Research Chair on Infrastructure Debt Investment Solutions', EDHEC Risk Institute-Asia, Singapore.

Esty, B. C. (2003). 'The Economic Motivations for Using Project Finance', *Harvard Business School*, **28**.

Hainz, C. and Kleimeier, S. (2006). 'Project Finance as a Risk-Management Tool in International Syndicated Lending', *Governance and the Efficiency of Economic Systems (GESY)*, Discussion Paper No. 183.

Kleimeier, S. and Megginson, W. L. (2000). 'Are Project Finance Loans Different from Other Syndicated Credits?', *Journal of Applied Corporate Finance*, **13(1)**, 75–87.

Mian, A. and Santos, J. A. C. (2012). 'Liquidity Risk and Maturity Management over The Credit Cycle'. Available at: https://scholar.princeton.edu/sites/default/files/SSRN-id2023516_0.pdf [accessed 9 March 2015].

Merton, R. (1974). 'On the Pricing of Corporate Debt: The Risk Structure of Interest Rates', *The Journal of Finance* **29**, 449–470.

Moody's Investor Service (2012). 'Default and recovery rates for project finance bank loans 1983–2010', Technical report, *Moody's Investors Service*, London.

Moody's Investor Service (2014). 'Default and recovery rates for project finance bank loans 1983–2012', Technical report, *Moody's Investors Service*, London.

Narbel, P. A. (2013). 'The likely impact of Basel III on a bank's appetite for renewable energy financing', *Institutt for Foretaks nomi*, Discussion paper.

Sorge, M. and Gadanecz, B. (2004). 'The term structure of credit spreads in project finance', *BIS Working Papers*, **159**.

Standard & Poor's Rating Services (2014). 'Lessons Learned from 20 years of Rating Global Project Finance Debt'.

Chapter Eleven

The Untapped Potential of Institutional Investors

David Nelson, Managing Director, Climate Policy Initiative

The general concerns about renewable energy finance generally fall into two broad categories: first, that there is not enough investment available to fund the renewable energy required under a transition to a low-carbon economy; and second, that investors demand too high a return, making the cost of renewable energy too expensive.

With US$86 trillion of assets under their control[1], institutional investors are one of the largest pools of investment capital available.

---

[1] This number represents an estimate of assets under management in OECD member countries as of 2010. This figure aggregates total assets managed by pension funds, insurance companies, investment funds and other forms of institutional savings including foundations and endowment funds, non-pension fund money managed by banks, private investment partnership and other forms of institutional investors. It includes book reserved pension plans and does not adjust for double-counting of assets managed by pension funds and insurance companies that are invested in mutual funds. Updated estimates would increase the total by at least US$5 trillion: pension funds grew from US$21.3 trillion in 2010 to US$24 trillion in 2012, insurance company assets grew from US$22 trillion in 2010 to US$24.2 trillion in 2012, and sovereign wealth funds grew from US$0.6 trillion in 2010 to US$1.1 trillion in 2014.

Further, many institutional investors — including insurance companies and pension funds — face long-term investment goals that often encourage them to accept lower returns in exchange for lower risks and longer-term investment certainty. Given the appropriate regulatory, technical and market conditions, renewable energy can provide exactly the type of cash flows and returns that institutions seek. Hence, there is apparently a perfect match in the making. Or is there?

In this chapter we examine the potential role of institutional investors in financing renewable energy. First, we address the issue of whether institutional investors are needed to fill a shortfall or gap in renewable energy finance, and how their role might differ from their current involvement. Next, we examine whether institutional investment could reduce the financing cost of renewable energy. Here it turns out that *how* institutions invest is much more important than *whether* institutions invest. Thus, we will explain how the route used to invest in renewable energy matters. We argue that direct investment in renewable energy projects shows greater promise in reducing renewable energy costs than investment in renewable energy corporations, like listed utilities or independent power producers. However, there are substantial barriers that restrict the ability of institutional investors to invest directly in projects. We conclude by examining these barriers and identifying potential solutions that could increase the potential for institutional investment.

Using Institutional Money to Fill the Gap

Much is made about the large amounts of capital required for a transition to a low-carbon economy, but in truth, the need is small relative to total infrastructure spend. In September 2014, the New Climate Economy Report estimated that a total of US$93 trillion would need to be invested in total infrastructure between 2015 and 2030 under a low-carbon transition (Global Commission on the Economy and Climate, 2014). This total represents only 5% more investment than the business-as-usual scenario to keep up with expected economic growth. Renewable energy itself accounts for less than 8% of this total infrastructure spend[2].

---

[2] New Climate Economy estimate based primarily on IEA's *Energy Technology Perspectives 2012*.

Thus, while the headline numbers for investment needed are large, the investment requirements are still well within the margins of the global financial system.

A report prepared by Climate Policy Initiative (CPI) as part of the New Climate Economy project goes further, covering all of the impacts that a transition to a low-carbon economy would have on the investment capacity of the global financial system (Climate Policy Initiative, 2014a). As described in Box 11.1, that report found that the transition to low-carbon electricity generation could benefit the global economy by as much as US$1.8 trillion.

Box 11.1: The financial impact of the transition to low-carbon electricity

To assess the impact of a potential transition to low-carbon electricity on the global economy, it is important to look beyond upfront capital costs. CPI's analysis looks not just at the investment required and the impact of a transition on the value of existing assets, but also more broadly at other factors that could affect the financial capacity of the global financial system, including operating expenses, risk, and the lifespan of investments. A savings in operating costs, for instance, could provide investors additional cash that could then be invested back into the economy. Lower risk frees up reserves and enables investment in further growth. And longer asset life means that investments need not be replaced as often, freeing cash for investment that would otherwise be needed for asset replacement.

When all of these factors are taken together, as in Fig. 11.1, the report found that transitioning to a low-carbon electricity system could actually increase the capacity of the global financial system by as much as US$1.8 trillion between 2015 and 2035.

More specifically, these overall benefit estimates capture the following dynamics in a move from business-as-usual to a two-degree pathway[3]:

(Continued)

---

[3] Our modeling is based on scenarios defined in the International Energy Agency's *Energy Technology Perspectives 2012*. We define the 'low-carbon transition' as the difference between the six-degree (business-as-usual) scenario and the two-degree, or 450 ppm, scenario. Scenarios and methodology are discussed further in the report.

Box 11.1: (*Continued*)

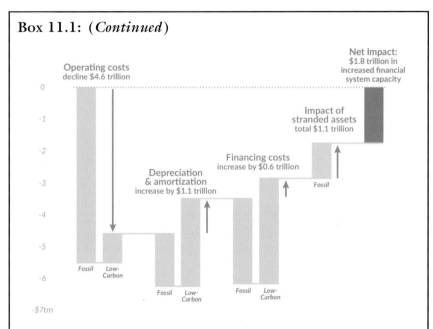

Fig. 11.1: Net financial impact of a transition from business-as-usual to low-carbon electricity generation. These figures are based on CPI Stranded Assets models (for oil, gas, and coal) and CPI analysis based on data from International Energy Agency (IEA), 2014: IEA 2012 (2DS scenario); and databases from Rystad and Platts. Depreciation and amortization, financing costs, and operating costs are undiscounted, accumulated expenses over the period from 2015 to 2035. Stranded assets represent a one-time reduction in asset value.

- Low-carbon energy infrastructure is less expensive to operate, primarily because of avoided operating costs associated with extracting and transporting coal and gas. Estimates operating savings would be significant, totaling US$4.6 trillion.
- The global electricity industry (including fuel extraction, generation, and transmission and distribution) would see more capital investment under a low-carbon pathway, because low-carbon energy tends to be more capital intensive than fossil fuel energy. Low-carbon investments tend to have slightly longer lives, somewhat offsetting the higher investment levels. Taken together we estimate that total depreciation

(*Continued*)

Box 11.1: (*Continued*)

and amortization (D&A) (the amount of the investment capital actually used up over a given timeframe) would increase by US$1.1 trillion between 2015 and 2035 — the net impact of a US$2.8 trillion increase in low-carbon capital (D&A) and a US$1.7 trillion decrease in fossil fuel D&A.

- Financing costs, which reflect both the level of investment and the riskiness of those investments, would increase by US$0.6 trillion. Many low-carbon electricity investments carry lower inherent risk than some of the fossil fuel investments they replace, and would particularly see lower costs of capital if the institutional and financial systems are fine-tuned to low-carbon investments rather than fossil fuel investments. However, total financing costs would still increase because of the larger quantity of capital investment under the two-degree pathway. Globally, existing fossil fuel assets that would otherwise be employed in electricity generation (including coal, oil, gas and power plants) would lose an estimated US$1.1 trillion in value during the low-carbon transition.

- The net impact of transition is an increase in available investment capacity of $1.8 trillion.

While the overall increase in investment for a low-carbon transition may be relatively small, the mix of investment within that total changes much more significantly. Investment requirements shift between countries and industries, between government and the private sector, between different kinds of risks, and, crucially, between different sets of investors. A low-carbon economy, for instance, may require a larger volume of low-risk infrastructure investment but fewer risky upstream energy investments. The result could be to strain debt markets while creating slack in equity markets, depending upon policy and other developments.

So, if there is no 'investment gap' in terms of the overall infrastructure investment required in a global low-carbon economy, is there an investment gap for renewable energy technologies in particular? Based on

investment estimates in IEA's *World Energy Outlook 2011*, we estimate
that US$7.2 trillion will need to be invested worldwide in non-hydro
renewable energy between 2011 and 2035, US$4 trillion of which
would be required in OECD countries (Climate Policy Initiative,
2013a). On an annual basis, as in Fig. 11.2, these needs are nearly
twice current investment levels. However, they are modest in the context of the global economy; consistent with the New Climate Economy
estimates cited above, renewable energy would represent less than 8%
of global infrastructure investment if fully funded at these levels.

Currently, renewable energy is financed through a mix of:

1. Direct investment in the equity and debt of renewable energy
    projects — this debt and equity is itself owned by developers, par-
    ent companies, banks, and other investors.

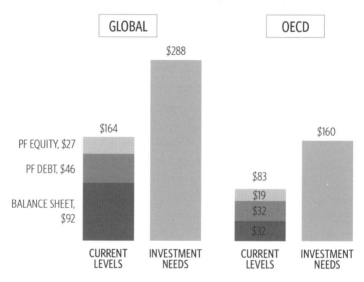

Fig. 11.2: Mix of current renewable energy investment vs annual investment needs.
Investment needs figures represent annual average of 2011–2035 cumulative invest-
ment needs for the IEA 450 Scenario, in 2010 billion US$. To compare with New
Energy Finance, this figure excludes estimated investment in hydro-electric power.
(Source: Climate Policy Initiative, 2013a. Data sources: International Energy Agency
2011, Bloomberg New Energy Finance 2012, Bloomberg New Energy Finance database,
CPI analysis.)

2. Corporations such as utilities and independent power producers use their own financial resources — that is, their balance sheet — often relying on the equity and debt of the corporation to finance these projects.
3. Governments — also major investors, often through the balance sheets of state-owned enterprises such as in China.

Institutional investors are already major investors in the corporations through ownership of stocks and bonds of these companies. Institutional investors also hold some of the debt and equity of renewable energy projects. If renewable energy build grows, there is likely to be significant opportunities for institutional investors to expand in each.

Institutional Investment as a Path to Lower-Cost Renewable Energy

The previous section suggests that financing renewable energy needs — even with a significant increase in the pace of build — is easily within the reach of global financial markets. Thus, it is the second of our two initial questions, the goal of low-cost finance, where the role of institutional investment becomes important.

Lowering the cost of financing renewable energy is a critical step in enabling broad deployment as part of a low-carbon transition. Because renewable energy is highly capital intensive, financing costs have a significant impact on the cost of energy generated from renewable sources — and institutional investors are a large potential source of low-cost capital, if they found renewables to be a good fit for their portfolios. Moving to more efficient investment vehicles could lower the cost of renewable energy by nearly 20%, compared to more traditional project finance models (Climate Policy Initiative, 2014b). The analysis in Box 11.1, showing a net benefit to the global economy, assumes that renewable energy is able to attract low-cost investment through these more efficient investment vehicles.

In other words, the main point is not whether institutions can fill an 'investment gap', but whether the apparent match between renewable energy investment characteristics and institutional investor needs can be used to reduce the cost of financing renewable energy. Here the answer appears to depend on how these investors choose to invest.

An institutional investor has three basic options for investing in renewable energy[4]:

1. *Investing in corporations* — through equity shares, corporate bonds, or other related investment vehicles — that then use this capital to invest in renewable energy projects. These can be publicly traded or be private investments, although we will focus on publicly traded investments as their greater liquidity and visibility make them easier for institutions to invest in. These corporations can be either pure play renewable energy companies, or more general energy or utility companies that have renewable energy in their portfolio.

2. *Direct investing in renewable energy projects,* either through equity ownership in the project, loans, other private placement project debt instruments made directly to the project, or a host of other similar variations.

3. *Investing in pooled investment vehicles,* such as investment or infrastructure funds, that invest in renewable energy projects. Again, these can be either debt or equity funds or a combination of both, and may be renewable energy pure plays or general infrastructure funds.

From an institutional investor perspective, the differences in the financial and market characteristics of these three investment options have a profound effect on how the investments fit within the portfolio and how much of their portfolio they could dedicate to these investments. In this section we estimate the potential investment capacity by institutional investors in each of these categories. However, before we present these estimates, it is important to note that the differences between these investment options also leads to a significant difference

---

[4] This analysis is excerpted from the Climate Policy Initiative (2013a).

in the impact that institutional investors might have on the financing costs of renewable energy through these investments. We summarize these differences in the following sections.

Corporate-level investments

When institutional investors invest in a company, they not only invest in the series of assets that the company owns, they also invest in the management, experience, and skills of the company itself. A significant portion of many companies' value lies not in the assets, but in the expectations that the company will be able to use these skills to create additional value from developing new assets, entering new markets, and enhancing the value of the set of assets it owns.

From an institutional investor and renewable energy perspective, this means that investors take on a series of risks, and potential benefits, that are in addition to the underlying project characteristics and cash flows. These risks include:

- *Reinvestment and dividend policy.* Will the corporation decide to keep the project cash flows to reinvest in new projects rather than paying out the steady dividend stream that the investor was expecting? If so, the investor can no longer depend upon the project cash flows, but must trust the corporate dividend policy.
- *Corporate strategy.* Will the management decide to change markets or focus away from the institution's original expectations? Since few renewable energy pure plays exist, and many are tied to the strategies of non-renewable parents[5], the risk might entail moving away from renewable energy-type investment profiles altogether.
- *General market risk.* The pricing for shares and bonds will move with market expectations. Although utility and renewable energy companies might be lower 'beta' companies (that is they will exhibit less price movement with respect to general share prices than the market in general), market volatility will continue to have

---

[5] For example, Iberdrola Renewables (subsidiary of Iberdrola) and NextEra (part of Florida Power and Light).

a significant effect. One of the benefits to institutional investors of direct investment in renewable energy projects, rather than investment through corporations, is that, if held through the life of the project, there should be close to no correlation of returns with the general market.

Of course, from an institutional investors' perspective, these effects are less pronounced with corporate debt than with equity, particularly if the corporate debt is held to maturity. However, the decisions that the corporation will make with respect to the required return of renewable energy projects and whether to invest in renewable energy or other projects will be based upon the market conditions and financial factors affecting their strategy, rather than that of the institutional investor. Therefore, even if investment in utilities or other corporations lowers the cost of capital for the company itself, it is unlikely to lower the cost of renewable energy so long as the corporation has a choice amongst a host of investment options.

Direct investment in renewable energy projects

As opposed to investment in corporations, direct investment in renewable energy projects creates an opportunity to structure the institution's investment to match the profile of the long-term institutional liabilities. But for this advantage to have an impact on the cost of capital for, and therefore the cost of energy from, a renewable energy producer, two conditions have to be met:

1. The institution typically needs to be actively involved in structuring the project, so that the cash flows they receive from the asset match the institution's long-term liabilities, and contribute to lowering their overall portfolio risk. If the asset is not structured in a way that lowers overall portfolio risk, it will not allow the institution to offer a lower cost of capital.
2. There must be enough competing potential investors with similarly low capital costs for institutions with structural advantages to share the benefits of their risk profile with the renewable energy

asset in the form of a lower cost of capital. If institutions with low capital costs are accepting higher market returns set by other project finance investors, they might simply capture the whole premium available for taking on liquidity risk, and not contribute to lowering the cost of capital for renewable energy projects.

There are a number of factors that limit the ability of institutions to invest directly into projects. As we will discuss later, a key question will be whether there is enough potential investment to change the renewable energy landscape, or whether this may only serve as a more profitable investment opportunity for institutions.

Pooled investment vehicles

Pooled investment vehicles can share many of the characteristics of either corporate or direct project investment. If an investment fund is large, well-researched, and traded over an exchange, the fund could eliminate both the liquidity and size constraints; however, in this case, like corporate investment, to trade over an exchange and offer liquidity, the fund will be unable to lock into project investments for long durations and will thus reduce the connection to underlying projects. Like corporate investment, this could undermine the potential cost advantage for renewable energy. Other fund designs could offer a better connection to the underlying assets — for instance by offering a 'buy and hold to maturity' strategy, where the fund agrees to hold an asset for its life in order to deliver predictable cash flows — but in so doing might need to sacrifice their ability to offer liquidity. Further, while these can be effective in increasing access to smaller pension funds and insurance companies by developing the teams, access to projects, and skills that might otherwise only make economic sense for very large funds to develop, developing these teams can be expensive, and the fees that such funds might need to charge could erode much of the economic benefit to either institutional investors or renewable energy projects. So far, the experience with pooled investment vehicles has been mixed. While pooled investment vehicles offer the potential to bridge the gap between corporate and project investing, some institutions express concern about high fees and the uncertain cash flow profiles of the current crop of pooled investment vehicles.

The Potential for Direct Investment in Renewable Energy by Institutions

The previous section showed why direct investment into renewable energy projects is the most promising of the investment paths in terms of matching investment needs and lowering renewable energy financing costs. However, direct investment in renewable energy projects faces many more challenges than corporate investment. Fig. 11.3 shows how various constraints reduce the potential direct renewable energy asset total holdings for developed world institutional investors from the almost US$90 trillion of assets they have under management, to only slightly more than US$250 billion.

As a starting point, estimates for the total stock of investments owned by institutions, commonly referred to as 'assets under management' (AUM), often include asset managers and mutual funds. A large share of these assets are actually managed for pension funds and insurance companies, and therefore represent double counting (as they are also included in the pension fund and insurance company AUM figures), while others are managed for individuals, who do not have the classic long-term investment horizon that would be appropriate for renewable energy. The remaining US$45 trillion that is owned by institutions with a potentially better profile for direct renewable energy project investment faces several constraints:

1. *Liquidity* — institutions must ensure that there will be enough cash to meet their liabilities (for example pension checks and life insurance payouts) under all circumstances. Therefore, they need a large degree of liquidity in their portfolios — that is investments that can be sold in a reasonable timeframe at a reasonably low transaction cost — to cover the most extreme set of cash demands from their policy-holders. Many face regulation that specifies the level of cash reserves or liquid investments they must have in their

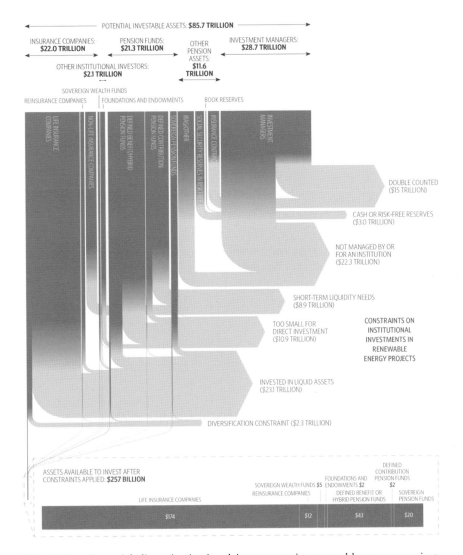

Fig. 11.3: Potential direct institutional investment in renewable energy projects (Climate Policy Initiative, 2013a)

portfolios; some are even prohibited from buying illiquid assets. Direct investments in long-lived infrastructure are fairly illiquid, being potentially difficult and costly to sell in times of crisis or unusual cash needs.

2. *Investment size and scale* — direct investment is more time consuming than investing in stocks, bonds or treasuries, requires specialist skills and can involve higher transactions costs. To make these extra costs worthwhile, deals often must be of a minimum size. Building a team to actually pursue these deals is also costly. As a result, institutions need scale to justify building a team and to cover the minimum deal size. Only the largest 150 or so institutions in the world are large enough to make this a viable business proposition. After considering their liquidity constraints, these largest institutions have just over US$2.5 trillion available to invest in illiquid assets including real estate, infrastructure and renewable energy.

3. *Diversification* — investors must diversify their portfolio to reduce the risk that one event or industry could go wrong and undermine the entire portfolio. Thus, institutions could not put all of their illiquid investments in renewable energy projects, but would also need to spread that investment among other alternatives including real estate, other infrastructure, and investments like hedge funds that might have lock in periods.

After each of these constraints, we estimate that US$257 billion, less than one half of one percent of total AUM will be available for direct investment in renewable energy projects. Each of these investors will have different perspectives on whether debt or equity is more attractive. Using the average mix of debt and equity investments for each type of investor, we estimate that US$191 billion will be available for project debt and US$66 billion for project equity. On an annualized basis, these figures correspond to US$8.8 billion and US$30.5 billion for project equity and project debt respectively[6].

We find fewer constraints in corporate investment and pooled investment vehicles, as shown in Table 11.1.

Every year institutions will be able to re-invest the dividends and cash flows from these projects. On average this money can be re-invested approximately every seven years, thus annual flows are about one seventh of this amount. Contrasting this investment potential with potential needs in Fig. 11.4, we find that if the mix of project

---

[6]These calculations are explained in further detail in Climate Policy Initiative (2013a).

Table 11.1: Potential total institutional investment portfolio held by asset class (excluding investment managers)

	CORPORATE Investments	PROJECT Investments	POOLED Investments
Equity	$354 bn	$66 bn	$136–272 bn
Debt	$335 bn	$191 bn	$230–290 bn

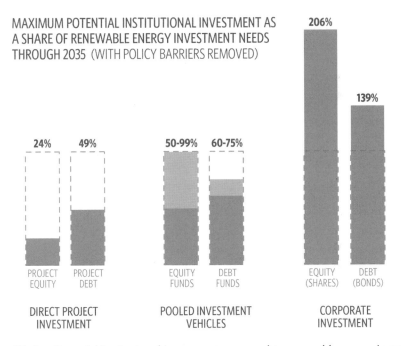

Fig. 11.4: Potential institutional investment compared to renewable energy investment needs by asset class

finance and corporate finance stays at current levels, even under perfect conditions institutions would not become large enough to dominate the market and in so doing bring down the cost of finance. To the extent that institutions enter this market, they are, therefore, likely to get higher returns than they would otherwise need for these types of investment characteristics; these investments are unlikely to reduce the cost of finance. On the other hand, institutions continue to have the potential to provide plenty of investment indirectly through corporate stocks and bonds.

Policy Barriers to Direct Investment in Renewable Energy by Institutions[7]

Beyond the portfolio constraints outlined in the previous section, other barriers limit the ability of institutions to achieve even the potential outlined here. These barriers include:

1. Policy barriers to renewable energy investing: both renewable energy policy and regulation of the institutional investors.
2. Investment practices of institutional investors: practices that affect how institutions make investment decisions.

Policy barriers to renewable energy investing

In the renewable energy world, policy is a fact of life. Until renewable energy options become among the lowest-cost form of providing energy, continued development and deployment of renewable energy will require policy-based incentives. Nearly every investor in this space identifies policy risk as the single biggest concern to investing in renewable energy.

Policy barriers facing institutions fall generally into three categories:

1. Policies designed to encourage renewable energy, but are implemented using mechanisms or incentives that either discourage institutional investors or favor other types of investors.
2. Policies addressing unrelated policy objectives — for instance, the security of financial markets — that are structured in ways that have severe unintended consequences on the ability of institutional investors to invest in renewable energy.
3. Energy policy and renewable specific policy that is lukewarm, inconsistent, or in other ways reflects an ambivalence of

---

[7] This section is excerpted from Climate Policy Initiative (2013a).

policymakers towards support for renewable energy investment and development.

Renewable energy policies that discourage institutional investors

So what renewable policy could discourage institutional investors? The most obvious starting point involves tax policy. As pension funds are tax-exempt investors, the use of tax credits as an incentive policy, such as US federal wind and solar tax incentives, can discourage their investment. In the best case, renewable energy projects will need to find a partner to monetize the tax credits at a transaction cost (and transfer of value to the tax investor), which could represent as much as 30% of the total value of the incentive (Climate Policy Initiative, 2012). In other cases, tax investors could take the place of the mezzanine or debt finance and reduce the investing opportunities that could attract institutions. In the worst case, institutions could be excluded from investing.

A second issue comes when policy support offers attractive economics, but creates more market risk than the investors seek. One example is short duration of support that induces market volatility and re-investment risk when the investors get back the investment. For instance, previous CPI analysis suggested that reducing the length of policy support by ten years raised the cost of projects by 11–15% (Climate Policy Initiative, 2011).

A third set of issues surface when incentive mechanisms are either complex or create risks that are more easily borne by other types of investors such as banks or utilities. A classic example is a switch in incentives from a feed-in tariff (FiT) that offers a fixed price for output from a project, to a feed-in premium (FiP) that offers a premium to the wholesale electricity market price. While the expected value of the FiT and FiP plus market price could be the same, revenues from a FiP will have more volatility. Utilities with large customer bases, energy trading businesses, and energy supply contracts will be in a better position to mitigate this risk than the institutional investor. Similarly, any incentive — such as renewable energy credit markets — that creates some volatility or market risk will, at the very least, require the typical institutional investor to enter into a contract to eliminate this risk, possibly giving away some incentive value in the process.

Policies unrelated to renewable energy that discourage institutional investing in renewables

Pension funds and insurance companies are often highly regulated. Their capital represents a large portion of society's safety net, and a broad range of government regulations impact them in both direct and tangential ways.

At the same time, access to secure and reliable energy and electricity is needed to ensure the proper functioning of a modern developed economy. So electricity markets are highly regulated as well.

Concerned with maintaining the safety net and the reliability of the energy supply system, policymakers can be forgiven for overlooking the impact of their regulation on the ability of these investors to invest in energy supply. Nevertheless, by doing so, they could be making both tasks more difficult and expensive to achieve. Examples of both energy market and financial regulation impact are plentiful. A few of the more topical ones include:

- *Energy Market — European electricity and gas market unbundling.* The EU's third energy package prohibits owners of a controlling interest of gas or electricity transmission assets from having a controlling interest in electricity generation or natural gas production. The policy is intended to prevent owners of transmission networks from operating and expanding their networks in a way that favors their own generation or production and thus distorts the EU energy market. While the policy has been developed to avoid the very real possibility of market distortions, institutional investment in renewable energy projects may be unintentionally damaged. Many institutional investors in projects require a high degree of asset control, so this regulation essentially forces them to choose between owning transmission or generation including renewables. Many already own some small transmission or pipeline assets and thus are excluded from investing in renewable energy projects anywhere in Europe.

- *Financial regulation — Solvency II.* New capital adequacy rules, similar to Basel III directed at banks, are intended to insure that European insurance companies have adequate financial reserves to account for the riskiness of their investment portfolios. The objective is to ensure the financial security of these companies. The rule sets reserve requirements for different asset classes, which as structured could make project investment in renewable energy — particularly project debt — considerably more expensive by requiring companies to hold more reserves against these projects. Interestingly, our interviews suggested that there is more concern about the potential for these rules to be extended to pension funds in the future than about the actual application of the rules to insurance companies.

  As Bloomberg New Energy Finance describes: 'Solvency II regulations governing the need for insurance companies to hold capital in supposedly liquid and/or low-risk instruments like public equities and government bonds will reduce their appetite for long-term investments for which there is no public market, even though such investments have well-understood yield characteristics and a well-developed private market' (Bloomberg New Energy Finance, 2013).

  Meanwhile several European pension funds interviewed by CPI highlighted their own concerns about potential regulations that may apply to them: 'Solvency II does not necessarily affect us, but the uncertainty about whether it will or whether future related regulation may be applied to us, makes us very concerned about the cost of having private placement debt in our portfolio' (Climate Policy Initiative, 2013a).

- *Financial regulation — accounting rules.* A recent trend in accounting has been the introduction of mark-to-market accounting ('fair value accounting' that takes into account current market value of investments) for investments to increase transparency. In broad strokes, mark-to-market accounting has driven pension funds in some countries towards higher allocations to fixed income securities, and encouraged greater use of liability-driven investing to immunize plan sponsors from large swings in funding status (Stone and Sweeting, 2005). However, mark-to-market accounting can be difficult to apply to illiquid investments with long holding periods. Countries vary in the timeframe that changes in market value need to be accounted for, but in some cases, there can be large differences in the short-term market value of an illiquid long-term asset and the expected value of the asset over its full life. These issues can be mitigated by allowing long-term investments to be valued in ways that reflect their true long-term economic value (Crowell Moring, 2008).

- *Environmental protection — planning rules.* Ironically, given that an important goal for renewable energy is protection of the global environment, protection of the local environment through difficult, expensive, and sometimes arbitrary planning processes can be an impediment to institutional investment. Delays by the process can be costly and uncertainty around the result — particularly if there is a risk of overturning a decision — can also be expensive.

- *Economic stimulus — bonus depreciation.* Bonus depreciation, where companies could offset large shares of investment against taxes when the investment was made rather than depreciating them across the life of the asset, has been used as a way to stimulate investment during financial crises and thus accelerate recovery. However, in the case of renewable energy that has been incentivized through tax credits, the result has been to reduce the taxes owed by many companies, and thus reduce the appetite for the tax credits generated from renewable energy projects. This decline in tax credit appetite may have increased the transaction costs associated with monetizing tax credits and made the incentives less attractive.

Inconsistent or lukewarm policy

The best-designed, most well-intentioned support by governments has little impact if that support is perceived to be short term and/or ambiguous. To encourage long-term investors to make long-duration investments requires unambiguous support by governments. As investors around the world highlighted to us, the risk of funding disappearing or policies being reversed has a chilling impact on the market.

Investment practices of institutional investors

External factors, such as policy constraints and external barriers, are not the only factors limiting institutional investors. Internal factors, such as the way that institutional investors respond to these barriers, and the way that they organize themselves to manage the portfolio have further impact.

Investor response to illiquidity

Many investors deem the risk of illiquidity in itself to be too high, and refuse to invest any of their portfolios in illiquid assets. Clearly, such investors would not be able to invest directly in any project type investments.

In general, we found that institutional investors have a difficult time analyzing and managing illiquidity in their portfolios. Given the problems with performing sophisticated liquidity calculations and the lack of trust that such calculations would have in the current market even if they were made, we found that even those funds that have decided to seek the additional premium are doing so cautiously.

Decisions to build direct investment teams

While there may be higher returns available for direct investment into projects, this type of investment requires a set of skills and business processes that many pension funds do not possess. Many pension funds manage most of their money through external managers. Thus, they have become adept at evaluating the relative quality of different investment managers, but will feel less in their comfort zone when evaluating particular project investments. In all likelihood they would need to hire different personnel, acquire transaction expertise, and change the organizational structure of their fund to support direct investment in projects. Doing all this can be quite daunting, and may be beyond the reach of many funds and their boards who may not see or believe the incremental value that may be created. The decision to build such a team, therefore, is very difficult and cannot be taken lightly.

Insurance companies, on the other hand, are generally larger and have a history of making direct private placement loans and other investments. Therefore, this step is much less daunting, as reflected in their greater presence in this space.

Sector diversification

Institutional investors and their external managers seldom break down sector limits to levels that would include renewable energy as a distinct category. Instead, they group these investments to reflect benchmarks or include industry classifications such as energy or utilities. The amount that can be invested in renewable energy can depend upon the sector grouping. For example, we have found instances of investors unwilling to invest more in renewable energy because they already had a portfolio replete with conventional power generation investments. Thus, grouping renewable energy with power generation, utilities, or energy could limit investment. Furthermore, a decision to overweight renewable energy, because it could appear attractive, could be complicated by the sector grouping and portfolio tracking methodology employed.

Evaluation of policy risk

Policy risks are continually changing. The problems of inconsistent or lukewarm renewable energy policies are discussed above. However, investor practices and perceptions of policy uncertainty may compound the impact of these issues on investment. Evaluation of these risks is difficult, particularly for investors for whom renewable energy, and the related policy, may be only a small share of the overall portfolio. The result is that investors do not have enough time to get comfortable with political and policy risk and may, therefore, not even consider investing in the sector.

The largest investors, however, may have teams and investors dedicated to specific sectors for whom understanding policy changes is one of their main tasks. These investors, therefore, are often more comfortable with risks. One result is that medium-sized funds, who might otherwise invest directly, may find it even more difficult to compete with their larger, better resourced, counterparts.

Setting overall portfolio investment objectives

The central problem for institutional investors is maximizing expected returns from their investment portfolio, while minimizing the risk that the cash available from the portfolio is insufficient to meet liabilities at any given time; in other words, lowering the cost of providing a pension or insurance for a given level of risk.

At the broadest level, this problem is often called asset/liability matching or ALM. ALM can be a complicated and analytically challenging task, employing sophisticated mathematical models, but even so, ALM is more of an art than a science. Crucially, the design of ALM modeling, and the input assumptions made, can dramatically alter the investment portfolio suggested by the ALM model. The output of the ALM exercise will usually suggest how much a fund will invest in corporate equities versus bonds, private equity, real estate, and so forth.

For potential renewable energy investment, the implications are significant. While ALM will say nothing specifically about renewable energy, it will impact the relative attractiveness of different asset classes within renewable energy and it may impact the team that the fund hires and whether or not it chooses to develop certain capabilities that would be required to invest in specific types of renewable energy investment. Thus, due to the more limited set of asset classes generally found in large pensions funds, some renewable energy investment opportunities, particularly project investments, may be overlooked:

- Since ALM modeling will always include public equities, investments in renewable energy corporate equity will be easy to make, as long as the corporation in question is large enough to be listed on an exchange, and, hopefully, be included in a stock market index.

- Corporate debt is also relatively easy, but perhaps slightly more difficult than equity. First, some funds concentrate their fixed income portfolio on sovereign debt, although low yields are driving more into corporate debt. Second, having a rating and being part of an index is more important for debt than for equity. Thus, institutions may be less inclined to invest in smaller companies not included in indices and may be discouraged by the high cost of obtaining ratings. As evidence for the advantage of large companies, many of the renewable energy pure play companies in Europe have been owned by utilities and have chosen to raise debt at the utility parent level rather than the renewable energy pure play.

- Project investments in either debt or equity are more difficult, as the ALM modeling may not specify investments by asset class. For instance, all direct investments in renewable energy, whether debt, equity, or a mix of the two, may be lumped in a single category of private equity or infrastructure.

Subdividing the portfolio into distinct, more manageable mandates

There are many different investment options and asset classes that can, in some way, fund capital investment in renewable energy. However, as we have argued, in the current regulatory and financial structure, the potential impact of institutional investors could be greatest in making project-level investments. At the ALM level the analysis and modeling does not delve much into decisions such as whether to invest in renewable energy, information technology, or consumer goods, rather it focuses on asset class issues and the general split between equity, debt, and maybe real estate, private equity, or infrastructure.

Institutional investors limit the number of asset classes — pension funds typically have three to six classes at this level, insurance companies may have more — because the data required grows exponentially as more asset classes are added, even while, some feel, the robustness and insight may diminish.

For asset classes such as unlisted, private placement debt, or where there is no readily available index or historical pricing information, calculating the expected performance relative to the general market is difficult, if not impossible[8].

Lack of specialized skills or teams for different types of renewable energy investment

While only the largest institutional investors can justify building direct investment teams, the good news is that many are busily doing so. Insurance companies have long been building deep and sophisticated direct investment teams and many have impressive portfolios of both equity and debt investments in projects including in renewable energy. The larger pension funds are somewhat late in the game, but a few are now beginning to build teams and investing directly into projects and infrastructure.

Yet, direct investing does not necessarily translate into direct investing in renewable energy, nor does it necessarily translate into investing as needed across the debt/equity spectrum. Unsurprisingly, the investment criteria and skill set required to invest in the equity of a project is somewhat different than those required to lend to the same project. The same goes for investing in renewable energy versus, say, telecommunications. Unless motivated by specific strategic decisions at the plan sponsor level[9], only the largest of the large funds can justify having a specific team dedicated to power generation debt, or clean technology equity. More typically, one team may handle all pri-

---

[8] While the data are scarce, there are efforts ongoing to improve the quality of data, particularly by the ratings agencies. Moody's has evaluated the default and recovery rates for project finance bank loans from 1983 to 2010, and S&P has conducted similar studies of the projects they have rated (Moody's, 2012; Standard and Poor's, 2009, 2010).

[9] One notable fund to make a significant strategic move towards renewable energy is PensionDanmark, which has quickly become one of the leading funds for renewable energy investment (Climate Policy Initiative, 2013b).

vate equity-type direct investments or all of infrastructure. While there are usually specializations within the team, the overall investment objectives of the team may not reflect the special characteristics of specific types of renewable energy investments. Generally, we observed two effects:

1. Pension funds often favor project equity to the exclusion of project debt. With all direct investing taking place in one team, the organization of the investment team often favors project equity almost to the exclusion of project debt. In these cases, the direct investment team is often given a target return rate that was typically higher than could be expected from debt investments.
2. Renewable energy may be at a disadvantage relative to other private equity or infrastructure assets. A private equity portfolio is likely to have aggressive return targets, while depending on the regulation, renewable energy is likely to offer a more stable and less risky investment return. As we heard from teams where renewable energy was handled within the private equity team, a team with private equity-type targets may find it difficult to dedicate a significant portion of the portfolio to renewable energy and may not value renewable energy for its stable cash flow profile.

Options for Increasing the Impact of Institutional Investment

One important finding stands out: even if all of the policy and investment practices are fixed to align with investment in renewable energy, there is unlikely to be enough direct project investment by institutions to dominate the market and reduce financing costs. On the other hand, there is plenty of investment available from institutions when funneled through liquid corporate investments; yet these investments, as currently structured, are unlikely to lead to lower renewable energy costs.

There are investment structures that provide liquidity, more direct access to cash flows, and can be quoted and traded on an exchange.

Real estate investment trusts (REITs), infrastructure funds, and master limited partnerships (MLPs) are prominent examples where illiquid assets are bundled together in corporate structures with steady cash flows in the form of dividends, and then traded in liquid markets. More recently, renewable energy and other infrastructure-type assets have been bundled into 'yieldco' structures that are traded on exchanges mainly to investors seeking steady dividend yields based on real underlying assets. NRG Yield, Greencoat Energy, Pattern Energy, and the recently announced NextEra YieldCo are all prominent examples.

While developing these first yieldcos is an important first step, current yieldco designs only move part of the way towards a structure that would optimize renewable energy finance and lower the cost of electricity from renewable sources (see Box 11.2 for more detail). To

---

Box 11.2: Current yieldco designs are beginning to establish the asset class, but their design fails to reach its full potential for reducing financing costs

The first set of yieldcos that have emerged recognize the opportunity to segregate low-risk assets into liquid securities that investors can easily access. Unfortunately, while these yieldcos establish the concept, their design does not fully take advantage of their potential to reduce financing costs for new renewable energy projects. Comparing existing yieldcos with the optimal features mentioned previously, we note a few key differences:

1. Many yieldcos have been designed with built-in expectations for growth[11]. Some profits are being retained instead of being fully distributed as dividends, in order to buy more assets. There may also be

(Continued)

---

[10] Some MLPs suffer from similarly high overhead costs if they make use of management incentives known as incentive distribution rights (IDRs). IDRs allocate an increasing fraction of free cash to the general partner with increasing cash payouts, providing an incentive for growth. Thus, while the limited partner yield may appear to be low, the cost of equity is actually much higher when general partner IDRs are considered.

[11] This choice has often been made in the US due to tax considerations as a large fraction of the benefits of many US renewable projects are provided through tax credits or deductions. The yieldco must have enough assets generating net tax liabilities to offset those credits and deductions. This requires them, primarily, to hold older plants that have long since used up their accelerated depreciation benefits and tax credits.

Box 11.2: (*Continued*)

expectations that the company will issue equity to further grow its assets, diluting current investments and creating uncertainty. The result is that while yields are currently low, the implied growth premium actually implies higher returns to compensate for the re-investment risk. Thus, these are structured closer to equity vehicles than would be optimal to minimize financing costs.

2. High costs and fees. In order to pursue growth, current yieldcos need a more sophisticated and expensive management team in place, increasing costs.

3. Yieldcos such as NRG Yield, have been built up using existing assets. The result is that the price, which will generally have been set when the original investment decision was made, will not reflect lower financing costs due to better transparency and access to project cash flows. Only when developers have the certainty that lower financing costs will be realized can they reflect the lower costs in project bids or prices. Without that certainty, prudent investment practice dictates that they do not consider future potential benefits to project economics in case they do not materialize. Under these circumstances, the value that comes from creating a yieldco will flow back to the company, but not to the consumer or to lower electricity prices. Only when developers have enough confidence — and potentially pre-contract arrangements — will yieldco development lead to lower energy costs.

---

minimize the effective average lifetime cost of energy from a project including both operating costs and required investment returns (also called the levelized cost of energy, or LCOE), the new type of yieldco investment class must do the following.

1. *Provide highly predictable long-term cash flows*

The yieldco:

- *Must pay out nearly all of the free cash it generates* from the underlying projects to the yieldco owners. Current yieldco or MLP designs retain 10–20% of cash to use for investment in future projects. This retention and potential investment creates uncertainty and risk for investors. The investor cannot rely on predictable cash flows to meet liabilities, but instead will have uncertainty about whether the yieldco or MLP management will make bad investments. To compensate for the risk, the investor will demand either a growth premium or an equity premium for the investment ultimately increasing the cost of finance for renewable energy.

- *Should be backed by long-term contracts* or FiTs that provide clear sight of future cash streams. Previous CPI analysis found that increasing the duration of contracts was the most effective policy tool for reducing the financing costs of renewable energy (Climate Policy Initiative, 2011).
- *Should own a diversified set of projects.* Owning diversified assets will reduce the risk associated with uncertainty around individual projects.
- *Should invest in assets that are in operation* or with iron-clad guarantees to reduce construction and development risk. Fixed operations and maintenance contracts can further enhance the attractiveness.

2. Provide liquidity in the investment

The yieldco:

- *Should be exchange-traded* or otherwise provide frequent transactions and pricing information. This information and the relatively low transaction costs will reduce the illiquidity penalty, and also enable smaller institutions to invest.
- *Should be large enough* to attract a large set of investors, as well as research and financial sector analysis. There needs to be enough interest in the security that brokerage firms will cover the company and provide recommendations. This research will enable smaller institutions with smaller investment teams to make decisions about whether or not to invest.

3. *Provide investment at low fees*

The yieldco:

- *Must have a light management structure* and low overhead costs lest these costs consume the advantage that the yieldco structure provides. One of the major problems that institutional investors cited — beyond the management risks of buying and selling assets — was the high fees that eroded the investment case. With the benefit driven by the 2% per year or so difference between corporate bond and project bond financing costs, these fees would need to be significantly lower than current funds.[10]
- *Should provide lower churn and less emphasis on long-term portfolio management,* so fees may be structured as an upfront cost rather than an annual cost.

4. *Become established as part of the portfolio of options for institutional investors*

- Institutional investor strategists and asset allocators use historical financial performance data. The yieldco asset class will need to establish itself as a distinct asset class with unique characteristics so that institutions can incorporate these characteristics into their asset allocation and risk models.

Conclusion

Institutional investors have the potential to play a significant role in providing capital for renewable energy. The match between renewable energy investments and the long-term investment needs of many institutions offers the possibility that, by making these investments, institutions could enhance their own risk-adjusted returns, lower the cost of financing renewable energy, or both. By providing low-cost capital to renewable energy projects, institutional investors could reduce the cost of renewable energy — and in so doing accelerate a transition to a low-carbon electricity system that could bring a significant net benefit to the global economy.

However, several barriers currently reduce the role and impact of institutional investors. Institutional investment in the equity and debt of corporations that build renewable energy — such as investor-owned utilities and developers — will fail to lower renewable energy costs as the investment case for new projects will be determined by the financial needs of the developer or utility rather than that of the institutional investor. Direct investment in renewable energy projects creates a path to lower costs by structuring the investment vehicle to match the needs of institutions. However, both energy policy and financial regulation often create barriers to direct investment by institutions, while the organization and investment practices of the institutions themselves create further barriers that can be difficult to remove.

The key may be to combine the best of both investment options, creating investment funds or corporations that have the liquidity, transparency and market access that stocks and bonds enjoy, while having the low-risk, well-defined, long-term cash flows that would serve the portfolios of institutions, large and small. Investment trusts, yieldcos, MLPs and infrastructure funds have already begun down this path, with promising results. However, these funds and structures continue to be designed around the needs of the parent corporations, developers or asset managers rather than institutional investors. The next step is to take these types of structures and design them explicitly for institutional investors. Our analysis suggests that with the appropriate design, and the related energy market regulation, these investment vehicles could cause a further significant decline in the cost of financing renewable energy.

On their own, institutional investors are unlikely to find and create the mix of financial and policy solutions that are required to reach the lowest cost renewable energy finance solutions. The ways forward — from improving policy and regulation, to creating effective pooled investment vehicles and encouraging new types of corporate investors — each deserve the attention of policymakers and the energy and finances industries. Yet any comprehensive solution that reduces the financing costs of renewable energy will require consideration and engagement of institutional investors, and if policymakers and the industry work together with institutions, the prize can be substantial.

References

Bloomberg New Energy Finance (2013). 'Financial regulation — biased against clean energy and green infrastructure?' Available at: http://www.bnef.com/ WhitePapers/download/278 [accessed 5 March 2015].

Bloomberg New Energy Finance (2012). 'Global Trends in Renewable Energy Investment 2012 — Data Pack'. Available at: http://fs-unep-centre.org/sites/default/files/attachments/unepglobaltrendsmasterdatapack2012.pdf [accessed 5 March 2015].

Climate Policy Initiative (2011). The Impacts of Policy on the Financing of Renewable Projects: A Case Study Analysis. Available at: http://climate-policyinitiative.org/publication/the-impacts-of-policy-on-the-financing-of-renewable-projects-a-case-study-analysis/ [accessed 5 March 2015].

Climate Policy Initiative (2012). 'Supporting Renewables While Saving Taxpayers Money'. Available at: http://climatepolicyinitiative.org/publication/supporting-renewables-while-saving-taxpayers-money/ [accessed 5 March 2015].

Climate Policy Initiative (2013a). 'The Challenge of Institutional Investment in Renewable Energy'. Available at: http://climatepolicyinitiative.org/publication/the-challenge-of-institutional-investment-in-renewable-energy/ [accessed 5 March 2015].

Climate Policy Initiative (2013b). 'San Giorgio Group Case Study: Jädraås Onshore Windfarm'. Available at: http://climatepolicyinitiative.org/sgg/publication/san-giorgio-group-case-study-jadraas-onshore-wind-farm-2/ [accessed 5 March 2015].

Climate Policy Initiative (2014a). 'Moving to a Low Carbon Economy: The Financial Impact of the Low Carbon Transition'. Available at: http://climatepolicyinitiative.org/publication/moving-to-a-low-carbon-economy/ [accessed 5 March 2015].

Climate Policy Initiative (2014b). 'Roadmap to a Low Carbon Electricity System in the U.S. and Europe'. Available at: http://climatepolicyinitiative.org/publication/roadmap-to-a-low-carbon-electricity-system-in-the-u-s-and-europe/ [accessed 5 March 2015].

Crowell Moring (2008). 'Mark to Market Accounting: Is it time to bend the rules?' Available at: http://www.crowell.com/NewsEvents/AlertsNewsletters/Financial-Lines-Directors-Officers-Management-Liability-Alert/Mark-to-Market-Accounting-Is-it-time-to-bend-the-rules [accessed 5 March 2015].

Global Commission on the Economy and Climate (2014). 'Financing a Low-Carbon Future'. Available at: http://newclimateeconomy.report/finance [accessed 5 March 2015].

International Energy Agency (2014). *World Energy Investment Outlook 2014*, IEA.

International Energy Agency (2012). *Energy Technology Perspectives 2012*, IEA.

International Energy Agency (2011). *World Energy Outlook 2011*, IEA, pp. 224–225. Available at: http://www.iea.org/publications/freepublications/publication/world-energy-outlook-2011.html [accessed 5 March 2015].

Moody's (2012). 'Default and Recovery Rates for Project Finance Bank Loans, 1983–2010'. Available at: http://www.moodys.com/research-documentcontentpage.aspx?docid=PBC_139381 [accessed 5 March 2015].

Organisation for Economic Co-operation and Development (2013a). 'OECD Pensions at a Glance, 2013'. Available at: http://www.oecd.org/finance/private-pensions/pensionmarketsinfocus.htm [accessed 5 March 2015].

Organisation for Economic Co-operation and Development (2013b). 'OECD Insurance Statistics'. Available at: http://www.oecd.org/daf/fin/insurance/oecdinsurancestatistics.htm [accessed 5 March 2015].

Sovereign Wealth Fund Institute (2014). 'Sovereign Wealth Fund Rankings'. Available at: http://www.swfinstitute.org/fund-rankings/ [accessed 5 March 2015].

Standard and Poor's (2010). 'Figuring the Recovery Rates when Global Project Finance Transactions Default', Global Credit Portal Article.

Standard and Poor's (2009). 'Project Finance Default Rates from 1992 to 2008 Reflect the Sector Ratings', Global Credit Portal Article.

Stone, J. and Sweeting, P. (2005). 'Mark-to-Market Accounting for Corporate Pension Plans', Fidelity Institutional Asset Management Whitepaper. Available at: http:// institutional.fidelity.com/publications_library/marktomarket_whitepaper.pdf [accessed 5 March 2015].

Chapter Twelve

The Spectacular Growth of Solar PV Leasing

Bruce Usher, Faculty Director, The Tamer Center for Social Enterprise, Columbia Business School

Albert Gore III, MBA Candidate, Columbia Business School

> More people, when given the option of paying more for dirty power or less for clean power will take paying less for clean power.
>
> Lyndon Rive, CEO of SolarCity

Origin of the Idea

The promise of solar power has long seemed just out of reach for the average homeowner. The primary deterrent has been the high upfront cost to purchase and install rooftop panels. An average residential solar system in the US costs between US$15,000–$35,000 (Shahan, 2014a), which includes equipment, installation, and gaining permits, a significant financial commitment for all but the wealthiest homeowners.

There are also several powerful psychological barriers to adoption. Solar is a relatively new phenomenon for residential use, and homeowners are wary about purchasing and installing sophisticated equipment about which they know very little. Misconceptions about the likelihood of technical problems and the cost of operating and maintaining systems mean that purchases of residential solar power systems have been limited to a small number of early adopters. By 2008, residential solar in the US was growing at less than 100 MW per year (Solar Energy Industries Association, 2014a).

These barriers to adoption of solar — upfront cost and uncertainty — are being overcome through a financial innovation known as solar leasing. This model was initially created for the commercial solar market, in order to accelerate the growth of solar installations on commercial buildings. The success of the solar leasing model in the commercial market soon transformed the residential solar landscape as well. The solar leasing model allows homeowners to shift the upfront cost of installation, as well as the ongoing risk of ownership of the system, to a third party. For this reason, it is sometimes referred to as third-party ownership, or TPO.

There are two variations of the solar leasing model currently in use. The first is a typical operating lease, in which a contract allows the homeowner to pay 'rent' on the equipment and receive all of the electricity generated by it. The second is called a power purchase agreement (PPA), which allows the homeowner to purchase the power provided by the system at a set price, generally below the price offered by the local utility. Despite these differences, the terms are sometimes used interchangeably to describe TPO in solar.

The solar leasing model has dramatically changed the US solar market in just five years — residential solar installations have grown over eleven-fold, and 70% of residential solar installations in three of the largest US solar markets (California, Arizona, and Colorado) now use the solar leasing model (Solar Energy Industries Association, 2013). Internationally, variants of the solar leasing model are driving similar growth rates in solar adoption in East Africa and Australia (Woody, 2012).

Financial Structure of the Leasing Model

In the solar leasing model (see Fig. 12.1), a homeowner agrees to have a solar energy system installed on the roof of his or her home,

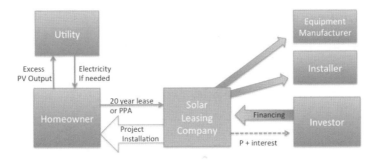

Fig. 12.1:   Finance structure of the solar leasing model

and signs a lease or long-term PPA with the solar leasing company to purchase the electricity generated by the system. The lease or PPA is generally fixed for the life of the contract, typically 20–25 years, and the price is set at a rate equal to or lower than the cost of electricity provided by the local utility, with escalation for inflation to account for increases in operation and maintenance costs. If the contract is designed as a PPA then it is performance based; the homeowner pays only for electricity generated by the solar energy system.

The solar leasing company acts as the project developer, arranging for financing and coordinating design, permitting, and construction of the system. Financing is typically provided by a commercial investor. In addition to receiving principal and interest payments, the investor also receives government tax and regulatory incentives for which the system is eligible. An independent installer will typically install the solar system, although the solar leasing company sometimes plays this role, and is responsible for system maintenance over the project life. The equipment manufacturer provides a long-term guarantee on the equipment, including a minimum performance guarantee.

The homeowner maintains a relationship with the local utility, buying electricity from the grid when the system is unable to deliver sufficient electricity — for example at night and on cloudy days — and selling electricity to the grid (referred to as 'net metering') when the system generates more power than can be used by the home. The actual terms of the purchase and sale of electricity varies by the state or region in which the project is located.

Advantages of Solar Leasing

For consumers

The primary advantage of the solar leasing model is that the home-owner receives the electricity generated by a solar project at a discount to current electricity rates, but is not required to pay any upfront capital cost for the system, and has no exposure to the risk of system underperformance. In most cases, solar leasing provides savings to homeowners in the first month, typically 10–20% less than their current electric utility bill. Furthermore, the homeowner has predictable electricity pricing over a long period, typically 20–25 years, although this can create a disadvantage in the rare situation where utility electricity prices decrease.

Residential homeowners in a solar leasing structure typically compare solar leasing terms to the outright purchase of solar energy systems. In this comparison, the long-term financial return to the homeowner from purchasing solar may be higher than using solar leasing, but the solar leasing model has significant advantages. To install and own a solar energy system, homeowners must secure financing or pay for the system themselves, secure permits, interconnection agreements with the local utility, and source tax equity and buyers of renewable energy certificates (if applicable). Furthermore, under the direct ownership model the homeowner typically bears the performance risk of the project. The long-term nature of solar projects results in a payback that is typically 11 years or longer (Chernova, 2012), with negative cash flow to the consumer during that period. Residential homeowners are especially sensitive to the long-term financial commitment associated with owning these systems — a majority of consumers in a research study said they made the decision based on shortest payback period, as opposed to net present value (NPV) or internal rate of return (IRR) (Sigrin, 2013).

Solar leasing has become a powerful innovation in the residential solar market because it presents a clear advantage for most homeowners. Solar leasing companies will install solar PV systems for little or no money down, with a contract that locks in electricity for many years at a fixed price that is lower than the current electricity price offered by the utility. The homeowner bears no responsibility for maintenance or repairs, thereby removing any product risk or ongoing cost of operations. Quite simply, by removing risks and offering savings, solar leasing aims to make residential solar an easy decision for homeowners.

For solar leasing companies

There are several advantages in the solar leasing model for developers of residential solar systems, especially as they achieve economies of scale. First, scale brings higher levels of operational efficiency in deploying technicians to install systems. Second, as developers make larger purchases from manufacturers, the price per panel goes down. Both of these factors lead to lower average cost per installation. Third, and perhaps most significantly, homeowners are providing space on their property for solar assets that the leasing company will control. Securing sites for solar projects in residential areas is challenging given the shortage of open space and high cost of real estate in most urban and suburban settings. With the solar leasing model, the customer solves the siting challenge by providing his or her rooftop, at no cost, for the project.

For investors

For investors, the solar leasing model aggregates many small solar projects through one financing vehicle — the solar leasing company — to simultaneously finance multiple systems. This reduces the cost to the investor of sourcing, evaluating and contracting with many small project owners, thereby reducing the cost of providing financing.

Another important benefit to investors in the US is the solar investment tax credit (ITC), which provides for a 30% tax credit for installed systems. The ITC is based on the total installed cost of the system, including both equipment and labor. Tax credit investors and solar developers typically establish a corporate entity such as a limited liability company (LLC) or limited partnership (LP) wherein the investor has a substantial but passive interest. This structure allows the tax benefit to pass through to the tax credit investor. Systems must be installed and placed in service for the full value of the tax credit to be earned, and the members of the partnership must retain ownership of the asset for a five-year compliance period. The risk of recapture is very low, and the solar ITC has been very successful in driving growth in the US solar industry, both in residential and commercial properties.

Lastly, the solar leasing model minimizes risk to all parties in the structure by allocating risk to the parties best able to manage it, for example by having the equipment manufacturer provide performance guarantees, and the lease originator bear the default risk of the customer.

Implementation Hurdles

Non-technical barriers to adoption

Customer inertia is the most significant barrier to adoption of solar leasing, as the traditional model of purchasing electricity from the utility has been effective and reliable for over a century. Furthermore, residential homeowners have difficulty understanding the value proposition of solar systems — 97% of US homeowners in a Harris poll overestimated the cost of installing solar (Gerdes, 2012). Addressing customer fears about complexity and reliability of solar energy systems is an implementation hurdle that solar leasing companies are overcoming through marketing and education.

Soft costs

Solar projects are comprised of equipment costs, primarily solar panels, inverters, controllers, racking and cables; and soft costs, including sourcing, labor, permitting, and customer acquisition costs. The cost of solar panels, the primary technology in every solar PV project, has declined dramatically, from US$76.67/watt in 1977 to US$0.74/watt today (Shahan, 2013a). Unfortunately, soft costs have not declined in tandem. In the US, a recent study concluded that soft costs now comprise 64% of the total price of residential systems. For example, supply chain costs total US$0.61/watt, installation labor US$0.55/watt, and customer acquisition costs US$0.47/watt, with the solar panels themselves at only US$0.74/watt (National Renewable Energy Laboratory, 2013).

In Europe, especially in Germany, soft costs are significantly lower than in the US, but they still make up a significant percentage of total project costs (Shahan, 2013b). Fortunately, ongoing reductions in soft costs are expected through development of policies and practices that reduce inefficiencies. A McKinsey study estimates that reductions in soft costs could cut the total installed cost per watt in half over the next five years (Frankel *et al.*, 2014).

Project construction and operation and maintenance (O&M)

Solar leasing companies must execute efficient construction of thousands of solar energy systems on host sites with economics that allow the company to earn a profit on the spread between the monthly payments from the homeowner and the cost of financing from the investor. This presents significant logistical challenges, given the many differences among rooftops, and the fact that installations are individually quite small. Furthermore, solar leasing companies are responsible for ongoing maintenance and repair to each and every system, including replacement of inverters every 10 to 15 years.

Credit risk

The solar leasing company is exposed to default risk of the customer in the event that the homeowner abandons the premises or refuses to pay for electricity generated by the system on their roof. Solar leasing companies mitigate this risk by performing a credit check on homeowners, normally requiring a FICO credit score of 680 or above to qualify for a solar lease, which represents the majority of American homeowners (Lamb, 2014). The solar leasing company also retains the right to remove the panels from the homeowner's premises in the event of a breach of contract, although in reality the cost of doing so is generally prohibitive.

Access to capital

Solar leasing companies require access to significant capital to finance the installation of systems. Investors are exposed to the credit risk of the solar leasing company, which can be mitigated by placing ownership of the underlying solar assets and leases in a bankruptcy remote investment vehicle. The cost of capital is declining for solar leasing companies as investors become more familiar with the model, which is further accelerating the rate of deployment. Institutional investors are also becoming more comfortable with risks related to reliability and weather fluctuations (Frankel *et al.*, 2014).

Sector Growth in the US

From commercial to residential

The solar leasing model was created in 2004 by SunEdison, a US company focused on the commercial solar market. SunEdison approached retailers with large stores with flat roofs, ideal for the installation of solar systems, with a compelling proposition — SunEdison would finance, install, and manage the solar system in return for the retailer entering into a 20-year PPA agreement at a small discount to prevailing commercial electricity rates.

Retailers were attracted to the solar leasing model, and leading companies like Staples Inc. entered into solar lease contracts on many stores. SunEdison grew rapidly until 2008, when the financial crisis in the US made it difficult to raise capital, at which point SunEdison was acquired by MEMC, a leading silicon chip manufacturer.

In 2008, several California-based companies began to apply the solar leasing model to the residential homeowner's market. California was an attractive opportunity for solar because of the California Solar Initiative Program launched in 2007 (see Fig. 12.2) as part of

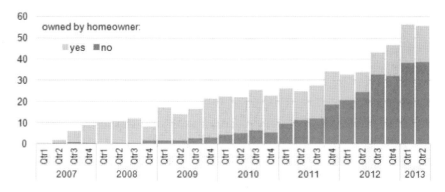

Fig. 12.2: Residential solar PV installed in California Solar Initiative Program (MW) (Source: U.S. Energy Information Administration, 2013)

Governor Schwarzenegger's Million Solar Roofs program to encourage adoption of solar energy. The program started slowly, as new residential solar systems had to be purchased directly by homeowners. The solar leasing model began to catch-on in late 2008, and by 2012 over two thirds of California residential installations were third-party owned, using solar leasing models (Climate Policy Initiative, 2013).

The dramatic growth in California launched solar residential leasing companies like SolarCity, SunRun and Sungevity into the national market, where the model quickly became the primary form of residential solar (see Fig. 12.3). The California market remains central to the growth in residential solar in the US. The sector has been growing steadily, as residential PV installations in the US were up 45% between the second quarter of 2013 and the second quarter of 2014 (Solar Energy Industries Association, 2014b). In fact, residential installation capacity outpaced commercial installation capacity in the US for the first time ever in the first quarter of 2014, 232MW to 225MW (Johnston, 2014), with California accounting for more than 50% of US residential PV installations during that time period.

Evolution of the Solar Leasing Model

There are now many variations on the basic solar leasing model, with some companies (i.e. SolarCity and Vivint) becoming vertically

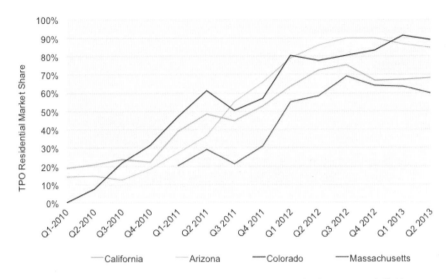

Fig. 12.3: Market share of the third-party ownership (solar leasing model) (Source: GTM Research)

integrated, and providing all services from lead generation → sales → financing → installation → monitoring. Other companies, including SunRun, NRG, and SunPower, partner with local companies to out-source installations, but provide financing and ongoing monitoring.

In recent years there has been a trend toward vertical integration of solar installers and finance providers. One reason for this shift is that there is a strong incentive for installers to handle financing, as they exercise control over the appraised value of a project from which the value of the tax credit is derived. Another reason is that the instal-lation market can be volatile and subject to shifts in margins, while financing provides a steady, reliable rate of return. The most recent advance in vertical integration is coming from companies like SolarCity, who are now seeking to manufacture their own solar pan-els. By supplying both its own equipment and its own financing, a solar leasing company can potentially secure a significant price advan-tage over competitors who rely on multiple supply chain partners with their own margins to maintain.

The sector is also consolidating, with the top-ten solar leasing companies controlling half the market (Munsell, 2014), and benefiting from the fact that the leading companies can leverage the huge referral potential of their fast-growing base of existing customers.

Growth in Solar Leasing Beyond the US

Germany

Installations of solar in Germany have grown dramatically due to a government policy requiring generous feed-in-tariffs (FiTs) for grid-connected systems. Solar generation meets nearly 30% of domestic power demand in Germany, but the top-three utilities own just 0.003% of installed capacity. German utilities have experienced significant financial losses as a result of these policies, and have lobbied for a cut in the FiT (Parkinson, 2012). In order to compete, German utilities are now looking to enter the solar leasing business. RWE Group, Germany's second largest utility, has teamed up with Conergy, a German solar company, to provide leased rooftop solar systems to customers. This comes after RWE lost 5% of its clients over the last three years, and the largest German utility, E.ON, lost 12% in the same period (Steitz, 2014).

China

The Chinese government has set a series of goals for solar installations. In 2007, the National Development and Reform Commission set a goal to grow installed solar capacity to 1.8 GW by 2020. This goal was increased in 2011 to 20–30 GW by 2020 (Shen and Wong, 2009). In 2014, the same commission set a new goal of 70 GW by 2017. This is both a reflection of the rapid growth in the intervening years, as well as a renewed focus of the government to move electricity generation away from coal (Bloomberg News, 2014).

In 2014, the National Energy Administration announced a key policy initiative to promote distributed solar generation using financing structures such as loan guarantees, leasing, and partnerships between banks and installers (Parkinson, 2014). It is too early to tell if solar leasing will succeed in the residential solar market in China as it has in the US, although the potential size of the residential market in China creates a tremendous opportunity. Solar leasing in China can also benefit from the cost advantages of local panel production — since 2011, China has produced the majority of the world's solar panels (Earth Policy Institute, 2013).

India

Solar power makes up a relatively small part of the energy mix in India. Large sections of the population live off-grid, and there has been significant growth in solar lamps and solar water heaters in rural areas. OMC Power and Selco are companies that lease solar powered lanterns to rural Indians who use them in place of kerosene lamps. In denser areas solar competes with heavily subsidized grid energy, but in areas where the primary source of electricity is diesel generators, solar is more cost competitive.

Simpa Networks established operations in Bangalore in 2011, with a financing model based on solar leasing called 'pay as you go'. Building on the success of Bharti Airtel and Royal Bank of India in establishing mobile payments through cell phones as a reliable way to provide financial services to the large unbanked population in India, Simpa allows customers to use their cell phones to access and pay for solar services. Customers purchase an access code via cell phone, which is then punched into the tamper-proof solar module. In January 2013, the Asian Development Bank invested US$2 million in equity capital in Simpa Networks to expand operations in India (Asian Development Bank, 2013).

Kenya

M-Kopa, based in Nairobi, Kenya, has applied the solar leasing model to East Africa. Established in 2011, M-Kopa developed solar products that are suited to off-grid households with several lights and a cell phone charger, connected to a solar panel with a battery and controller. The system also includes a mobile payments device by which

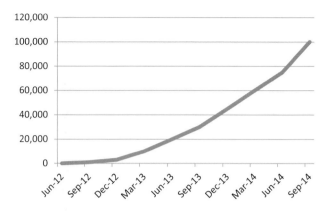

Fig. 12.4: M-Kopa customers in Kenya (Source: M-Kopa website data)

consumers can make payments using mobile money. M-Kopa's varia-tion on the solar leasing model is for customers to make a modest upfront payment followed by monthly payments over one year, at the end of which the customer owns the system. As of September 2014, M-Kopa has grown to reach 100,000 households in Kenya (see Fig. 12.4). M-Kopa's products allow off-grid African households to save money as compared to current spend on kerosene lanterns, while also improving lighting and charging mobile phones.

Advances in the Financing of Solar Leasing Companies

Securitization

Solar leasing companies have begun to raise capital using securitiza-tion, the issuance of notes backed by the cash flows generated from a bundle of solar projects. Securitization reduces investor risk by diversi-fying over many projects, while increasing investor liquidity by aggre-gating many small projects into one larger investment vehicle. For solar leasing companies, securitization reduces the cost of capital.

Solar leases are attractive assets for securitization, offering stable, long-term cash flows, creating attractive risk-adjusted returns for investors. In 2013 SolarCity, the leading US solar leasing company, issued the first securitization of a portfolio of solar leases. Credit

Suisse underwrote the issuance of a US$54 million portfolio of solar leases on 5,033 distinct solar systems totaling 44 MW. The notes had a maximum term of 13 years, and carried an interest rate of 4.80%. SolarCity subsequently achieved a breakthrough in July 2014 with an innovative master lease provision to avoid triggering repayment of tax credits in projects that end up in foreclosure (Wiltermuth, 2014). This allowed the company to issue three more securitizations from their pool of solar leases, creating a very low-cost source of financing for further project development.

Yieldcos

Broadly defined, a yieldco is a publicly traded company that is formed to own operating assets that produce cash flow. The cash flow is distributed to investors as dividends. To establish a yieldco, an energy company contributes power projects to the yieldco on a tax-free basis in exchange for stock and cash. The yieldco then sells stock to the public in an initial public offering (IPO). Investors are attracted to yieldcos because they provide access to dividend yielding, low-risk operating assets, while also allowing for liquidity in the event the investor wishes to sell their shares. As a result of high investor demand for yieldco shares, this structure has become an attractive source of financing in the US solar sector, providing large amounts of very low-cost capital.

In July 2014, SunEdison became the first solar leasing company to establish a yieldco, called TerraForm Power. At IPO, TerraForm Power owned solar projects with 808 MW of capacity and raised US$599 million. Subsequent to the IPO, TerraForm added two large California utility-scale projects, bringing capacity up to 1,637 MW. SunEdison plans to launch the first emerging market yieldco with solar projects in Africa and Asia (Perrault, 2014).

What's Ahead?

Solar leasing is a financial innovation that has dramatically accelerated the growth in residential solar installations, first in the US and now in many other countries. This relatively simple financial structure has eliminated the two primary barriers to adoption of residential solar — upfront cost and uncertainty — without the need for additional government incentives. Its very success is driving down the cost of solar installations, as increased volumes are creating economies of scale, leading to further demand and lower costs, in a virtuous circle of development.

Ironically, the declining cost of installing solar on residential homes is forecast to reduce the demand for solar leasing going forward (Shahan, 2014b). With lower costs, homeowners have less incentive to use the third-party ownership model, and are more likely to simply purchase systems outright as payback periods shorten. Furthermore, as homeowners become more comfortable with solar technology, they will begin to view it as a reliable appliance, at which point more people are likely to choose to buy equipment as opposed to leasing. As an analogy, car leases currently make up 20–25% of US auto sales (Henry, 2013).

In parallel with solar leasing, solar companies are now testing loan programs with residential homeowners, offering solar loans in the range of 4–6%. Annual residential default rates are lower than utility default rates or Standard and Poor's AAA corporate bond default rates (Clean Power Finance, 2014), providing an attractive risk/return profile for fixed-income institutional investors. As solar loan costs decline, homeowners are also likely to accelerate the acquisition of residential solar energy systems using solar loan programs.

The combination of lower installed costs and lower cost of capital is leading to rapid expansion of residential solar power. As the first generation of solar-backed securities and yieldcos are deployed, institutional investors are becoming more comfortable pricing the risks of the technology, potential regulatory changes, and creditworthiness of lessors and borrowers. Access to institutional capital is further decreasing the overall cost of residential solar, further increasing the scale and speed at which residential solar is deployed.

Looking ahead, the success of solar leasing and the introduction of innovative solar loan programs, financed with low-cost institutional capital through securitization and yieldco structures, will continue to drive dramatic growth in the residential sector.

References

Asian Development Bank (2013). 'Affordable Pay-As-You-Go Solar Power for India's Energy-Poor Homes'. Available at: http://www.adb.org/sites/default/files/pub/2013/affordable-solar-power-india-energy-poor-homes.pdf [accessed 28 September 2014].

Bloomberg News (2014). 'China Targets 70 Gigawatts of Solar Power to Cut Coal Reliance'. Available at: http://www.bloomberg.com/news/2014-05-16/china-targets-70-gigawatts-of-solar-power-to-cut-coal-reliance.html [accessed 10 September 2014].

Chernova, Y. (2012). 'The Economics of Solar Power for Your Home'. Available at: http://online.wsj.com/news/articles/SB10000872396390444506004577615662289766558 [accessed 11 September 2014].

Clean Power Finance (2014). 'CPF Investor Kit'. Available at: http://www.cleanpowerfinance.com/wp-content/uploads/2014/06/CPF-Investor-Kit-4JUN14.pdf [accessed 10 October 2014].

Climate Policy Initiative (2013). 'Improving Solar Policy: Lessons from the solar leasing boom in California'. Available at: http://climatepolicyinitiative.org/wp-content/uploads/2013/07/Improving-Solar-Policy-Lessons-from-the-solar-leasing-boom-in-California.pdf [accessed 15 September 2014].

Earth Policy Institute (2013). 'Annual Solar Photovoltaics Production by Country, 1995–2012'. Available at: http://www.earth-policy.org/datacenter/xls/indicator12_2013_2.xlsx [accessed 22 October 2014].

Frankel, D., Ostrowski, K. and Pinner, D. (2014). 'The disruptive potential of solar power'. Available at: http://www.mckinsey.com/insights/energy_resources_materials/the_disruptive_potential_of_solar_power [accessed 14 September 2014].

Gerdes, J. (2012). 'Solar Power More Competitive Than Decision-Makers or Consumers Realize'. Available at: http://www.forbes.com/sites/justingerdes/2012/05/24/solar-power-more-competitive-than-decision-makers-or-consumers-realize/ [accessed 22 September 2014].

Henry, J. (2013). 'Lease or Buy: More U.S. Customers Say Lease'. Available at: http://www.forbes.com/sites/jimhenry/2013/07/31/lease-or-buy-more-u-s-customers-say-lease/ [accessed 10 October 2014].

Jenkins, J. (2009). 'Soaking Up the Sun: Solar Power in Germany and Japan'. Available at: http://thebreakthrough.org/archive/soaking_up_the_sun_solar_power [accessed 1 October 2014].

Johnston, A. (2014). 'SolarCity, Vivint Solar Top US Solar Residential Installers In Q1 2014'. Available at: http://cleantechnica. com/2014/07/06/solarcity-vivint-solar-top-us-solar-residential-installers-q1-2014/ [accessed 2 October 2014].

Lamb, L. (2014). 'What is a good credit score?' Available at: http://credit. org/blog/what-is-a-good-credit-score-infographic/ [accessed 5 October 2014].

Munsell, M. (2014). 'Top 10 Installers Eclipse 50% of US Residential PV Market in Q1 2014'. Available at: http://www.greentechmedia.com/ articles/read/top-10-installers-eclipse-50-of-us-residential-pv-market-in-q1-2014 [accessed 15 September 2014].

National Renewable Energy Laboratory (2013). 'Benchmarking Non-Hardware Balance-of-System (Soft) Costs for U.S. Photovoltaic Systems, Using a Bottom-Up Approach and Installer Survey — Second Edition'. Available at: http://www.nrel.gov/docs/fy14osti/60412.pdf [accessed 14 September 2014].

Parkinson, G. (2012). 'Euro utilities declare war on solar PV'. Available at: http://reneweconomy.com.au/2012/euro-utilities-declare-war-on-solar-pv-57935 [accessed 10 October 2014].

Parkinson, G. (2014). 'China Solar Leasing to Contribute to the Impending Solar Boom'. Available at: http://cleantechnica.com/2014/09/05/ china-solar-leasing-solar-boom/ [accessed 10 September 2014].

Perrault, M. (2014). 'SunEdison Plans 2nd YieldCo, This One For Asia'. Available at: http://news.investors.com/technology/092914-719368-sunedison-announces-plans-for-another-YieldCo-following-terraform-power-ipo.htm [accessed 12 September 2014].

Shahan, Z. (2013a). 'Solar Power's Massive Price Drop'. Available at: http://cleantechnica.com/2013/05/24/solar-powers-massive-price-drop-graph/ [accessed 11 September 2014].

Shahan, Z. (2013b). 'DOE Calls For More Support Bringing Down The Soft Costs Of Solar, Could Be You!' Available at: http://cleantechnica. com/2013/12/05/doe-calls-support-bringing-soft-costs-solar-infographic/ [accessed 7 September 2014].

Shahan, Z. (2014a). 'What Is The Current Cost Of Solar Panels?' Available at: http://cleantechnica.com/2014/02/04/current-cost-solar-panels/ [accessed 9 September 2014].

Shahan, Z. (2014b). 'Solar System Ownership to Eat into Solar Leasing Pie in 2015'. Available at: http://cleantechnica.com/2014/07/01/solar-leasing-solar-power-purchase-agreements/ [accessed 1 October 2014].

Shen, R., and Wong, J. (2009). 'China solar set to be 5 times 2020 target-researcher'. Available at: http://www.reuters.com/article/2009/05/05/china-solar-idAFPEK12384620090505 [accessed 2 October 2014].

Sigrin, B. O. (2013). 'Financial Modeling of Consumer Discount Rate in Residential Solar Photovoltaic Purchasing Decisions'. Available at: http://repositories.lib.utexas.edu/bitstream/handle/2152/21759/SIGRIN-THESIS-2013.pdf?sequence=1 [accessed 8 September 2014].

Solar Energy Industries Association (2013). 'Solar Market Insight 2013 Q3'. Available at: http://www.seia.org/research-resources/solar-market-insight-2013-q3 [accessed 11 September 2014].

Solar Energy Industries Association (2014a). 'Solar Market Insight 2013 Year in Review'. Available at: http://www.seia.org/research-resources/solar-market-insight-report-2013-year-review [accessed 11 September 2014].

Solar Energy Industries Association (2014b). 'Solar Market Insight Report 2014 Q2'. Available at: http://www.seia.org/research-resources/solar-market-insight-report-2014-q2 [accessed 11 September 2014].

Steitz, C. (2014). 'Desperate German utilities will try to become solar leasing companies'. Available at: http://www.reuters.com/article/2014/09/03/germany-utilities-solar-idUSL6N0QD2XU20140903 [accessed 28 September 2014].

U.S. Energy Information Administration (2013). 'Most new residential solar PV projects in California program are not owned by homeowners'. Available at: http://www.eia.gov/todayinenergy/detail.cfm?id=12991 [accessed 23 September 2014].

Wiltermuth, J. (2014). 'SolarCity deal lights way for securitization'. Available at: http://www.reuters.com/article/2014/07/29/structured-finance-solarcity-bonds-idUSL6N0Q049O20140729 [accessed 11 October 2014].

Woody, T. (2012). 'California's Sungevity Moves Into Australian Solar Market'. Available at: http://www.forbes.com/sites/toddwoody/2012/04/19/californias-sungevity-moves-into-australian-solar-market/ [accessed 10 October 14].

Chapter Thirteen

Crowdfunding: Ready for the Big League?

Karl Harder, Managing Director, Abundance Generation
Sam Friggens, Independent Economist

In 2012 when a wind turbine started spinning in the historic village of St Briavels on the border of England and Wales, it was more than just another small step towards a clean energy system in the UK. The turbine lays claim to be the first renewable energy project in the world to be financed through crowdfunding — the 21st century phenomenon that involves large numbers of individuals coming together via the Internet to directly raise money for projects or ventures of their choosing. A total of £1.4 m was collectively invested by hundreds of people who now stand to receive annual financial returns of 6–8% over a period of 20 years as electricity is generated. The achievement signified the evolution of crowdfunding from a niche based on donations and rewards to an investment mechanism capable of delivering new sources of private finance to fund the energy infrastructure of the 21st century.

A small but increasing number of crowdfunding companies now provide the online platforms to connect individual investors to renewable energy investment opportunities in this way. At the time of writing (January 2015, this is a fast-moving space) Abundance Generation led the UK market, having facilitated £10m of investment in ten wind and solar projects from 1,500 people in two years. In the US, Solar Mosaic had raised over US$9 million for solar projects in a number of states including California, Florida and New Jersey. In France, Lumo had successfully funded a number of local pilot projects and was set to formally launch following the introduction of new crowdfunding regulation there. Within a relatively short period of time these companies have built the online infrastructure and financial processes essential to their operations, shaped emerging regulatory regimes, and established an intellectual framework rooted in notions of choice, ethics, disintermediation and the democratisation of finance[1]. Above all, they have proved renewable energy crowdfunding can deliver tangible outcomes on the ground.

Renewable crowdfunding is also demonstrating its potential to resonate with broader social and economic objectives and appeal to both politicians and campaigners alike. In the UK in 2013, the then Minister of State for Energy Greg Barker stated his belief that crowdfunding is an 'innovative and potentially scalable source of funding' (Marsh, 2013). In the US, fossil fuel divestment campaigner Bill McKibben has written and tweeted about renewable crowdfunding opportunities, pointing out the double benefit of pulling funds out of fossil fuel companies at the same time as investing in renewables (McKibben, 2013).

Despite this early success, a cursory comparison of the relatively small amounts raised to date with the huge sums needed to transform the global energy system (see Chapter 3) shows the distance renewable crowdfunding has yet to travel before it makes a serious dent at national or global scales. This chapter discusses the potential of crowdfunding to grow as a source of capital for renewable energy infrastructure. It outlines some of the factors likely to influence this process.

---

[1] The term disintermediation is used here to mean removing the 'middle-men' or intermediaries from financial decision-making so that people directly choose where their money is invested.

What is Crowdfunding and How Does it Work?

Different explanations have emerged as to the origins of crowdfunding. One reference point sometimes held to be the first example of a modern online crowdfunded project is the raising of US$60,000 by fans of British rock-group Marillion to fund a US tour in 1997. This interpretation sees crowdfunding as an essentially new phenomena defined by use of the Internet and the organic coming together of like-minded individuals to financially support a common cause. By contrast, other interpretations emphasise crowdfunding's links with earlier forms of decentralised finance; viewing it not as a radical break from the past but as a natural evolution of older mechanisms reformulated and modernised for the digital age. In this spirit, a recent World Bank report has described how crowdfunding 'began as an online extension of traditional financing by family and friends; communities pool money to fund members with business ideas' (infoDev/ The World Bank, 2013, p.8).

Indeed a broader historical perspective offers rich pickings in identifying early forms of capital raising that display at least some, if not all, the characteristics of modern-day crowdfunding. In the 19th century, for example, newspaper publisher Joseph Pulitzer used appeals in the *New York World* to raise US$100,000 from 125,000 people in six months to fund the completion of the pedestal to the Statue of Liberty. As a reward, the name of every contributor was later published in the newspaper (BBC News, 2013; US National Park Service, 2014). In the 18th century the Irish Loan Funds first developed by Irish nationalist and author of *Gulliver's Travels*, Jonathan Swift, involved the pooling of philanthropic donations to fund millions of small-scale loans to poor households. In the absence of collateral, repayment obligations were enforced through mechanisms of trust and social capital; borrowers were required to present a guarantee from two neighbours who were immediately notified if a repayment was missed (Hollis and Sweetman, 2001). Even further back, the 17th century coffee-houses of the City of London can be seen as arenas for an earlier form of disintermediated capitalism; places of exchange where investors and investees met face-to-face in the absence of financial intermediaries, to directly trade the first shares in commodities and companies.

At present, there is no universally accepted definition of the term 'crowdfunding' or other related concepts such as peer-to-peer lending. In this chapter we define crowdfunding broadly, in line with the approach set out by the European Commission: crowdfunding is understood to be an overarching term for any open call to the wider public to raise funds for a specific project or business via the Internet, whether through donations, equity or debt (European Commission, 2014). We also recognise the distinction made by the UK regulator, the Financial Conduct Authority, between different forms of debt crowdfunding: peer-to-peer lending is based on non-tradable and non-transferable loan agreements, whilst debt-based securities like debentures are unlisted but remain exchangeable (FCA, 2014).

Some renewable energy crowdfunders are experimenting with models based on equity and rewards. In 2014 Dutch platform Windcentrale raised €1.3m in just 13 hours by offering shares in exchange for an agreed quantity of 'free' clean electricity every year. The higher the retail price of electricity, the greater the value of this free electricity will be. In many countries the use of share offers to raise equity from local people for community energy projects is a mechanism that has been used for many years (the UK's first cooperative renewable project, Baywind in Cumbira, dates back to 1997). The transition to launching such offers online now means a much wider group of potential investors can be accessed.

We would argue, however, that it is debt crowdfunding that represents the real opportunity for renewable energy infrastructure, due to the natural match between the project finance requirements of developers and the stable low-risk returns sought by ordinary investors. As Bloomberg New Energy Finance recently put it, 'clean energy crowdfunding is much more of a debt play than an equity play' (BNEF, 2012). In the UK, the Abundance model is based on debentures, which are debt-based securities that represent a loan to the project company and entitle the holder to a payment every six months. The role of Abundance in this process is administrative: to undertake due diligence on projects, facilitate the sale and purchase of debentures between project and investor, and provide the forum for communication relating to the project throughout its life. Investment occurs directly between the investor and the project company, and only after the project has all the necessary consents to proceed. The project company is ultimately responsible for the delivery and main-tenance of the project and for repaying its investors.

What Benefits Does Renewable Energy Crowdfunding Bring?

The attraction of debt-based crowdfunding for renewable energy lies in its capacity to meet the needs of project developers, local commu-nities and investors alike.

For developers of small renewable energy projects — typically a few megawatts in size or less — accessing debt finance has always been a major challenge. The reasons for this are varied and well-documented but include the perception that community energy is niche and high-risk, and the fact that new small developers such as cooperatives often lack the balance sheet and track-record required by most investors (Julian and Olliver, 2014). The financial crisis of 2007–2008 made this situation worse, initially by the disappearance of virtually all bank lending to small businesses and more recently as a result of Basel III regulations squeezing lines of credit to projects that are inherently long term in nature. In this context, crowdfunding mechanisms that provide new sources of patient capital are likely to prove indispensa-ble[2]. A secondary potential benefit for developers is a reduction in planning risk as a result of increased local involvement and support.

For communities, the opportunity to host appropriately sized local energy infrastructure is often seen as an attractive concept, but one that is difficult and risky to put into practice. Debt-based crowd-funding provides a solution to this problem. It allows experienced professional developers to undertake the complex work needed to build and operate projects, whilst at the same time giving people liv-ing in the local community the opportunity to invest at an appropriate

---

[2] Patient capital refers to capital invested for the medium or long term.

point in the development process: after the highest risk planning stages are complete. The benefits and sense of ownership that flow from community projects are retained but without asking more of local people than they are able to give. In addition to financial returns, these wider community benefits can include reduced energy bills for local residents and the use of project revenues to fund initiatives such as local energy efficiency drives and ecological restoration. Investment in local energy infrastructure is also seen as a way to retain wealth in the local economy, because money that would otherwise have flowed out through energy bills is recycled back through investor returns.

For individuals looking to invest their money, debt-based renewable crowdfunding offers an attractive and suitable asset class that has previously been out of reach. Many forms of electricity generation infrastructure offer relatively low-risk returns but the UK's framework for supporting renewable energy means that projects under five megawatts in size have the additional benefit of receiving government-backed inflation-linked revenues. The returns that result from this arrangement typically reach 6–9% per year and are more reliable than many other types of investment. Before the advent of debt crowdfunding, retail investors had little access to these kinds of opportunities. Investment in renewables or other types of infrastructure has typically been limited to specialist funds or cooperative share offers — options that often involve higher risks, exposure to stock market volatility and significant barriers to entry (such as high minimum investment thresholds). By comparison, debt-based renewable crowdfunding has a lot to offer investors — including those with no personal interest in renewable energy.

The appeal of renewable energy crowdfunding is not limited to the financial bottom line however. By directly connecting those with money to those who need it, crowdfunding offers an alternative to the mainstream approach to finance that has dominated for over a century. The emergence of a global financial system in the 20th century was characterised by complexity and a professional intermediary class of bankers and fund managers. The idea that technology can be used to bypass these intermediaries ('disintermediation') and democratise finance in the process is an important intellectual underpinning of the crowdfunding movement. From this perspective, if people take back control of their own money and invest it transparently and tangibly in the real economy, ethics can be reintroduced into financial decision-making. Where the financial capitalism of the 20th century produced institutions stripped of objectives beyond the pursuit of profit, disintermediated capitalism has the potential to make markets social again, and help to build an economy more reflective of its constituent parts.

Together, these benefits are effectively 'the pitch' for renewable energy crowdfunding. They are the reasons for thinking it is a scalable model capable of making a significant contribution to financing clean energy infrastructure in the decades ahead.

How Big Could it Get?

The most comprehensive publicly available assessment of global crowdfunding activity illustrates the rapid growth achieved in recent years. A 2013 Industry Report by research analyst firm Massolution estimated that US$5.1bn was raised across all types of crowdfunding in 2013 — a figure up 80% from US$2.7 billion in 2012 (Massolution, 2013). Roughly half was associated with investment crowdfunding and much of this was via lending or debt-based instruments. Geographically, crowdfunding is at present almost exclusively a developed world phenomenon (North America and Europe accounted for over 90% of the 2012 total) but there are signs this is changing, with activity in other parts of the world now growing at a fast pace. In jurisdictions where crowdfunding is more established it is beginning to register in the minds of those with a macroeconomic outlook. In the UK, a recent Bank of England assessment of national lending trends recognised the increasing importance of peer-to-peer lending and crowdfunding sources of businesses finance (Bank of England, 2014).

The share of total crowdfunding investments specifically attributable to renewables has not been systematically quantified, but it is almost certainly very low, not least because renewable crowdfunding is such a recent phenomenon. A simple aggregation of the publicised investment totals from the main renewable crowdfunding platforms in Europe and North America suggests the total raised to date for renewables is in the tens of millions of pounds rather than anything higher. This equates to around 1% of all crowdfunded capital raised across the globe in 2013, and it is a tiny fraction of the huge sums needed to fund a global clean energy transition. Whether renewable crowdfunding can close this gap in any meaningful way will depend on the extent to which recent growth trends can be maintained.

Looking to the future, a number of recent reports have attempted to provide indications of the broad quantities of capital potentially available. According to Bloomberg New Energy Finance, just 1% of current US retail investment in savings accounts, money markets and US treasuries would provide US$90 billion for clean energy crowd-funding, with 0.5% of the bond market adding a further US$190 billion (BNEF, 2012). In developing countries, the World Bank has estimated that ordinary people will have the potential to invest US$96 billion each year by 2025 (based on the assumption that families with incomes of US$10,000 p/a will save as well as consume), of which over half will be from China (infoDev/The World Bank, 2013). Whilst these figures should not be interpreted as actual predictions of future investment levels from renewable energy crowdfunding, they do serve to make the basic point that the money is out there, if only a mechanism can be found to access it.

In exploring whether renewable crowdfunding could be such a mechanism, two case studies are instructive.

The first is Zopa, a UK peer-to-peer lending platform that has facilitated well over £500 million pounds of lending from a community of 50,000 lenders since its launch in 2005. It is growing strongly (over a third of total lending through the site occurred in 2013) and in doing so is demonstrating the trajectory that individual platforms can achieve by offering retail investors the chance to directly select where their money goes. Recently Zopa also facilitated tens of millions of pounds of lending from institutional investors, mirroring the actions of peer-to-peer lenders in the US who have teamed up with Wall Street funds attracted by yield and new opportunities for securitisation (Alloway, 2013). Such moves have proved controversial in light of the evident tension with the principal of disintermediation, but they are at the same time contributing to the rapid scaling up of the platforms involved. Where such an approach is adopted, a core challenge will be to strike a balance between retail and institutional investors that retains the integrity of the crowdfunding concept and resists the temptation to offer different terms to different types of investors. With this caveat in mind, Zopa's experience to date suggests the existence of crowdfunding sites each raising billions of pounds a year is a near-term possibility.

The second case study is the German Energiewende, or Energy Transition, which aims to rapidly replace fossil fuels and nuclear energy in Germany with renewables over the coming decades. In 2014 Germany generated around 30% of its electricity from wind, solar, hydro and biomass (Fraunhofer Institute, 2014). A core feature of this transition to date has been the decentralised nature of the renewable energy infrastructure built and the extent to which this has been driven by decentralised finance. Almost half of Germany's installed renewable energy capacity is currently owned by private citizens and farmers, which represents tens of billions of euros of retail investment over the last decade[3]. This has been achieved through a variety of mechanisms including limited partnership Burgerwindparks (citizen wind farms) and cooperative models, often supported by government-backed low-interest loans. Germany's experience shows that with right framework and structures in place, it is possible for distributed capital to be aggregated at a significant scale for investment in energy infrastructure. Whilst such achievements result in part from distinctly German perspectives on autonomy, energy and the environment, there is evidence that higher levels of direct financial participation are possible elsewhere. In the UK a recent survey by the Institute of Mechanical Engineers (2013) indicated that a third of British people would like to personally invest in community

---

[3] Statistics from Germany's *Renewable Energies Agency* show that around €150 bn was invested in German renewables between 2003–2012 (*Agentur Fur Erneuebare Energien*, 2014a), and that 46% of this was owned by private individuals and farmers in 2012 (*Agentur Fur Erneuebare Energien*, 2014b). Assuming an equity ratio of 20%–50% suggests €14 bn–€35 bn directly invested in equity by citizens and farmers over this time.

renewable projects. That this rarely happens in practice is as much a failure of public policy as it is of public sentiment.

The Context and Conditions for Growth

Expanding the pool of people willing to take more direct control of their money will be an essential precondition for the scaling up of renewable energy crowdfunding. The case studies above provide some anecdotal evidence that this is possible, but a broader and per- haps more important issue is whether trends emerging in tandem with the Internet's integration into society are fringe phenomena or early indicators of a more fundamental restructuring to come. According to Harvard Business School Professor Shoshana Zuboff, new digital technologies are impacting our sense of self and expectations about the world in fundamental ways. 'We have a new society of individuals', she says. 'People are more experienced, have more disposable income, more education, more information, leisure, connectedness, travel than at any other time in human history. And because I feel a unique sense of self, I want to have control over my own life, I want to make my own choices, I want to make a life which reflects my uniqueness' (BBC, 2013). Such changes can be seen playing out in business, where standardised products like music albums have been overtaken by our ability to create personalised products online, and in manufac- turing, where innovations like 3D printing promise to revolutionise the level of customisation that will be possible in the production of consumer goods. If this perspective proves accurate and the mass production of the 20th century gives way to greater personalisation in the 21st, then it is hard to see the world of finance avoiding a com- parable transformation of its own. New mechanisms like crowdfund- ing that are disintermediated, personalised and ethical will be well poised to challenge the centralised and opaque structures of old.

A further factor likely to affect the attractiveness of renewable crowdfunding investments is the macroeconomic context for saving, and the range of savings products available to retail investors. Ever since the 2007–2008 financial crisis many countries have seen infla- tion exceed base interest rates, which has in turn eroded the value of money kept in current and savings accounts. Yet people persist with the strategy of keeping much of their money in these accounts in part because the mainstream financial services industry has failed to provide suitable next-step options with better returns at relatively low risk. All too often the choice for savers is perceived as between cash and shares, yet the risk and volatility of the stock markets means the latter is simply a step too far for many. As long as this remains the case, there will be an opportunity for alternative savings products to step into the gap, particularly those that offer relatively stable inflation-linked returns such as renewable energy debentures. Until recently in the UK, tax structures to encourage saving (such as individual savings accounts (ISAs)) reflected the dichotomic choice savers faced between cash and shares. However these structures are now being opened up to included crowdfunding investments too, which will in turn help to increase the number of investors in renewable energy crowdfunding.

Crowdfunding platforms themselves also have work to do. Their pitch may be attractive in terms of returns, stability and ethics, but practical barriers to expanding the pool of investors still need to be overcome. One of the clearest examples of this (and most frequent charges from critics of crowdfunding) is the lack of liquidity. Capital markets are volatile and unsuitable places for many retail investors, but they at least provide an opportunity to turn assets into cash quickly when needed. By contrast unlisted crowdfunding products cannot be traded on these markets, meaning other mechanisms are needed to provide liquidity. Abundance's solution has been to set up an online bulletin board that allows renewable energy debentures to be directly bought and sold between registered individuals. It is comparable to eBay, and is intended to enable people to efficiently trade previously hard-to-trade items, creating an alternative to traditional public markets. At the time of writing (January 2015), this has operated effectively for over a year, but many investors will require confidence that such mechanisms are both effective and here to stay before going ahead with an investment.

To raise capital in the quantities indicated by Bloomberg and the World Bank, a greater number of suitable projects will also be required alongside an increase in the number of willing investors. In theory, an economy set on a low-carbon pathway should provide plenty of opportunities here. However approaches to energy system decarbonisation vary between jurisdictions, and a focus on large-scale top–down infrastructure rather than smaller community and municipality sized projects could still mean it is challenging in practice to expand the pool of suitable projects for crowdfunding platforms. One solution to this problem would be for developers of utility-scale projects to team up with crowdfunding platforms to raise part of the required debt directly from retail investors; an arrangement that would signify a major step forward in the evolution of renewables crowdfunding. In either case, the role of government in establishing a financial framework that provides predictable revenues is critical. In this sense crowdfunding investors are no different from other types of investors: asset financing will not materialise without enough certainty and incentives in place.

The issue of regulating crowdfunding reflects the same inherent tension as regulating other disruptive new business models. It is desirable where it creates markets, builds credibility and protects against rogue elements, but if done badly it risks quashing the very innovation it seeks to support. In countries where crowdfunding has already emerged, regulatory frameworks are still being established.

In the US the key piece of federal legislation relating to crowdfunding is the 2012 JOBS Act, which includes provisions to exempt crowdfunding from previous federal securities laws, in turn enabling non-accredited investors to invest up to certain limits[4]. Yet as at the time of writing, these provision had still not been operationalised, leaving a patchwork of different rules across the country with individual states implementing their own exemptions and requirements. In any case, the JOBS Act provisions are proving controversial. Some fear the federal requirements will be too restrictive and costly to unleash the full potential of crowdfunding; others are concerned that consumer protection measures are insufficiently strong, particularly in relation to equity crowdfunding.

---

[4] In the US a non-accredited investor is an investor who does not meet the net worth requirements for an accredited investor under Securities & Exchange Commission regulation.

In the EU there is no EU-wide legislation specifically targeted at crowdfunding, although the European Commission has outlined its intention to monitor progress and report back on the need for further action in 2015 (European Commission, 2014). In the meantime a number of Member States are developing their own approaches to regulation, risking a fragmented approach across the continent. In the UK a new framework came into force in 2014. Whereas previously some platforms were regulated by the Financial Conduct Authority and others were not, now all platforms offering debt and equity crowdfunding must comply with standards relating to marketing, risks and capital reserves. Retail investors buying 'non-readily realisable securities' (a category that includes renewable energy debentures as well as mini-bonds and equity investments) must be either professionally advised, certified as sophisticated, or confirm they will not invest more than 10% of their net investible assets (FCA, 2014). France also adopted a new legal framework for crowdfunding activities in 2014, to a generally positive reception from French crowdfunding platforms (Dekker, 2014). The growth of crowdfunding and the scale it can achieve will depend on the effectiveness of these new regulatory regimes and the responsiveness of regulators to changing conditions in the future.

From Small Acorns ...

Renewable energy crowdfunding has come a long way in a short time. In just a few years a small but growing number of online platforms have started giving ordinary people the opportunity to benefit from the long-term stable returns that investment in clean energy infrastructure brings. A new source of private finance for projects has been created and tens of millions of pounds have already been raised. The crowdfunding models used to do this provide new ways to engage communities and offer new opportunities for individuals to take control of their finances. For all these reasons, renewable energy crowdfunding is attracting political as well as public interest, and a number of countries are putting regulation in place to encourage the growth of crowdfunding of all types.

What can we expect to see in the coming years to indicate that renewable energy crowdfunding is coming of age? The establishment of more platforms in more countries will signify a greater supply of projects and healthy competition for an increasing number of investors. Platforms operating across a number of countries are likely too, and as the market matures in this way, the cost of capital will come down, making crowdfunding a more attractive option for project developers. The size of projects will increase and partnerships between platforms and developers of utility-scale projects will facilitate raises of tens or even hundreds of millions of pounds. For investors, the emergence of secondary markets will provide the confidence that they can make long-term investments whilst retaining the liquidity that they need. Overall, the share of retail investments funnelled through intermediated funds will reduce and the share invested directly via online platforms will grow.

This is not to suggest scaling up is inevitable or a problem-free path. How will investors respond when a high-profile project fails to deliver? Will regulators strike the right balance between consumer protection, innovation and encouraging new sources of private finance? Can crowdfunding platforms develop effective secondary markets and adapt to a much larger scale of project? Each of these issues will require the right response to enable the full potential of renewable energy crowdfunding to be realised. If this happens, a movement that started small in the historic village of St Briavels in the autumn of 2012 could be the beginning of something big for the future of renewable energy finance.

References

Agentur Fur Erneuebare Energien (2014a). 'Investitionen In Erneuerbare-Energie-Anlagen In Deutschland 2000–2013'. Available at: http://www.unendlich-viel-energie.de/mediathek/grafiken/investitionen-in-erneuerbare-energien-anlagen [accessed 21 September 2014].

Agentur Fur Erneuebare Energien (2014b). 'Eigentumsverteilung An Erneurbaren Energien–Anlagen 2012'. Available at: http://www.unendlich-viel-energie.de/mediathek/grafiken/eigentumsverteilung-an-erneuerbaren-energien-anlagen-2012 [accessed 22 December 2014].

Alloway, T. (2013) 'Peer-to-peer lending comes of age as Wall Street muscles in'. Available at: http://www.ft.com/cms/s/0/d6903c54-4447-11e4-8abd-00144feabdc0.html#axzz3GWcmD2Cn [accessed 18 October 2014].

Bank of England (2014). 'Trends in Lending'. Available at: http://www.bankofengland.co.uk/publications/Documents/other/monetary/trendsjuly14.pdf [accessed 26 September 2014].

BBC News (2013). 'The Statue of Liberty and America's Crowdfunding Pioneer'. Available at: http://www.bbc.co.uk/news/magazine-21932675 [accessed 21 September 2014].

BBC Radio 4 (2013). 'The World Turned Upside Down'. Available at: http://www.bbc.co.uk/programmes/b03cd572 [accessed 26 September 2014].

BNEF (2012). 'All Renewable Energy — Research Note. Extraordinary popular solution: funding from crowds?' Available at: https://www.bnef.com/InsightDownload/7188/pdf/ [accessed 26 September 2014].

Dekker, L. (2014) 'France's first mover advantage in crowdfunding legislation: a separate legal status for crowdfunding platforms', Crowdfund Insider. Available at: http://www.crowdfundinsider.com/2014/06/41106-frances-first-mover-advantage-crowdfunding-legislation-separate-legal-status-crowdfunding-platforms/ [accessed 12 September 2014].

European Commission (2014). 'Unleashing the Potential of Crowdfunding in the European Union', Communication From The Commission To The European Parliament, The Council, The European Economic and Social Committee And The Committee Of The Regions, Brussels.

FCA (2014) 'The FCA's regulatory approach to crowdfunding over the internet, and the promotion of non-readily realisable securities by other media', Policy Statement PS14/4, London.

Fraunhofer Institute (2014). 'Electricity production from solar and wind in Germany in 2014'. Available at: http://www.ise.fraunhofer.de/en/downloads-englisch/pdf-files-englisch/data-nivc-/electricity-production-from-solar-and-wind-in-germany-2014.pdf [accessed 26 September 2014].

Hollis, A. and Sweetman, A. (2001). 'The Lifecycle of an Irish Microfinance Institution: The Irish Loan Funds', *Journal of Economic Behaviour & Organization*, **46**, 291–311.

infoDev/The World Bank (2013). 'Crowdfunding's Potential for the Developing World', Washington DC.

Institute of Mechanical Engineers (2013). 'Poll finds 64% of the public is concerned about blackouts'. Available at: http://www.imeche.org/news/institution/all/2013/06/13/energy_poll_blackouts [accessed 26 September 2014].

Julian, C. and Olliver, R. (2014). *Community Energy: Unlocking Finance and Investment — The Way Ahead*, Respublica, UK.

Marsh, S. (2013). 'Expert roundup: Q&A with Greg Barker', *Guardian*. Available at: http://www.theguardian.com/local-government-network/2013/jun/29/greg-barker-local-energy-live-chat [accessed 12 September 2014].

Massolution (2013). 'The Crowdfunding Industry Report 2013CF Excerpt'. Available at: http://www.crowdsourcing.org/editorial/2013cf-the-crowdfunding-industry-report/25107?utm_source=website&utm_medium=text&utm_content=LP+bottom&utm_campaign=2013CF+Launch [accessed 21 September 2014].

McKibben, B. (2013) 'Solar Mosaic: Kind of a big deal for clean energy', *Grist*. Available at http://grist.org/climate-energy/solar-mosaic-kind-of-a-big-deal-for-clean-energy/ [accessed 12 September 2014].

US National Park Service (2014). 'Joseph Pulitzer'. Available at: http://www.nps.gov/stli/historyculture/joseph-pulitzer.htm [accessed: 21 September 2014].

Index